THE TASTE OF COURAGE

The drama, the humor, the horror, and sometimes the tenderness of men and women confronting their greatest ordeal speak through this absorbing narrative of World War II, told in eyewitness accounts by soldiers, housewives and journalists in the many countries involved.

Volume 1: The Blitzkrieg carries the story from the invasion of Poland through Dunkirk and the Battle of Britain to the end of the Italian Empire in North Africa and the intervention of Germany in Greece and the Middle East.

THE TASTE OF COURAGE
THE WAR, 1939-1945
VOLUME I: THE BLITZKRIEG
Edited by DESMOND FLOWER and JAMES REEVES

A BERKLEY MEDALLION BOOK
PUBLISHED BY
BERKLEY PUBLISHING CORPORATION

Published by arrangement with Harper & Row Publishers
BERKLEY MEDALLION EDITION, MAY, 1971
SBN - 425 - 03374 - 0
BERKLEY MEDALLION BOOKS are published by
Berkley Publishing Corporation
200 Madison Avenue
New York, N. Y. 10016
BERKLEY MEDALLION BOOKS ® TM 757,375
Printed in the United States of America
SECOND PRINTING

ACKNOWLEDGMENTS

Grateful acknowledgment is made to the following for permission
to reprint selections included in this book:

Brandt & Brandt
  I Was There by Admiral William D. Leahy. Published by
  McGraw-Hill Book Co.
  Admiral Halsey's Story by William F. Halsey and Joseph Bryan.
  Published by McGraw-Hill Book Co.
  Hitler and His Admirals by Anthony Martienssen. Copyright
  1949 by Anthony Martienssen.
  Defeat in the West by Milton Shulman. Copyright 1948 by Mil-
  ton Shulman.
Cassel & Co. Ltd.
  Sunk by Mochitsura Hashimoto. Copyright 1954 by Henry Holt
  & Co., Inc.
Constable & Co. Ltd.
  Retreat, Hell! by William Camp. Copyright 1943 by William
  Martin Camp. Published by Appleton-Century-Crofts, Inc.
Curtis Brown, Ltd.
  Still Digging by Mortimer Wheeler. Copyright © 1955 by Eric
  Robert Mortimer Wheeler. Published by E.P. Dutton & Co.
  The Green Beret by Hilary St. George Saunders. Reprinted by
  permission of the author's estate.
  The Spirit in the Cage by Peter Churchill.
The John Day Company
  The Invisible Flag by Peter Bamm.
Dodd, Mead & Company
  Going to the Wars by John Verney. Copyright © 1955 by John
  Verney.

TO THE
30,000,000
DEAD

INTRODUCTION

THIS is a documentary conspectus of the worst war in history, beginning at the German invasion of Poland on 1 September 1939 and ending with the last Japanese surrenders in September and October 1945. But it is not a history of the war: that has been written—by Sir Winston Churchill and by other historians, official and unofficial. This book could not have been written by one man, for it is an attempt to put together a chronicle of how it actually felt to be alive twenty years ago; to see, to hear, to smell, to feel the war at first hand. As service men and women, politicians and diplomats, workers in the resistance movements and victims of aggression, as men and women in civil occupations, and even as children, millions were aware of the war as a world-wide cataclysm hanging over the whole of life. Some, comparatively few but still numerous, wrote down their experience of that part of the war in which they were immediately involved; this book is a mosaic of such records. The contributors are world leaders, soldiers, sailors and airmen, journalists, firemen, hospital staff, factory workers, peasants—anyone who has written down in the spirit of an eye-witness or a participant his impressions of some aspect of war experience, of greater or lesser significance.

What must impress the reader of these pages is the vastness of the war: its totality, the extent to which it penetrated like an evil contagion into every corner of the inhabited world. As Marshal Pétain, the misguided master of Vichy, remarked at one stage—'Now for the first time the whole world is at war.' In these pages will be found the views and feelings of housewives in London, Berlin, Moscow and Tokyo: their problems, joys and sorrows are much the same. Here, too, we present the views of British and Germans facing one another at El Alamein, of Russians and Germans creeping forward through the frozen ruins of Stalingrad, of Americans and Japanese inching through a sodden Pacific jungle. All these, and many more, were men and women committed the world over to a problem from which none could escape once the politicians had decreed that the shooting should begin. This second World War produced heroism comparable with anything which had gone before, cowardice, inefficiency, brilliance, greatness, and a dedication to one object—on whichever side it might be—of more people that have ever before been involved in a single, terrifying catastrophe.

One of us responsible for this volume was concerned in 1937 with the production of a similar book describing the first World War: it was called *Vain Glory*. In our present task we find a difference. About the second World War there was little either vain or glorious. It was a bitter, sordid affair—for even the horrors of Passchendaele had an heroic dignity which cannot be equalled. It was not in vain, since it was begun to remove the evil men of Nuremberg, and in that at least it succeeded. But, to the surprise of those who found themselves involved in it, it developed into a display of hard-hitting brutality—sparing neither men, women, nor children—which only the mythical depredations of Genghis Khan may have challenged.

If there is ever a third world war, it will no doubt be a very clean job of destruction started at a range of thousands of miles by technicians suitably protected below ground and pressing a knob. But when the first scientific flurry is over, the destruction will be so great that it will be left to the surviving men, women and children to stick it out and somehow try to get the mess through to a conclusion.

In compiling this book we have paid our respects to military prowess—the actions of the professional soldiers who have triumphed with all the skill to which their lives have been devoted; but the victims of any war are the people: people in uniform, people out of uniform, people fighting, and people fleeing. There will be nowhere to flee next time, so this book offers a record of what may be the last of its kind: for better or for worse.

D. F.   J. R.
Headley, Hants   Chalfont St. Giles, Bucks

CONTENTS

MAPS

ACKNOWLEDGMENTS

WE wish to express our gratitude to the individuals, libraries, and other bodies listed below, all of whom have been of the greatest possible assistance in the preparation of this book. The authors and publishers of the extracts used are acknowledged in full between pages 355 and 359.

> The American Embassy Library
> The Guildhall Library
> The Imperial War Museum Library
> The Information Bureau, Chatham House
> The Book Information Bureau, National Book
>   League
> The Walter Hines Page Memorial Library
> The War Office Library
> Mr. J. A. Williams

We would also like to thank the many publishers and literary agents who have lent us new books in typescript, proof, or bound copy form, a kindness which has allowed the inclusion of much recently-published material. We also wish to thank Mr. T. R. Nicholson for his great editorial help in the closing stages of the preparation of the book for the printer, Mrs. Herta Ryder, who throughout has kept under her control the vast amount of material which accumulated, and Mr. Antony Brett-James for his assistance in checking proofs.

D. F.   J. R.

NOTE

The contributions to this book are chosen from documentary sources. In one or two cases, where no eyewitness account is available, a reliable historian has been drawn upon for the record. Fiction has only been used when the Editors are satisfied that the writer was present at and witnessed the events which he has woven into his narrative. The war and its ramifications were so great and so many that some aspects have not been mentioned in these pages. To those on all sides whose work has not been recognized, we offer our apologies and hope that they will find some satisfaction in the overall picture of the vast struggle.

D. F.   J. R.

IDENTIFICATION
OF EXTRACTS

IN order to discover the source of any extract, the reader should note the number of the page on which it begins and its heading and first words, and then refer to the section entitled *Key to the Sources of Extracts* (pages 347 to 352). There, following the page number and brief identification of the passage, will be found a key number. Reference to this key number in the following section, entitled *Sources* (pages 355 to 359), will reveal the title, author, publisher and publication date of the work drawn upon.

The italicized passages between extracts have been interpolated by the Editors to provide a consecutive narrative.

Signatures: A very few extracts are not signed. These are the small minority of completely impersonal passages written by historians, inserted, when of a sufficiently high standard, for lack of first-hand material. Of the signed extracts, a few are anonymous; for example, 'British gunner'. In these cases the Editors have been unable to ascertain the writer's identity, or else the writer has wished to remain anonymous. In some cases the signatures of servicemen do not include ranks. These are omitted either because the appropriate rank could not be ascertained, or because it was thought more effective to omit them. Where a rank is given, it changes appropriately in the cases of the most famous men, and in other cases remains the same throughout, the rank likely to sound most familiar or natural to the reader being given. These are broad principles, but individual circumstances may have had to dictate some exceptions, at the expense of rules of consistency.

... THERE is a great danger in this war. But if we are among those that get back, we shall have nothing to tell. I have had adventures—pioneering mail lines; flying the Andes; being forced down among rebellious Arabs in the Sahara. But war is not a true adventure. It is a mere *ersatz*. Where ties are established, where problems are set, where creation is stimulated—there you have adventure. But there is no adventure in heads-or-tails, in betting that the toss will come out life or death. War is not an adventure. It is a disease. It is like typhus.

Antoine de Saint-Exupéry

If it be Life that awaits, I shall live forever unconquered: If Death, I shall die at last strong in my pride and free.

Scottish National Memorial

1

THE COMING OF WAR

In the summer of 1939 Hitler's Germany, having annexed Austria and Czechoslovakia with the acquiescence of the rest of the world, turned eastward towards Poland. On 31 March, Britain, ending the policy of appeasement, had joined France in a guarantee of Poland against aggression. On 23 August Hitler secured Soviet connivance to his designs on the Poles. The stage was set.

WE WANT WAR

THE bloodless solution of the Czech conflict in the autumn of 1938 and the spring of 1939 and the annexation of Slovakia rounded off the territory of Greater Germany in such a way that it then became possible to consider the Polish problem on the basis of more or less favourable strategic premises.

General Jodl to the Gauleiters, 1943

I wanted to make sure for myself, and on 11 August I went to Salzburg. It was in his residence at Fuschl that Ribbentrop informed me, while we were waiting to sit down at the table, of the decision to start the fireworks, just as he might have told me about the most unimportant and commonplace administrative matter. "Well, Ribbentrop," I asked him, while we were walking in the garden, "what do you want? The Corridor or Danzig?" "Not any more," and he stared at me through those cold *Musée Grévin* eyes. "We want war."

Count Ciano, Italian Foreign Minister, 1939

POLAND

An Act of Aggression is Arranged: 26 August 1939

Mehlhorn's voice grew more excited as he told me that
Heydrich had asked him to come to his office and, surprisingly, had confided to him one of Hitler's secret orders.
Before 1 September, if possible, an absolutely irreproachable cause for war had got to be created, one that
would stand in history as a complete justification and
would brand Poland in the eyes of the world as the aggressor against Germany. It had therefore been planned to
dress troops in Polish uniforms and attack the Gleiwitz radio transmitter. Hitler had assigned Heydrich and Admiral
Canaris, Chief of Army Intelligence, to carry out this
operation. However, Canaris was so repelled by the order
that he had managed to withdraw and Heydrich alone was
in charge of it. Heydrich had explained to Mehlhorn the
details of the plan. The Polish uniforms were to be supplied at Keitel's command by the O.K.W.—the Supreme
Command of the Armed Forces.

I asked Mehlhorn where they would get the Poles who
were to wear these uniforms. "That's just it," Mehlhorn
replied. "That's the devilish thing about this plan: the
'Poles' will be convicts from the concentration camps.
They're going to be armed with proper Polish weapons,
but most of them will just be mown down, of course.
They've been promised that any who get away with it will
have their freedom immediately. But who's going to
believe such a promise?"

Mehlhorn paused. Then he said, "Heydrich has put me
in command of the attack." He gripped my arm hard:
"What am I to do?" he asked. "Heydrich has given me
this assignment to get rid of me. I know it. He wants my
death! What can I do?"

Now it was my turn to be silent. What advice could I
possibly give? Finally I said, "The whole thing is insane.

One can't make world history by tactics of that kind. The thing couldn't possibly be kept secret, not for long, anyway. Somewhere, somehow, it'll all come out. You must keep clear of it though. Try to talk your way out. Make some excuse—say you're ill—or just simply refuse. Whatever happens through your refusing that sort of order, it'll be preferable to the consequence of your carrying it out."

> Walter Schellenberg,
> German Foreign Intelligence Service

Most Secret

Directive No. I for the Conduct of War: 31 August

1. Now that all the political possibilities of disposing by peaceful means of a situation on the Eastern Frontier which is intolerable for Germany are exhausted, I have determined on a solution by force.

2. The attack on Poland is to be carried out in accordance with the preparations made for "Fall Weiss", with the alterations which result, where the Army is concerned, from the fact that it has, in the meantime, almost completed its dispositions.

   Allotment of tasks and the operational target remain unchanged.

   The date of attack—1 September, 1939.

   Time of attack—04.45 [inserted in red pencil].

   This time also applies to the operation at Gdynia, Bay of Danzig, and the Dirschau Bridge.

3. In the West it is important that the responsibility for the opening of hostilities should rest unequivocally with England and France. At first, purely local action should be taken against insignificant frontier violations.

> Adolf Hitler

Proclamation to the Armed Forces: 1 September

The Polish Government, unwilling to establish good

neighbourly relations as aimed at by me, wants to force the issue by way of arms.

The Germans in Poland are being persecuted with bloody terror and driven from their homes. Several acts of frontier violation, which cannot be tolerated by a great power, show that Poland is no longer prepared to respect the Reich's frontiers. To put an end to these mad acts, I can see no other way but from now onwards to meet force with force.

The German Armed Forces will with firm determination take up the struggle for the honour and the vital rights of the German people.

I expect every soldier to be conscious of the high tradition of the eternal German soldierly qualities and to do his duty to the last.

Remember always and in any circumstances that you are the representatives of National Socialist Greater Germany.

Long live our people and the Reich.

                                                    Adolph Hitler

BRITAIN

A Letter to America: 3 September 1939

It was a brilliantly sunny morning.

At ten o'clock the wireless said, "Stand by for an announcement of national importance." It was about our ultimatum and the time-limit of eleven o'clock. At quarter-hour intervals they announced that the Prime Minister would "make an announcement of national importance at 11:15"; in between they played things like the Berceuse from *Jocelyn* and at the zero hour they were disseminating a talk by Mrs. Somebody on "How to Make the Most of Tinned Foods: Some Useful Recipes". . . .

11.15 a.m.

I am speaking to you from the Cabinet Room at 10

Downing Street. This morning the British Ambassador in Berlin handed the German Government a final note stating that, unless we heard from them by eleven o'clock that they were prepared at once to withdraw their troops from Poland, a state of war would exist between us. I have to tell you now that no such undertaking has been received, and that consequently this country is at war with Germany.

You can imagine what a bitter blow it is to me that all my long struggle to win peace has failed. Yet I cannot believe that there is anything more or anything different that I could have done and that would have been more successful.

Up to the very last it would have been quite possible to have arranged a peaceful and honourable settlement between Germany and Poland, but Hitler would not have it. He had evidently made up his mind to attack Poland whatever happened, and although he now says he put forward reasonable proposals which were rejected by the Poles, that is not a true statement.

The proposals were never shown to the Poles, nor to us, and, though they were announced in a German broadcast on Thursday night, Hitler did not wait to hear comments on them, but ordered his troops to cross the Polish frontier. His action shows convincingly that there is no chance of expecting that this man will ever give up his practice of using force to gain his will. He can only be stopped by force.

We and France are to-day, in fulfilment of our obligation, going to the aid of Poland, who is so bravely resisting this wicked and unprovoked attack on her people. We have a clear conscience. We have done all that any country could do to establish peace. The situation in which no word given by Germany's ruler could be trusted, and no people or country would feel themselves safe, has become intolerable. And now that we have resolved to finish it, I know that you will all play your part with calmness and courage.

At such a moment as this the assurances of support that

we have received from the Empire are a source of profound encouragement to us.

Now may God bless you all. May He defend the right. It is the evil things that we shall be fighting against—brute force, bad faith, injustice, oppression, and persecution—and against them I am certain that the right will prevail.

Neville Chamberlain

. . . . His voice was firm, with an undertone of great sadness, and at certain moments you could hear indignation deepening the timbre. Immediately afterwards came the general directions what to do in air-raids, etc. I locked up, gave Mrs. C. the key, and accepted a lift from our landlord to Westminister Cathedral where I was going to the twelve o'clock Mass.

And hardly had we set out when, doggone it, the sirens started warbling, and the whistles shrilling and the A.R.P. wardens patrolling the streets. We got past about a hundred doorways, and all the people indoors were coming out to see the war start, and standing around craning their necks at the sky as if that would help. Finally a warden pulled us over to the kerb and advised us to take cover, assuring us that it was a genuine warning with about ten minutes allowed for taking cover. Mr. P., whose *sang-froid* is immense, remained in his car, but I elected to duck for the nearest likely place, because I'd had time to think about trying to explain to you how I came to be near Victoria at all, and I felt slightly conscience-stricken. Anyway, I crossed the street to that block of L.C.C. flats which you'll remember on the left coming away from Victoria—council houses with archway entrances. The paved courtyard inside was filling with people of the flats, each with that small square cardboard box that everybody carries now—the effect of an enormous picnic with each one carrying his own sandwiches—and we were all sent down to the laundry, a nice cool long room lined with tubs and well sandbagged on the outside. There were about fifty of us, men and women. They were all, of course, very poor

and "common" people and they were all pretty well convinced that "that man", with his well-known instinct for
the dramatic, was about to put over a really convincing
reply to the Ultimatum. And they were as cool as cucum-
bers—just as gallantly matter-of-fact as you'd expect them
to be. One young girl was sniffling a bit, and her friends
were jollying her out of it. The men busied themselves in
shifting a pile of sandbags. There was no joking, no talk to
speak of; the only expression on their faces was one of
deep disapproval—the incredulous, "shocked" disapproval of a man who is serene enough in his own mind to
feel morally outraged without feeling flustered.

Beatrice L. Warde

Mobilization: Britain

The plan was this. In the event of the international situation deteriorating to such an extent that the Government felt it could not carry on without the backing of the
54th (County of London) H.A.A. Regiment, R.A. (and
perhaps some other units of the Territorial Army as well),
the summons would be passed down through channels of
ever-diminishing grandeur until it reached the permanent
staff at the drill hall, Putney; the permanent staff would
then ring up the keymen, and the keymen would ring up
the sub-keymen, whose duty it was to inform what I can
only call the sub-submen. The use of the word "inform"
rather than "ring up" is noteworthy here. For whereas all
sub-keymen were on the phone, such was by no means the
case with all sub-submen, so that to the sub-keyman fell
the responsible and arduous duty of getting out his car and
actually calling in person at the doors of those whose
names were inscribed on his folder. It will be seen that the
position of sub-keymen was one of great trust—though,
looking back, it is hard to resist the conclusion that
possession of a telephone *and* a car may have been more
of a recommendation for the post than a good bearing,
say, or steadiness on parade.

Despite, or in ignorance of, these arrangements, Hitler

continued his aggressive preparations against Poland, and on 24 August 1939 the call came. I wish I could say that I answered it with flashing eyes and a gesture of defiance. But when the sergeant rang me up at my office and told me to report at the drill hall without delay, my first feeling, as I remember it, was that this really was going a bit too far. Was this, I wonder, the instinctive reaction of others in A.A. units of the T.A.? We had recently got back from a month's "embodiment"—a fortnight on operational gun positions "just in case" and a fortnight at practice camp—and twenty-eight days in khaki seemed, in those far-off days, about as much as could reasonably be demanded of any private citizen. To be rung up with this peremptory order at 2:30 in the afternoon, in the sanctity of one's own office, was getting very near downright impertinence.

"Oh, but look here, Sergeant, this is getting beyond a joke. I mean, I've got my work to do, you know."

I don't claim that these were my actual words. It is possible that, on reflection, I may have substituted the shorter form, "Yes, Sergeant." But I know what I was thinking.

I remember laying down the receiver and looking slowly round the office. It seemed much the same. The sun still streamed through the window on the papers on my desk, the half-written letter, the note to ring up So-and-so at four, the memo about to-morrow's meeting. On the window-sill lay the brown-paper parcel containing the new pullover to which I had treated myself during the lunch hour. Across the street a man suspended in a cradle of ropes and planks was busily cleaning the windows of the building opposite. Everything was just as it had been two minutes ago; only now it had no significance. It was incredible that I should have been concerned, a few short moments ago, with the phrasing of a letter that seemed to belong to so remote a point in time, to have been written by so dim and irrecoverable a personality. This sense of being suddenly cut off from one's own past, and future, is the strongest recollection I have of this peculiar day.

On the way home to pick up my car and my gear the feeling of numbness evaporated and a certain excitement came over me. After all, I was a sub-keyman. My own moment of shock was over, and I was now to be the bringer of startling news to others—always a pleasurable occupation. "Get cracking, Gunner Bones," I should say. "It's war!" And Gunner Bones, remembering that his only pair of boots was at the cobbler's, would pale beneath his tan, while I stood calm and collected on his doorstep. These unworthy thoughts sustained me through most of the journey, save for a grim moment as my bus passed the ground of my club and I remembered that I was due to play tennis there that evening, with perhaps a swim to follow. Tennis! The Lord alone knew when my next game would be. . . .

My recollections of rounding up my sub-submen and driving to the drill hall are vague. But a few random pictures remain of the drill hall itself. I remember a scene of some confusion. I remember sitting on my kit-bag, with that sensation of slight sickness one used to get on the first day at school, wishing, quite simply and unheroically, that I was back home again, and I remember falling in in full marching order and then falling out again to get stripped to the waist for a medical inspection. I remember the M.O. asking whether I felt all right as I halted in front of him, and dismissing me with a kindly nod when I assured him that I felt fine, thank you. I also remember reflecting, as I struggled into my uniform again, that if my own doctor had got me stripped to the waist and then declined even to lay a stethoscope against my chest I should rapidly have taken my custom elsewhere. But this, of course, was war—or pretty near it.

Somebody was shouting my name. What now? Could it be that they had decided to get along without me? "Bit of a muddle. Didn't mean to trouble a busy man like you, sir. Get off home as soon as you like." However, it turned out to be not quite that. They told me the sergeant wanted me.

"Yes, Sergeant?"

"Ah, there you are. Is that stinking old red car outside yours?"

"The thirty-two-horse La Salle?"

"I don't care what it is. Is it yours?"

"Yes, Sergeant."

"Then say so. You're to take the Battery Commander down to the gun site."

"The Battery Commander? Crikey!"

"He's ready now."

"Yes, Sergeant."

There's glory for you. Just the Battery Commander and me—leading the van. They piled his kit in the dickey, somebody stuck an *Air Defence of Great Britain: Priority* label on the windscreen, and we were off.

This was, without question, my finest hour. Never again throughout the war did I feel so important—never again, to be truthful, did I feel important at all; but just at this moment I felt terrific.

1440433 Gunner Ellis, H. F.

Mobilization: New Zealand

We had a week before the men came in. The huts were barely finished, showers and ablution stands not completed; but the carpenters took their kits with them one evening and the drafts to form the 3rd Rifle Battalion, the Machine-gun Battalion, a Field-Ambulance, and an A.S.C. Company came in by special trains. Most were ending a long journey. All were in old civilian clothes and many were far from sober. As I watched some of my men trudge in I remarked to Gordon Washbourn, "This is going to be the best infantry in the world."

On the first night we did nothing more than give them their army numbers, feed them, and get them to bed; in beds, for the one and only time in their service, made up by the officers and the N.C.Os. All slept very well. Next day, with the aid of a big chart showing the establishment of a rifle battalion, we organized and allotted jobs.

The rifle companies were made up by their Provinces, but Headquarters Company was not so easy. Officers kept rushing into the Orderly Room, consulting the chart, and

dashing out to collect another driver or signaller or
water-cart man or range-finder or some such, those
already acquired being left seated in puzzled groups under
the strictest injunctions not to stray. Gradually the parade
ground emptied as the completed platoons were moved
away, some already being asked to do so in step; and
about midday there were only a few stragglers left who
collected and sat themselves down together. Frank Davis
and I checked our chart and discovered that we had omitted to provide for the anti-aircraft platoon, which had no
officer. There should have been fourteen in that platoon. I
went out and counted the survivors. There were fourteen,
so establishment was completed, though as a matter of
fact this was the only platoon up to strength. Several days
later I found three innocents sunning themselves behind
one of the huts and found that somehow they had been
missed altogether and were apparently quite happy about
it. They promptly became riflemen.

Three months later we embarked at Lyttleton in the
first transport to leave New Zealand for the war. In the
meantime the mob which had tramped in that afternoon
had become a battalion, very young, very partially trained,
but already possessing its own memories and beginning to
be proud.

Brigadier Howard Kippenberger

The Reason for Fighting

*From a broadcast prepared by George Bernard Shaw,
but banned by the Minister of Information.*
. . . . What am I, a superannuated non-combatant, encouraging young men to fight against? It is not German
National Socialism: I was a National Socialist before
Mr. Hitler was born. I hope we shall emulate and surpass
his great achievements in that direction. I have no prejudice against him personally: much that he has written
and spoken echoes what I myself have written and said.
He has adopted even my diet. I am interested in his career
as one of the great psychological curiosities of political

history; and I fully appreciate his physical and moral courage, his diplomatic sagacity, and his triumphant rescue of his country from the yoke the Allies imposed on her after her defeat in 1918. I am quite aware of the fact that his mind is a twentieth-century mind, and that our governing class is mentally in the reign of Edward III, six centuries out of date. I can pay him a dozen compliments which I could not honestly pay to any of our present rulers.

My quarrel with him is a very plain one. I happen to be what he calls a Nordic. In stature, in colour, in length of head, I am the perfect blond beast whom Mr. Hitler classes as the salt of the earth, divinely destined to rule over all lesser breeds. Trace me back as far as you can; and you will not find a Jew in my ancestry. But I have a friend who happens to be a Jew. His name is Albert Einstein: and he is a far greater human prodigy than Mr. Hitler and myself rolled into one. And the nobility of his character has made his gift an unmixed benefit to his fellow-creatures. Well, Adolf Hitler would compel me, the Nordic Shaw, to insult Albert Einstein; to claim moral superiority to him and unlimited power over him, drive him out of his house, exile him, be punished for miscegenation if I allow a relative of mine to marry a relative of his, and finally to kill him as part of a general duty to exterminate his race. Adolf has actually done these things to Albert, bar the killing, as he carelessly exiled him first and thus made the killing impossible. Since then he has extended the list of reprobates from Semites to Celts and from Poles to Slavs: in short, to all who are not what he calls Nordics. If he conquers these islands he will certainly add the Irish to the list, as several authorities have maintained that the Irish are the lost tribes of Israel.

Now this is not the sort of thing that sane men can afford to argue with. It is on the face of it pernicious nonsense; and the moment any ruler starts imposing it as a political philosophy on his nation or any other nation by physical force, there is nothing for it but for the sane men to muster their own physical forces and go for him. We ought to have declared war on Germany the moment his police stole Einstein's violin. When the work of a police force consists not of suppressing robbery with violence but actually committing it, it becomes a recruiting ground for the most infernal blackguards, of whom every country has its natural-born contingent. Unless such agents are very strictly disciplined and controlled, their heads are turned by the authority they possess as a State police; and they resort to physical torture as the easiest way to gratify their tastes and execute their function at the same time. How is that discipline and control to be maintained? Not by an autocrat, because, as Napoleon said when he heard of the defeat of his navy at Trafalgar, an autocrat cannot be everywhere. And when his police get out of hand and give his prisons and concentration camps a bad name, he has to back them up because he cannot do without them, and thus becomes their slave instead of their master.

George Bernard Shaw

GERMANY

War broke quietly and as if under a cloud. There were no frenzied people in the streets such as we had read about in 1914. No flags, no processions. No cheering and marching troops and flowers. The streets of Berlin seemed empty and there were no troops to be seen. There was only a particularly dull sense of waiting, which gradually faded, and then, with the finish of the "siege" of Poland, completely changed to a wild excitement.

Werner Harz, journalist

There was only one topic of conversation in the homes and cafés during those last days of August 1939, the Non-Aggression Treaty with Russia. It had come as a complete shock to all of us. Ever since the Reichstag fire in February 1933, Communism had been expelled from Ger-

man political life. Members of the Communist Party had
been bitterly pursued and put in prison. Russia was
declared the arch-enemy. In February 1933 we had been
told that Russia had prepared a revolution in Germany,
and had it not been for Hitler we would all have been
swallowed up in the Communist régime, and now, after six
years of hate campaign, the Press suddenly declared
unanimously that Russia had no wish to export her
ideology to Germany. Nor did Germany wish to export
National Socialism to Russia. The world, our Press said
firmly, was wide enough for both ideologies to flourish
side by side. . . . Our feelings now were a jumble of relief
and astonishment at the quick change. Towards Hitler we
had nothing but admiration and respect. A man who had
the courage to step over the abyss between Germany and
Russia to prevent war was a man worthy of the highest
praise.

Mr. Wolter told us all to read the writings of
Machiavelli. "Get a copy of Machiavelli's book *Il Prin-
cipe*," he told me. "Keep yourself up to date. Learn about
politics, my dear comrade-assistant. The key is 'no
morals'; forget the Salvation Army; be ruthless and have
no remorse. No price is too high for peace for your home-
country." He said all this in a stern voice with a half-
twinkle in his eye. Then he became gentler and added:
"You know, in the long run this ruthlessness may be best.
It's more merciful than a long 'decent, human' war, don't
you agree?"

I agreed.

"In time you will get used to seeing the flag with the
hammer and sickle flying in the Unter den Linden," said
Mr. Wolter ironically.

On 1 September, 1939, however, my personal views
changed. The radio and newspapers announced the attack
on Poland.

"You look like the Mater Dolorosa," Mr. Wolter said
to me that morning. "You want your sons to live, don't
you? Well, how can they live if Germany is to be cramped

up—*ein Volk onhe Raum* [a people without living room]? Twenty years after the Treaty of Versailles and we are still separated from our own people by the Polish Corridor! Danzig is a German town. If the Poles won't give it back to us voluntarily, then, all right, we march in and take it. . . .

"It's all trash when they accuse Germany of being responsible for the first World War, and say we must be punished. They talk of freedom to us, but where is freedom when a big town like Danzig can't come back into its Fatherland? Do you seriously think we would have got the Rhineland back if we hadn't marched into it?; or Austria?; or Czechoslovakia?; and our Army?; and our rivers; we weren't even masters of our own rivers till Hitler came! Now we have got our Army and no more foreign restrictions in our country." He looked at me with a certain pity. "But, of course, you women don't understand politics. You have to be hard and strong to grasp such things. Women have the brains of babies over politics. My wife is just the same."

Somehow I just had to answer back. "But up till now Hitler has done everything peacefully. I *do* admire his foresight and diplomacy, as long as it means peace. But this is war!"

Mr. Wolter commented, "No need to worry at all. You take my word for it, this war against Poland will be just a Blitzkrieg. It will be over in a flash."

                              Else Wendel, housewife

I regarded England's and France's interference and declaration of war as nothing else but a formality. There was no doubt that as soon as they realized the utter hopelessness of Polish resistance and the vast superiority of German arms they would begin to see that we had always been in the right and it was quite senseless to meddle in our private business. But of course we had to let these warmongers know that this was the last time that Germany would stand for any sort of foreign interference. It was only as a result of their guarantee of something that wasn't their business that the war had ever started. If Poland had been alone she would certainly have given in quietly.

Otherwise, we had no quarrel with France or England. Our West Wall was perfectly secure, and we never thought that we would have to invade these countries or fight them actively.

Fritz Muehlebach, Storm Trooper

AMERICA

The only interest here, as everywhere, is the war, and I believe that we really can keep out of it. Fortunately there is no great sentiment in this country for getting into it, although I think almost everyone wants to see England and France win.

Harry L. Hopkins, Presidential adviser, to his brother
Emory, October 1939

. . . . Americans in 1939 were fortified with the experience that the previous generation had conspicuously lacked, the experience of involvement in European war, and they wanted no more of it. The impulse to let "Europe stew in its own juice" was a very powerful one, and an entirely understandable one, for there were too many Americans who considered that their country's only reward for coming to the aid of Britain and France in 1918 was to be given the name of "Uncle Shylock". (As Roosevelt remarked many times, "We fortunately never had a chance to find out what our 'reward' would have been if Germany had won that war.") Thus isolationist sentiment in 1939 was not limited to Americans of German birth or descent, or to those who loved German music and admired German science and industry, or to those who were pure pacifists: it was representative of the entire American people save for a diminutive minority of those who believed that a victory for Hitler would put the security of our own country and our own constitutional democracy in deadly peril.

Harry L. Hopkins

INVASION

The ordering of general mobilization came almost on top of Britain's and France's guarantee of Poland; reservists were called up, vehicles and troops mobilized and ammunition distributed. We loaded our tanks and trucks on to the train and travelled for three days to Paprad in Slovakia, where we waited about ten miles from the Polish border. Several of us went up to the frontier to reconnoitre, and after the third day we got orders to move up during the night. At dawn we crossed into Poland.

The whole thing was so like an occupation or a manoeuvre that we could hardly believe this was really war; it all seemed too well-ordered and familiar. There was virtually no resistance, and for days on end we advanced towards the Polish Ukraine. There were rumours of sharpshooters and partisans, but I never saw or heard anything of them, except for the occasional sound of a shot in the distance. There was a certain amount of sporadic fighting when we got to the river barriers, but the Luftwaffe had already cleared the way for us. Their Stuka dive-bombers were deadly accurate, and as there was no opposition they had it all their own way. The roads and fields were swarming with unhappy peasants who had fled in panic from their villages when the bombing began, and we passed hundreds and hundreds of Polish troops walking dejectedly towards Slovakia. The Poles seemed to be completely apathetic, and there were so many prisoners that nobody bothered to guard them or even tell them where to go.

Lieutenant Barow Tassilo von Bogenhardt,
6th Motorized Regiment

On 5 September our corps had a surprise visit from Adolf Hitler. I met him near Plevno on the Tuchel-Schwetz road, got into his car and drove with him along the line of our previous advance. We passed the destroyed Polish artillery, went through Schwetz, and then, following closely behind our encircling troops, drove to Graudenz, where he stopped and gazed for some time at the blown bridges over the Vistula. At the sight of the smashed artillery regiment, Hitler had asked me, "Our dive-bombers did that?" When I replied, "No, our Panzers!" he was plainly astonished. Between Schwetz and Graudenz those elements of 3 Panzer Division not needed for the encirclement of the Poles were drawn up: these included the 6th Panzer Regiment and the 3rd Armoured Reconnaissance Battalion with my son Kurt. We drove back through parts of 23 and 2 (Motorized) Infantry Divisions. During the drive we discussed at first the course of events in my corps area. Hitler asked about casualties. I gave him the latest figures that I had received, some one hundred and fifty dead and seven hundred wounded for all the four divisions under my command during the Battle of the Corridor. He was amazed at the smallness of these figures and contrasted them with the casualties of his own old regiment, the List Regiment, during the first World War: on the first day of battle that one regiment alone had lost more than two thousand dead and wounded. I was able to show him that the smallness of our casualties in this battle against a tough and courageous enemy was primarily due to the effectiveness of our tanks. Tanks are a life-saving weapon. The men's belief in the superiority of their armoured equipment had been greatly strengthened by their successes in the Corridor. The enemy had suffered the total destruction of between two and three infantry divisions and one cavalry brigade. Thousands of prisoners and hundreds of guns had fallen into our hands.

General Heinz Guderian

Warsaw: The End

Upon the capitulation of the city on 29 September, we left the special trains for a few days and travelled to Warsaw by road. Our three-day stay in the capital made one of the deepest and most disturbing impressions on me of all my war experiences. I was shocked at what had become of the beautiful city I had known—ruined and burnt-out houses, starving and grieving people. The nights were already unpleasantly chilly and a pall of dust and smoke hung over the city, and everywhere there was the sweetish smell of burnt flesh. There was no running water anywhere. In one or two streets isolated resistance by Polish nationalist bands was being continued. Elsewhere everything was quiet. Warsaw was a dead city.

                                            Walter Schellenberg

When signing the instrument of capitulation, the Polish general said: "A wheel always turns." He was to prove right in the end, though hardly—as far as the subsequent fate of his fatherland was concerned—in the sense his words had been meant to convey.

                                    General Erich von Manstein

THE SOLDIER'S CATECHISM

If it moves, salute it.
If it doesn't move, pick it up.
If you can't pick it up, paint it.

2

PHONEY WAR AND WINTER WAR

For six months after the conquest of Poland, land and air warfare in Europe virtually came to a standstill, with the exception of Russia's campaign against Finland. An uneasy truce prevailed on the Western Front, where the French and the British Expeditionary Force, despatched to France a week after war broke out, faced the Germans, each side sitting behind its fixed fortifications.

PHONEY WAR

The Birth of a Catch-phrase

FOR some reason which still seems inexplicable public imagination in this country* had been captured by the phrase employed by Senator Borah when he referred to the European war as a "phoney" war. It was true that after the devastation of Poland the Germans had refrained from undertaking any air offensive against the Western powers. Nor had the German armies as yet made any move to invade the Low Countries or to break through the Maginot Line. But even to the most casual observer familiar with the working of Hitler's mind it was obvious that Hitler was waiting for two developments. First, he hoped that Germany's overwhelming superiority in the air and in mechanized equipment, as evidenced in the invasion of Poland, would persuade Great Britain and France that

* The United States (Ed.)

39

a negotiated peace granting Germany, as a first step, hegemony over Europe would be preferable to the probability of annihilation and occupation. Second, should this hope fail, he knew that the winter months would give his propaganda and subversive agencies much valuable time in which to break down the morale of the French armies. In this manner he would improve his chances for a military pushover as soon as the approach of summer made weather conditions more propitious for an all-out offensive.

Why any considerable segment of public opinion in the United States should have regarded the war as a "phoney" war in view of constantly accumulating evidence of Hitler's military strength, and in view of the ruin which Poland had already suffered, must always remain a mystery. Moreover, many people appeared to feel, like Senator Borah, that the failure of Great Britain and France to undertake the offensive was somehow reprehensible. This feeling was almost sadistic. It had in it something of the "boos" howled out by the spectators at a prize-ring when the two contestants are not putting on as bloody an exhibition as they have paid to witness.

                Sumner Welles, U.S. Under-Secretary of State

Britain: Comment

In a Blackpool pub:
    "Nothing doing yet."
    "Looks like another bloody hundred years' war."
    "Rummest bloody war I ever knew."
    "Fighting with bloody pamphlets."
    "Strikes me they've both got the wind up."
    "It's a war of nerves."
    "Nerves my arse. It's boring me bloody well stiff. No football neither."
From Cardiff:
    "It's hard to believe there's a war on at all."
    "I shan't be happy until I see a really satisfactory casualty list."

"Why don't they start something?"

"A couple of real air raids is what we want."

From Harrow:

"This is a funny war; wish they would do something."

"It's another trick of Hitler's. He thinks we shall get so bored with doing nothing that we shall start bombing, and then he can say we began it."

"It's just another way of waging a war of nerves."

Black-out

A woman: "There's no need for all this darkness."

Another: "It's the same as everything they do—daft. They started rationing coal, and now they can't get shot of it, and they're asking you to buy as much as you can. Same with fish, and butter, and bacon; I don't know what things are coming to."

Pub manageress:

"Wasn't Tuesday an awful night? I couldn't see a thing because the rain got on my glasses, and what with the black-out I walked into the sandbags under the clock, just by there. It hurt my leg, and it isn't better yet. That's a week ago, and I haven't been out since. It makes you frightened to go out, doesn't it, in case you get hurt again?"

Other women who are frightened:

"I'm all alone, with no one beside me, and it's terrible if they black-out before anyone comes back."

"This black-out is simply cruel. I daren't go to chip shop of a night, and t'boss does like chips for his supper."

"This darkness gets on my nerves. I don't know what to do with myself of an evening, when my husband is out. I can't go out anywhere unless he comes to fetch me. I wouldn't dare to come home alone in the dark—why, I'd never find my way."

"I'm afraid of being molested. One of our girls was, going home from work last night."

"It's all right for you; you're married. But I can't go out any more at night. I'm disgusted with this black-out."

An insurance manager in Blackpool, married, forty:

"Had a nice night last night. Tommy bloody Handley on the wireless again; read every book in the house. Too dark to walk to the library, bus every forty-five minutes, next one too late for the pictures. 'Freedom is in peril'—they're telling me!"

South Croydon porter:

"I fell off the platform the other night. Clean over the edge I fell. Thought I had turned far enough left and I hadn't. Mind you, there was a fog at the time."

A bus conductor in Macclesfield:

"The number of times I been fooled wi' coins since black-out. . . . Last week I paid up four and sixpence from me wages."

Amateur Inventors

Backroom scientists of a research group under the War Ministry consider suggestions for new weapons.

"Come on," I said. "Keystone Komics. Let's get going."

They came and sat at my table and Joe produced the Keystone Komics file. The Komics were bright ideas which had been sent in to Mair. Joe and Tilly and I used to run through the week's bag every Wednesday.

Some of them were sent in by departments who'd received them and wanted Mair's view or wanted to be rid of them. But the others were from all over the place. The thing which always puzzled me was how these people got to know the address.

Joe opened the file and took out the first one.

"Poisoned barbed wire," he said. "You scratch yourself on it and die in agony two hours later. Any bidders?"

"What's the poison?" I said. "Curare?"

"Oh, he doesn't go into *that*," said Joe. "He says he isn't a scientist himself. He just has ideas."

"If I had ideas like that I'd see a doctor," I said. "Out."

Joe put the letter aside and picked up the next.

" 'Specification of the Barnes Retractable Bayonet. The

bayonet is carried in a housing in the forepiece of the rifle. When the bayonet is required, a button is depressed and the bayonet is forced forward into the "Ready" position by a strong spring, and locks itself rigidly. After use it can be pressed back into the housed position where it is retained by a catch.' "

I said, "I like 'after use'. Nice phrase."

Tilly said, "It's not a bad idea, though. Saves carrying the bayonet separately or having it sticking out all the time."

" 'An experimental model, fitted to a sporting rifle, works perfectly'," Joe read. " 'The device costs very little.' He's sent a drawing of it."

We looked at it. It was quite a workmanlike drawing.

"I think it's a darned good idea," said Tilly. He was always a perfect customer for the Komics.

"Hardly that," I said. "If it works and doesn't jam or break or mind being buried in mud or anything like that, it might have been a good idea before the war. That's about the size of it."

"Why?"

"Well, damn it, we can't start re-equipping the whole army with joke bayonets. Anyhow, if the poor devil but knew it, what's really wanted is a bayonet that will open a bully beef tin without cutting you. Send him a nice note though, Joe."

"Sure," said Joe, "and a free entry form for next week's competition. *A bas* the Barnes Bayonet." He pulled out a big blueprint. "The next's a radio thing which Williams has sent across. Leave that to the Old Man?"

"Yes. He wants to see all the radio. What is it?"

"Search me," said Joe. "I'm not a radio man myself. I saw something about the Heaviside Layer and decided it was out of my class. Now *this* is much more my sort of thing: 'Dear Sirs, I have always been interested in birds. . . .' " He stopped and laughed a lot. "Can you beat it?"

"Funny joke," I said. "What's he invented?"

" 'It occurs to me,' " read Joe, " 'that migrating birds are one of the few agencies which can enter enemy occupied territory without arousing suspicion.' "

"Oh God!" I said. "Which does he want them to take? Little bombs round their necks or bacteria?"

Joe looked on down the page. "You've got it," he said, looking up. "Or nearly. Plant diseases. Out, I take it?"

"Yes. Y'know it's amazing what *dirty* ideas people get. That using animals one is a hardy annual, and it always gets me. There was the chap who trained dogs and wanted to teach them to take explosive booby traps across to the enemy."

Nigel Balchin

The Venlo Incident

In the late autumn of 1939, Holland was still a neutral country. Captain Payne Best, a British intelligence officer stationed there, was trying to make contact with a mysterious German "general" who was said to be at the head of an underground resistance movement in Germany aimed at displacing Hitler and coming to terms with the Allies. Captain Best had several abortive clandestine meetings just over the frontier in Holland with German officers who claimed to represent the "general". In fact these officers were loyal, and were party to a plan to kidnap Captain Best and his associates and carry them off to Germany. On 9 November, Captain Best, Major Stevens and Lieutenant Klop of the Dutch Army were again due to meet the German officers near Venlo, a Dutch frontier town. Owing to the prevailing quiet, the events which followed created a great uproar.

All the way down from The Hague we had noticed that military precautions had been intensified and we had been held up at every road block and tank barrier. Even now, between Venlo and our café, we were stopped twice. The first time the sentry said something about having orders to allow no cars to pass, and although Klop showed him his authority, insisted that he must first go to the guard-room and speak to the N.C.O. in charge. Both Stevens and I, I believe, felt alike and hoped that he would come back with the news that we could go no farther; but in a few minutes he was with us: "Everything is all right. The N.C.O. had a message for me which had been phoned through from the office. Carry on."

The second sentry did not actually stop us, but only made signs that we should drive slowly. He was stationed at a bend in the road just before we entered the straight along which one had a view of the frontier. Somehow or other, it seemed to me that things looked different from what they had on the previous days. Then I noticed that the German barrier across the road which had always been closed was now lifted; there seemed to be nothing between us and the enemy. My feeling of impending danger was very strong. Yet the scene was peaceful enough. No one was in sight except a German customs officer in uniform lounging along the road towards us and a little girl who was playing at ball with a big black dog in the middle of the road before the café.

I must have rather checked my speed, for Klop called out, "Go ahead, everything is quite all right." I felt rather a fool to be so nervous. I let the car drift slowly along to the front of the café on my left and then reversed into the car park on the side of the building farthest from the frontier. Schaemmel was standing on the veranda at the corner and made a sign which I took to mean that our bird was inside. I stopped the engine and Stevens got out on the right. My car had left-hand drive. I had just wriggled clear of the wheel and was following him out when there was a sudden noise of shouting and shooting. I looked up, and through the windscreen saw a large open car drive up round the corner till our bumpers were touching. It seemed to be packed to overflowing with rough-looking men. Two were perched on top of the hood and were firing over our heads from sub-machine guns; others were standing up in the car and on the running-board, all shouting and waving pistols. Four men jumped off almost before their car had stopped and rushed towards us shouting: "Hands up!"

I don't remember actually getting out of the car, but by the time the men reached us I was certainly standing next to Stevens, on his left. I heard him say, "Our number is up, Best." The last words we were to exchange for over five years. Then we were seized. Two men pointed their guns at our heads, the other two quickly handcuffed us.

I heard shots behind me on my right. I looked round and saw Klop. He must have crept out behind us under cover of the car door which had. been left open. He was running diagonally away from us towards the road; running sideways in big bounds, firing at our captors as he ran. He looked graceful with both arms outstretched —almost like a ballet dancer. I saw the windscreen of the German car splinter into a star, and then the four men standing in front of us started shooting, and after a few more steps Klop just seemed to crumple and collapse into a dark heap of clothes on the grass.

"Now, march!" shouted our captors, and prodding us in the small of our backs with their guns, they hurried us, with cries of "Hup! Hup! Hup!" along the road towards the frontier. As we passed the front of the café I saw my poor Jan held by the arms by two men who were frog-marching him along. It seemed to me that his chin was reddened as from a blow. Then we were across the border. The black and white barrier closed behind us. We were in Nazi Germany.

Captain S. Payne Best

WINTER WAR

Russia invaded Finland at the end of November in order to occupy territories considered strategically necessary for her security. Such a move could only be directed against Germany, yet so unpopular was Russia and so unprovoked her aggression that Allied sympathy for the Finns resulted in preparations to send them active help. Such help was also being given, less openly, by the Ger-

mans. This extraordinary state of affairs was concluded by the signing of peace between Russia and Finland in March 1940.

An Analysis of the Russian Failure

If the general impression of the performance of the Soviet Union in the Finnish War had not been so unfavourable, Germany would hardly have under-estimated the war potential of the Russian giant to the extent she did.

On what was this view of the Red Army, produced by the Winter War, based?

The most striking factor was no doubt the disproportion between the enormous effort and the small result achieved. Even in the first week of the war, unexpectedly large forces were thrown against Finland. . . . About half of the regular Russian divisions in Europe and Western Siberia had been mobilized for the Finnish War. Including the specialist formations, the enemy's strength amounted to nearly a million men, of whom part possessed a certain experience of war from the Polish campaign.

It was a characteristic mistake of the Red High Command to start military operations without paying necessary attention to the basic factors in the war against Finland, the character of the theatre of war and the strength of the enemy. It is understandable that the latter was under-estimated because of our obvious material weakness. It is more remarkable that the Russian High Command did not realize that its army organization was too cumbersome in northern country and winter conditions. How could troops coming from plains, even if they were accustomed to severe winters, be expected to fight in a barren wilderness the like of which they had never seen? The failure to estimate our powers of resistance shows the lack of foresight with which their plan of war had been drawn up, and also the blind faith of the Russians in the unlimited possibilities of modern technique.

That every order must first be approved by the political

leaders necessarily led to delay and confusion, not to
speak of a lessening of initiative and fear of responsibility.
The political commissars were undoubtedly a driving force
to be reckoned with. This became apparent in the first
phase of the war when they had to restore order in detach-
ments whose discipline had suffered through unsuccessful
attacks, and also when it was a question of forcing unwilling troops to attack. The fact that surrounded units
refused to surrender in spite of cold and hunger was
largely due to the political commissars. Soldiers were prevented from surrendering by threats of reprisals against
their families and the assurance that they would be killed
after torture if they fell into the hands of the enemy. There
were innumerable cases where officers as well as men preferred suicide to surrender.

The Russian officers were generally brave men who
were little concerned about casualties, but in the higher
ranks there were signs of a kind of inertia. This displayed
itself in the formalism and simplicity of the operative plan,
which excluded manoeuvring and was obstinately pursued
to victory or defeat. The Russians based their art of war
on weight of material, and were clumsy, ruthless and ex-
travagant. There was a striking absence of creative
imagination where the fluctuations of the situation demanded quick decisions. The commanders were often
unable to follow up initial successes.

The Russian infantryman showed himself brave, tough
and frugal, but lacking in initiative. Contrary to his Finnish adversary, he was a mass fighter who was incapable
of independent action when out of contact with his officers or comrades. Especially in the beginning, the Russians for this reason went in principally for mass attack,
which often resulted in the attackers being mown down to
the last man by a few well-placed automatic weapons. In
spite of this, one attacking wave after another would
follow, with a similar result. It happened in the initial
fighting in December that the Russians would advance in
close formation, singing, and even hand in hand, against
the Finnish minefields, apparently indifferent to the explo-

sions and the accurate fire of the defenders. The fatalistic submission which characterized the infantry was astonishing. The Russian soldier was not very susceptible to outward impressions and in every situation quickly regained his composure. Even if political terror played its part, the real explanation is to be found in the Russian people's hard struggle against nature, which in the course of ages had created a capacity for suffering and deprivation, a passive courage, and a fatalism incomprehensible to Europeans, and which has had, and continues to have, an important part in political development.

In this connection, the Russians' phenomenal ability to dig themselves in deserves special mention. It seemed second nature with them, and they were masters of engineering. In spite of long military service, the Russian infantry showed a number of defects. Their musketry with automatic arms and rifles was very poor. Though many of the divisions against us came from wooded country, the troops were unable to manoeuvre successfully and fight in forests. As they lacked compasses, even orientation presented difficulties, and the forests, the ally of the Finnish fighter, filled them with terror. Here the "White Death" (*Bielaja Smert*), the Finnish commando in his winter garb, harried them. But the greatest weakness of the troops was their lack of familiarity with skis. Even though they started systematic training of their troops immediately after the outbreak of the war, this meant little, because the technique of ski-ing, especially as practised in war, cannot be mastered in a few weeks.

In the Tsarist army the artillery had, from a technical as well as from a tactical point of view, been regarded as an *élite* arm. Now its level had naturally sunk because of the lack of education of the Officer Corps. But the material had kept up well to modern development. This was illustrated by the astonishingly great mass of modern artillery of great rapidity of fire and range as well as by the apparently inexhaustible stocks of ammunition.

In spite of tactical deficiencies, it was the enormous mass of artillery which formed the base of the Russians' activity on the Isthmus, but their artillery, such as it was, was not capable of meeting the demands of a war of movement.

There can be no question but that their armour was a disappointment to them. Already, the country in Finland made the dense and deep advances favoured by Russian tactics impossible. Instead, they had to work with smaller numbers attached to the infantry, and at what price? The total of tanks captured or destroyed by us was one thousand six hundred, which amounted to half of those opposed to us. In other words, a quarter of the Red Army's modern armour, not to mention the loss of three to four thousand politically picked and technically trained specialists. It should be mentioned, however, that the cooperation of armour with infantry improved considerably in the latter phase of the war. Their twenty-eight- and forty-five-ton tanks, armed with two guns and four or five machine-guns, contributed decisively to their penetration of our lines.

In spite of their crushing superiority—they had about two thousand five hundred planes—Russian air power was not to prove a factor of decisive importance. Its activity against ground troops was, especially in the beginning of the war, hesitant, and it was not able to break the defensive spirit of the nation. Total air war was in our country met by a calm and intelligent population whom danger merely steeled and united more strongly. The destruction was nevertheless considerable, for about a hundred and fifty thousand explosive and incendiary bombs were dropped with a total weight of seven thousand five hundred tons. Seven hundred civilians were killed and twice that number injured.

The Russians failed completely in their strategic task of severing our channels with the outside world and in producing chaos in our communications. Shipping traffic had been concentrated in Turku, which was subjected to sixty air attacks without becoming paralyzed. It is difficult to understand why the Russians had not for this purpose based light naval forces in Baltic ports, but the explanation may be that they had from the beginning counted on a lightning victory. Our only railway connection with the outside world was the line Kemi-Tornio, which carried most of our exports as well as our imports of war material. This line remained intact until the end of the war.

That their effort in the air did not produce corresponding results is unquestionable, and what did it cost them? According to figures from General Headquarters, 684 planes were shot down, but a later examination of war reports show that the actual number was 725. If one includes the "unconfirmed" cases, the figure rises to 975.

The Finnish Air Force at the outbreak of war possessed ninety-six machines, a large part of which were antiquated. The total number of our planes during the whole of the war numbered 287, of which 162 were fighters. Our losses amounted to sixty-one, corresponding to 21 per cent of the total.

In men, our losses were 24,923 killed, missing and died from wounds, and 43,557 wounded.

It is unlikely that the exact Russian losses will ever be revealed, but they can at least be estimated in the light of known facts as approximately two hundred thousand killed.

Two causes contributed to these heavy losses, and should be especially noted—i.e. the severe winter and the deficiencies in the medical service. The continuous cold caused the death of thousands of wounded while awaiting succour.

There is no doubt that the experiences of the Finnish campaign were made full use of by Marshal Timoshenko in his reorganization of the Red Army. In his own words, to our Military Attaché in Moscow, "The Russians have learnt much in this hard war in which the Finns fought with heroism."

Marshal Mannerheim

ALL QUIET ...

The Siegfried Line

Even before the end of the Polish Campaign, III Corps·
was transferred to the west, and at the beginning of October we arrived in the sector north of Trier. My elder
brother was serving as a platoon commander in a reserve
division near Saarbrücken, and I was able to visit him.
This gave me an opportunity of inspecting the famous
West Wall, or Siegfried Line, at first hand.

I soon realized what a gamble the Polish campaign had
been, and the grave risks which were run by our High
Command. The second-class troops holding the Wall were
badly equipped and inadequately trained, and the defences
were far from being the impregnable fortifications pictured by our propaganda. Concrete protection of more
than three feet was rare, and as a whole the positions were
by no means proof against heavy-calibre shelling. Few of
the strong points were sited to fire in enfilade and most of
them could have been shot to pieces by direct fire, without
the slightest risk to the attackers. The West Wall had been
built in such a hurry that many of the positions were sited
on forward slopes. The anti-tank obstacles were of trivial
significance, and the more I looked at the defences the less
I could understand the completely passive attitude of the
French.

Apart from sending some local patrols into the outlying
areas (very "out-lying") of Saarbrücken, the French had
kept very quiet and left the West Wall alone. This negative
attitude was bound to affect the fighting morale of their
troops, and was calculated to do much more harm than
our propaganda, effective though it was.

General von Mellenthin

Boxing Day

The B.E.F. has had two Christmases—one white, one green. On the Maginot Line, sharp frost created rime on the woods and grass so thick that it resembled a fall of snow. A dense mist has at times shrouded their positions so that you could not see much more than forty or fifty yards ahead. Christmas morning was quiet. The sound of folk-songs drifted over from the German lines. But the truce, if truce there was, was probably more accidental than purposeful. Little activity beyond patrols and intermittent gunfire, which lasts only a few minutes, as a rule, has marked the festive season.

The bulk of the B.E.F. has had a different Christmas. In our other positions on the Belgian frontier frost suddenly changed to a wet mist, and Christmas Day and today saw rain falling. French children romped round British Christmas trees, colonels presented toys, and thousands of French youngsters will not forget the first Christmas of this war, nor their parents either, nor we.

J. L. Hodson, British war correspondent

Montgomery in France

My own divisional area was south of Lille. My operational task was to work on defences which were being undertaken in order to prolong the Maginot Line behind the Belgian frontier. Until 10 May Belgium was a strictly neutral country. Apart from the defensive tasks, I concentrated on training the division for the active operations which I was certain must come. My soul revolted at what was happening. France and Britain stood still while Germany swallowed Poland; we stood still while the German armies moved over to the West, obviously to attack *us* later on; we waited patiently to be attacked; and during all this time we occasionally bombed Germany *with leaflets*. If this was war, I did not understand it.

I well remember the visit of Neville Chamberlain to my

division; it was on 16 December 1939. He took me aside
after lunch and said in a low tone so that no one could
hear, "I don't think the Germans have any intention of attacking us. Do you?"

I made it quite clear that in my view the attack would
come at the time of their own choosing; it was now winter
and we must get ready for trouble to begin when the cold
weather was over.

3 Division certainly put that first winter to good use
and trained hard. If the Belgians were attacked, we were
to move forward and occupy a sector astride Louvain
behind the River Dyle. I trained the division for this task
over a similar distance moving westwards, i.e. backwards
into France. We became expert at a long night move, and
then occupying a defensive position in the dark, and by
dawn being fully deployed and in all respects ready to
receive attack. This is what I felt we might have to do; and
it was.

. . . . During the winter G.H.Q. arranged for divisions to
send infantry brigades in turn down to the active front in
the Saar, holding positions in front of the Maginot Line in
contact with the German positions in the Siegfried Line. I
went down there in January 1940 to visit one of my
brigades and spent a few days having a look round. That
was my first experience in the war of the French Army in
action; I was seriously alarmed, and on my return I went
to see my Corps Commander, and told him of my fears
about the French Army and what we might have to expect
from that quarter in the future. Brooke had been down
there himself and had formed the same opinion.

The popular cries in the Maginot Line were: *Ils ne
passeront pas* and *On les aura*.

But the general attitude did not give me any confidence
that either of these two things would happen. Brooke and
I agreed not to talk about it to our subordinates; I believe
he discussed the matter with Gort.

I got into serious trouble during that first winter of the
war. It happened in this way. After a few months in
France the incidence of venereal disease in 3 Division

gave me cause for alarm. To stop it I enlisted the aid of the doctors and even the padres; but all efforts were unsuccessful and the figures increased. Finally I decided to write a confidential letter to all subordinate commanders in which I analysed the problem very frankly and gave my ideas about how to solve it. Unfortunately a copy of the letter got into the hands of the senior chaplains at G.H.Q., and the Commander-in-Chief (Gort) was told of my action. My views on how to tackle the problem were not considered right and proper and there was the father-and-mother of a row. They were all after my blood at G.H.Q. But my Corps Commander (Brooke) saved me by insisting on being allowed to handle the matter himself. This he did in no uncertain manner and I received from him a proper backhander. He said, amongst other things, that he didn't think much of my literary effort. Anyhow it achieved what I wanted, since the venereal disease ceased.

General Montgomery

Live and Let Live

"Live and let live" was still the policy in the Saar, and anybody who loosed off a rifle was thought to be thoroughly anti-social. Twenty years of peace-time training made one hesitate to take life; and there was a marked reluctance among the Jocks to raise one's rifle to one's shoulder and have a shot at an unprovocative German. Twice in April the Germans went through the motions of an attack, and the second time overran some French posts on our flank; this was considered to be extremely bad form, and not to be imitated.

Bernard Fergusson

Leaflet Raids

In the earliest stages of the war we were not allowed to bomb anything on land, and our only possible targets were therefore warships, which we could attack only by day. Our losses from enemy fighters and flak were prohibitive and we therefore desisted before we had done ourselves or the enemy much harm. Meanwhile the Whitleys and Wellingtons were put to the questionable employment of dropping pamphlets all over Europe, a game in which we never had the slightest faith. My personal view is that the only thing achieved was largely to supply the Continent's requirements of toilet paper for the five long years of war. You have only to think what any man of sense would do with an obviously enemy pamphlet when he picked it up, how he would regard it, and how he would react to the statements in it. Our reaction to enemy pamphleteering had always been to jeer and at the most to keep some of their leaflets as souvenirs. News to occupied territory was another matter.

Years before, the idiotic expansion of secret files at the Air Ministry once drove me to send a minute round pointing out that at the rate we were going we should be making newspapers secret next. But never did I think to see the day when not only were newspapers made secret, but moreover newspapers expressly produced for the sole purpose of being delivered as rapidly as possible and by any and every means to the enemy. Yet they still had to be handled under all the complicated secret document procedure on our bomber stations and, in spite of repeated applications, we could never get these instructions withdrawn. Many of these pamphlets were patently so idiotic and childish that it was perhaps just as well to keep them from the knowledge of the British public, even if we did risk and waste crews and aircraft in dropping them on the enemy.

Air Vice-Marhsal Arthur Harris

First Air Raid: Paris 1940

At dawn the siren sounded. By the second wail we were up and dressing, so quickly does one's mind readjust to past experience. In the lobby the night *concierge* was stretching and rubbing his eyes. We went out into the street. Chimney pots and the trees of the Champs Elysées black against a grey sky. The crackle of anti-aircraft guns. People in doorways and on the pavement. Men in dressing-gowns and slippers, smoking cigarettes. Women in every stage of dress and undress, some of them exercising lap dogs. Bored little girls in curl papers.

Someone said: "There they are", and pointed directly overhead. Eyes turned upward and voices hushed. In the silence the drone of engines plainly audible. Then, we saw them. Five dark birds flying close formation. Clusters of air bursts, pink in the morning sun, surrounded them. A prayer that at least one burst might find its target, but with slow, deliberate progress the marauders passed safely out of sight. A little later the all-clear sounded.

Colonel Charles Codman, U.S. Army

In February 1940, Mr. Sumner Welles, U.S. Under-Secretary of State, was sent by President Roosevelt on a fact-finding tour of the belligerent nations of Europe.

Mussolini: February 1940

My first impression was one of profound astonishment at Mussolini's appearance. In the countless times I had seen him in photographs and in motion pictures and in the many descriptions I had read of him I had always gained the impression of an active, quick-moving, exceedingly animated personality. The man I saw before me seemed fifteen years older than his actual age of fifty-six. He was ponderous and static rather than vital. He moved with an elephantine motion; every step appeared an effort. He was heavy for his height, and his face in repose fell in rolls of flesh. His close-cropped hair was snow-white. During our long and rapid interchange of views he kept his eyes shut a considerable part of the time. He opened them with his dynamic and often-described wide stare only when he desired particularly to underline some remark. At his side was a large cup of some hot brew which he sipped from time to time.

Mussolini impressed me as a man labouring under a

tremendous strain. One could almost sense a leaden oppression.

Impressions of Germany: March 1940

When our interview was over Goering insisted upon showing me the vast and innumerable rooms of his palace. It would be difficult to find an uglier building or one more intrinsically vulgar in its ostentatious display. The walls of the reception rooms and of the halls were hung with hundreds of paintings. Many examples of the best Italian and old German masters were placed side by side with daubs by modern German painters. He had made a speciality of collecting Cranachs. Two of them I recognized as being from the collection in the Alte Pinakothek in Munich.

In the entrance hall, lined like the first reception room with glass vitrines, there were displayed gifts presented to the Marshal by foreign governments. In this collection were shown a large number of objects recently given to him by the Government of Japan. Goering told me that he had personally arranged the placing of every object in the house.

In March the twilight sets in early in North Germany. It was already getting dark as we came out through the entrance gate of Goering's preserve. I had ample time for meditation on the long drive back to Berlin.

Various things had become fully clear. The key to the question whether Hitlerism was going to dominate Europe, and possibly succeed in dominating the rest of the world, was to be found in Berlin and nowhere else. It was far more evident than I had previously realized that Mussolini's influence, if it had ever possessed even some slight weight, had vanished. It had all along been more than obvious that both the British and French Governments had kept on appeasing until, if they were to retain even a semblance of independence, they could appease no longer. But never before in the history of Europe had the Western powers fought a more wholly defensive war than that in which they were now engaged. The allegations of

Hitler, Ribbentrop and Goering that the Western powers wanted the war might have had some deceptive effect in 1914. They were farcical in 1939.

There was only one power on earth which could give Hitler and his associates pause. That would be their conviction that, in a war of devastation forced upon Europe by Germany, the United States, in its own interest, would come to the support of the Western democracies. Equally clearly, however, there was at that moment not the remotest chance that our Government could tell the Nazi Government that this would prove to be the case. The great majority of the American people were altogether confident that they could keep out of the war. No executive in Washington with any sense of his responsibility to the American electorate, or with any regard for his constitutional limitations, could assume the authority for bluntly informing the Government of the Third Reich that the United States would support Great Britain and France should Germany persist in her policy of world conquest. And yet it was only that threat which would have the remotest chance of averting the greatest calamity that the modern world had known.

As we drove through the dreary Berlin suburbs, night was just settling down. Long queues were patiently standing in the streets, as they had been when I had earlier passed through, waiting to obtain provisions or to enter a motion-picture theatre. It struck me that the temper of the Berlin people had radically changed during the years since I had last been there. Even in the inflation days and in the days of desperate poverty of my last visits the crowds in the streets had seemed good-natured. One saw smiling faces. Through the miles of Berlin streets that I traversed on this final visit I never saw one smiling face.

Hitler: 1940

He said: "I am fully aware that the Allied powers believe a distinction can be made between National Socialism and the German people. There was never a greater mistake. The German people to-day are united as one man and I have the support of every German. I can see no hope for the establishment of any lasting peace until the will of England and France to destroy Germany is itself destroyed. I feel that there is no way by which the will to destroy Germany can itself be destroyed except through a complete German victory. I believe that German might is such as to make the triumph of Germany inevitable, but, if not, we will all go down together." And here he added the extraordinary phrase, "Whether that be for better or for worse."

He paused a moment and then said textually, rapidly, and in high and raucous pitch, "I did not want this war. It has been forced upon me against my will. It is a waste of my time. My life should have been spent in constructing and not in destroying."

Sumner Welles

3

THE WAR AT SEA,

1939-1940

The war at sea began on the same day as the war itself with the sinking of the liner Athenia *by a U-boat. There was never any "phoney" war for the men at sea. German submarines and aircraft immediately began to attack Allied and then neutral merchant vessels, though the main German effort was still to come, in 1941–43.*

At this early stage, combats involving heavy warships were the most prominent, largely because the Germans at once sent their pocket battleships to sea as commerce raiders. The Graf Spee *was the most successful of these.*

THE SINKING OF THE *ROYAL OAK:* SCAPA FLOW, OCTOBER 1939

IN September 1939 one of the "canoes"* operating east of the Orkneys found herself off the Pentland Firth, the passage between Scotland and the Orkneys. A strong westerly current caught the boat and swept her through the turbulent narrows. Finding that his engines were not powerful enough to pull him free, the captain, making a virtue out of necessity, carefully surveyed the movement of ships and the defences in the area. On his return he made a detailed report to Doenitz, who at once saw the

* U-boats (Ed.)

possibilities of a special operation. After much deliberation he ordered one of his best young officers, Lieutenant Gunther Prien, to report on board the depot-ship *Weichsel* at Kiel.

As Prien entered the Commodore's cabin he found Doenitz in conference with his own flotilla-commander and Lieutenant Wellner, the captain of the "canoe". Charts lay spread on the table before them and Prien's eye was immediately caught by the words "Scapa Flow". The Commodore addressed him.

"Do you think that a determined C.O. could take his boat into Scapa Flow and attack the ships there? Don't answer now, but let me have your reply by Tuesday. The decision rests entirely with you, and without prejudice to yourself." It was then Sunday. Prien saluted and withdrew, his heart beating fast. He went straight to his quarters and settled down to a thorough study of the problem. He worked away hour after hour, calculating, figuring, checking and re-checking. On the appointed day he stood once again before the Commodore.

"Yes or no?"—"Yes, sir." A pause. "Have you thought it all out? Have you thought of Emsmann and Henning who tried the same thing in the first World War and never came back?" "Yes, sir." "Then get your boat ready."

The crew could make no sense of the preparations for their next patrol. Why were they disembarking part of their food supplies and taking so little fuel and fresh water with them? Apart from giving essential orders the captain was uncommunicative, and on the appointed day the U-boat slipped quietly through the Kiel Canal into the North Sea. The nights were dark, the seas running high. While on passage the crew watched their captain closely; although funnel-smoke was sighted several times he never attempted to attack. At last, early in the morning of 13 October, the Orkneys were in sight. Prien gave the order to dive and when the U-boat was resting easily on the sea-bed, he ordered all hands to muster forward. "To-morrow we go into Scapa Flow", he began, and went on talking quietly, making sure that every man knew what he had to

do. Then he ordered every available man off watch to turn
in; they would need all their strength when the time came.

At four o'clock in the afternoon the boat came to life
again and the cook served a specially good meal. Jokes
were bandied about and Prien wrote in his log: "The
morale of the ship's company is superb." At 7.15 all
hands went to diving-stations, and the chief engineer
began to lift the boat off the bottom; the ballast-pumps
sang and the boat began to move as the motors stirred into
life. Prien took a first cautious glimpse through the
periscope. All clear. He gave the order to surface. The
wind had dropped but the sky was covered with light
clouds; although there was a new moon, the Northern
Lights made the night almost as bright as day.

Log of the U-47

. . . . We are in Scapa Flow.

14.10.39. It is disgustingly light. The whole bay is lit
up. To the south of Cava there is nothing. I go farther in.
To port, I recognize the Hoxa Sound coastguard, to which
in the next few minutes the boat must present itself as a
target. In that event all would be lost; at present south of
Cava no ships are to be seen, although visibility is extremely good. Hence decisions:

South of Cava there is no shipping; so before staking
everything on success, all possible precautions must be
taken. Therefore, turn to port is made. We proceed north
by the coast. Two battleships are lying there at anchor,
and further inshore, destroyers. Cruisers not visible, therefore attack on the big fellows.

Distance apart, three thousand metres. Estimated
depth, seven and a half metres. Impact firing. One torpedo
fired on northern ship, two on southern. After a good
three and a half minutes, a torpedo detonates on the
northern ship; of the other two nothing is to be seen.

About! Torpedo fired from stern; in the bow two tubes
are loaded; three torpedoes from the bow. After three
tense minutes comes the detonation on the nearer ship.

There is a loud explosion, roar, and rumbling. Then come columns of water, followed by columns of fire, and splinters fly through the air. The harbour springs to life. Destroyers are lit up, signalling starts on every side, and on land, two hundred metres away from me, cars roar along the roads. A battleship had been sunk, a second damaged, and the other three torpedoes have gone to blazes. All the tubes are empty. I decide to withdraw, because: (1) With my periscopes I cannot conduct night attacks while submerged. . . . (2) On a bright night I cannot manuoevre unobserved in a calm sea. (3) I must assume that I was observed by the driver of a car which stopped opposite us, turned around, and drove off towards Scapa at top speed. (4) Nor can I go farther north, for there, well hidden from my sight, lie the destroyers which were previously dimly distinguishable.

At full speed both engines we withdraw. Everything is simple until we reach Skildaenoy Point. Then we have more trouble. It is now low tide. The current is against us. Engines at slow and dead slow; I attempt to get away. I must leave by the south through the narrows, because of the depth of the water. Things are again difficult. Course, 058°, slow—ten knots. I make no progress. At full speed I pass the southern blockship with nothing to spare. The helmsman does magnificently. Full speed ahead both, finally three-quarter speed and full ahead all out. Free of the blockships—ahead a mole! Hard over and again about, and at 02.15 we are once more outside. A pity that only one was destroyed. The torpedo misses I explain as due to faults of course, speed and drift. In tube 4, a misfire. The crew behaved splendidly throughout the operation.

Lieutenant Gunther Prien

THE BATTLE OF THE RIVER PLATE: DECEMBER 1939

.... On the 11th and 12th the *Graf Spee* continued on

a south-westerly course towards the Plate Estuary. By the 12th Langsdorff* reached what he estimated would be the shipping lane and he took the *Graf Spee* along it with the intention of patrolling to and fro across it during the night.

If, by the following day, 13 December, nothing had been sighted, he intended to turn right round and cross the South Atlantic again to an area off the West African coast near the Gulf of Lagos. There he would search along and either side of the peacetime shipping lanes.

So it came about that shortly before dawn on Wednesday, 13 December, 1939, the *Panzerschiff Admiral Graf Spee* was cruising at fifteen knots on a course of 155 degrees in a position 34° 27' south, 49° 55' west. She had destroyed nine British ships, totalling 50,089 tons, without the loss of a single life. The man who made that proud claim, *Kapitän zur See* Hans Langsdorff, was at that moment in his sea cabin on the bridge, his task as a commerce raider nearly finished and his life, at the age of forty-two, almost over.

The British Warships Close In

At noon Commodore Harwood made a signal to Captain Parry in the *Achilles* and Captain Bell in the *Exeter*, which gave, in a few words, his plan for battle. It was brief and it was clear.

Harwood's small force, which would be outgunned from the start, could only sink or cripple a pocket battleship by superior tactics. There would be no scope for the unexpected move which would take the enemy unawares that Nelson had employed at the Nile; but there was just as much scope for mistakes.

The Commodore planned to attack immediately by day or by night, and he would split his force into two divisions—the *Exeter*, with her heavier 8-inch guns forming one, and the *Ajax* and *Achilles*, with their less effective

* Captain of the *Graf Spee* (Ed.)

and shorter ranged 6-inch guns, forming the other. Both divisions would attack from slightly different directions, so that each could spot the other's fall of shot (flank marking) and also force the enemy to divide his attention. This splitting of his main force was unorthodox—it would have been more usual to keep the three ships concentrated—but it might keep the enemy guessing.

. . . . The rest of the hunting groups were in the following positions:

Force H (*Sussex* and *Shropshire*) sweeping off the West African coast, more than four thousand miles away.

Force I (*Eagle*, *Cornwall* and *Gloucester*) were at Durban, more than four thousand one hundred miles away, short of fuel after a wild goose chase into the Indian Ocean.

Force K (*Ark Royal* and *Renown*), the most powerful hunting group in the South Atlantic, were off Pernambuco, two thousand miles northwards.

Force X (*Hermes* and the French cruisers *Dupleix* and *Foch*) with the *Neptune*, *Hardy*, *Hostile* and *Hero*, were still farther north off St. Paul Rocks.

The *Cumberland* was at the Falkland Islands; and the *Dorsetshire* was on the eve of sailing from Simonstown to relieve the *Exeter*. The submarine *Severn* was halfway between St. Helena and Bahia, on her way to the Falklands, and the submarine *Clyde* was approaching Dakar.

That, then, was the scene in the South Atlantic on 12 December, 1939, the eve of the Battle of the River Plate.

13 December

The captain of the *Graf Spee* . . . thought at first that he had been sighted by only one cruiser and hence turned immediately to attack. Too late he realized the true situation, and a running fight ensued throughout the day.

The Crippling of the *Exeter*

From Captain Bell's report: . . . *After the eighth salvo B turret received a direct hit from an 11-inch shell and was put out of action. The splinters also killed or wounded all the bridge personnel with the exception of the Captain, Torpedo Control and Firing Officers, and wrecked the wheelhouse communications. . . .*

. . . . The *Graf Spee*, after firing four salvoes of base-fused shells, switched over to impact fuses "in order to obtain the greatest possible damage to the lightly-armoured turrets and super-structure and through hits on its hull to reduce the ship's speed".*

One of these shells landed on B turret just between the two guns, ripping off the front armour plate and killing eight men at the front of the gunhouse.

They had fired seven broadsides and the Number Ones of the two guns were just about to ram home the next rounds when the shell burst. All the lights went out, leaving the gunhouse in darkness, and dense, acrid fumes started to burn the nostrils and throats of the stunned survivors.

Sergeant Arthur Wilde, R.M., groped for the Number Ones who should have been either side of him, but they were not in their seats. Then he saw daylight coming in through the left rear door of the gunhouse, which had been blown open, and he made his way out on deck.

"As I was going aft," Wilde reported later, "Marine Attwood called for me to assist him with Marine W. A. Russell. I turned and saw Russell had lost a forearm and was badly hurt in the other arm.

"Attwood and I assisted Russell down to the port 4-inch gundeck, and as we reached it there was another violent explosion which seemed to be in the vicinity of B turret. I dropped to the deck, pulling Russell with me.

"After the splinters had stopped I cut off two lengths of signal halyard, which were hanging loose, and put a clove hitch for a tourniquet around both of Russell's arms above the elbows.

"I went to the Sick Bay and told someone that I had left

* Later in the action she reverted to base-fused shells.

Russell sitting against the funnel casing, port side. I proceeded down to the waist and turned forward, intending to
go to B magazine and shell room, but was ordered back as
the gangway was blocked by C.P.O. Evans, who was at-
tending to a man who was seriously injured around the
legs. . . .

"Some time later I collected Marines Camp, Attwood
and Thomas, and we went back to B turret to see what
could be done. I observed several small fires, some of
which were put out by sand, the fire hydrants being dry.

"Marine Thomas drew my attention to a small fire near
the left elevating standard, and I sent him for water and
sand. Then, remembering I had seen water in the starboard waist, I went down for some. When I returned
Lieutenant Toase, assisted by Marine Thomas, had extinguished the fire and we proceeded to take the cordite
from both rammers and pass it overboard. . . ."

While this was being done, the badly wounded Russell,
his clothing blood-stained and his arms still bound with
signal halyard, walked round making cheering remarks
and, in the words of Captain Bell, "encouraging all by his
fortitude". (He stayed on deck until after the action, when
he collapsed.)

But although the shell had hit B turret, the worst
damage was done on the bridge just above: a withering
shower of splinters, like spray from a big sea, had been
flung up at more than the speed of sound and cut through
the thin armour and window openings, ricocheted down
from the metal roof and killed or wounded nearly every
man standing on the bridge.

Within a fraction of a second the *Exeter* was changed
from a perfectly handled fighting ship to an uncontrolled
machine. The wheelhouse was wrecked; all communications to the engine room and Lower Steering Position were
cut. Captain Bell had been wounded in the face. Among
the dead were the Navigating Officer, plotting staff and
the men standing either side of Captain Bell.

 . . . . By now the forward part of the ship was slowly
flooding. Water streamed out of a shattered fire main and

from hoses pouring water on to the fo'c'sle fire; and the sea was spurting in through splinter holes caused by the hit on the anchor and the many near misses. The flow was increased by the forward thrust of the ship, which was now steaming at full speed.

From Captain Bell's report: . . . *Two more 11-inch hits were received, one on A turret, putting it out of action, and one which penetrated the Chief Petty Officer's flat, where it burst, causing very extensive damage. . . .*

Just before the Chief Petty Officer's flat was hit another shell, not mentioned in the above report, hit the Navigating Officer's cabin, passed through the Armament Office, killed five telegraphists and went on for sixty feet before bursting on the barrel of 'S-one' (Starboard one) 4-inch gun, killing or wounding several more men.

The foremost ready-use locker, containing 4-inch shells, immediately caught fire and the ammunition started bursting, sending up showers of debris and splinters. At that moment a man ran up to Midshipman Cameron, in command of the 4-inch guns, and warned him that the fore topmast was just about to fall down.

"I gave the order to clear the fore end of the gun deck," Cameron reported later. "As it did not appear to be coming down immediately I started the crews working again."

The men in A turret had fired between forty and fifty rounds when, at this moment, an 11-inch shell hit the right gun. Once again the explosion tore at the armour plate on the front of the turret. Inside all the lights were put out and fumes streamed in.

Petty Officer Pierce tried to get through to the bridge by telephone, but it was wrecked. Ordering the telegraphists to stay at their posts, he climbed out of the gunhouse to go up to warn the bridge, but finding it had already been wrecked he went back to the gunhouse to tell the men to abandon it.

By this time an 11-inch shell had burst in the Chief Petty Officers' flat and started a bad fire above the 4-inch magazine. After checking that it was being dealt with, Midshipman Cameron returned with Ordinary Seaman

Gwilliam to find the 4-inch ready-use locker still burning from the earlier hit.

"There were still several live shells in the bottom of the locker. Without any hesitation, Gwilliam removed his greatcoat and attempted to smother the flames with it," Cameron reported later. "At the same time somebody else threw a bucket of sand over it. The flames were extinguished and we proceeded to throw over the side what was left in the locker.

"Gwilliam reported to me that there were still several cans of petrol underneath the port catapult. These we threw overboard.

"As the fire on the messdecks was still raging, I got more hands on to the job of carrying buckets to it. At the same time Lieutenant Kemball and I kept the remainder occupied in breaking up blocks of holystone in an effort to make sand out of them. . . .

"At this time an effort, which subsequently proved to be successful, was being made to get the planes over the side, they having been badly holed and showering out quantities of petrol."

The shell which burst in the C.P.O.'s flat did so much damage that the *Exeter* later had to discontinue the action. It penetrated the light plating of the ship's amidships, as if it were cardboard, cut through three bulkheads and then burst on the lower deck above the 4-inch magazine and the torpedo-gunner's store, blasting a hole measuring sixteen feet by fourteen feet.

The *Exeter*'s tall topmasts were still in danger. Flying splinters had cut through many of the wire shrouds supporting them, and when finally the triatic stay joining the heads of the two masts was severed they had started to whip so violently that all the main aerials parted and the ship's wireless link with the Commodore was cut. As soon as the sets had gone dead Chief Petty Officer Telegraphist Harold Newman began the dangerous and laborious job of rigging jury aerials.

The topmasts were so tall that they undoubtedly helped the *Graf Spee*'s gunners in finding the range; and had the

weather not been exceptionally calm they almost certainly
would have toppled down.

A Tribute

"You English are hard. You do not know when you are
beaten. The *Exeter* was beaten, but would not know it!"

Captain Langsdorff

Commodore Harwood's tactics were successful; the
Graf Spee *suffered considerably, and her captain became*
convinced that the cruisers would not have pressed home
their attack so persistently if they were not expecting im-
mediate support from heavier ships.

Damaged, and a considerable distance from his home
bases, Langsdorff decided to make for a neutral port
where he could carry out temporary repairs before attempting to break through once more into the North
Atlantic and so back to Germany. Unaware of the pro-
Allied feeling in Uruguay, he shaped course for Montevideo.

Graf Spee reached Montevideo on the evening of the
same day, 13 December, and began a prolonged diplomatic argument in an effort to remain in port beyond the
legal seventy-two hours. Meanwhile skilful British propaganda created the impression of a large fleet in the
vicinity of the La Plata estuary waiting to annihilate the
Graf Spee. H.M. Ships *Ark Royal* and *Renown* were
reported to be at Rio de Janeiro while in reality they were
many thousands of miles away. The cruiser force had in
fact been reinforced by only one more ship, another
cruiser, H.M.S. *Cumberland*.

Langsdorff signaled his appreciation of the situation
and his intentions to Berlin. On 16 December Raeder consulted Hitler:

Report of the Commander-in-Chief, Navy, to the
Führer on 16 December 1939:

The C.-in-C., Navy, reports that at least two weeks

are needed to make the *Graf Spee* seaworthy, and that
the Government of Uruguay has granted only seventy-
two hours. The Foreign Office is requested to continue
efforts to obtain an extension of the time allowed; this
appears hopeless, however, as Britain and France are
exerting great pressure, and Uruguay will conform to
their wishes. Uruguay is unreliable as a neutral, and is
not able to defend her neutrality.

The Commander's telegram of 16 December follows:

1. Strategic position off Montevideo: Besides the
cruisers and destroyers, *Ark Royal* and *Renown*. Close
blockade at night. Escape into open sea and break-
through to home waters hopeless.
2. Propose putting out as far as neutral boundary. If
it is possible to fight our way through to Buenos Aires,
using remaining ammunition, this will be attempted.
3. If a break-through would result in certain destruction of *Graf Spee* without opportunity of damaging
enemy, request decision on whether the ship should be
scuttled in spite of insufficient depth in the estuary of
the La Plata, or whether internment is to be preferred.
4. Decision requested by radiogram.

Commander, *Graf Spee*

The text of the instructions follows (sent as
Radiogram 1347/16 to *Graf Spee*):
1. Attempt by all means to extend the time in
neutral waters in order to guarantee freedom of action
as long as possible.
2. With reference to No. 2: Approved.
3. With reference to No. 3: *No* internment in
Uruguay. Attempt effective destruction if ship is scuttled.

Raeder

Note: The envoy in Montevideo reports in the afternoon that further attempts to extend the time limit were without result.

Confirmation was therefore sent by radiogram to the Commander of the *Graf Spee* that the instructions in Radiogram 1347 with reference to No. 2 and No. 3 remain in force.

The text of the radiogram is as follows:

As envoy reported impossibility of extending time limit, instructions according to Radiogram 1347/16 Nos. 2 and 3 remain in force.

Sent at 00.40 on 17 December.

On the following morning, watched by a vast crowd of sightseers, *Graf Spee* put to sea. The British ships cleared for action, but, before they could engage the enemy, their spotting aircraft reported that the *Graf Spee* had been scuttled and blown up by her own crew.

The End of the *Graf Spee*

. . . At 20.54, as the sun dipped below the coastline, a sudden flash of flame leapt from the ship, followed by a vast double explosion. The centre of the *Graf Spee* seemed to dissolve into swirling black smoke which twisted upwards in tortured spirals towards the darkening sky.

The pocket battleship's crew, scattered in the tugs, the barge and the *Tacoma*, stood to attention, giving the Nazi salute. . . .

But the first rumbling reverberation had not lost itself in receptive space before another curtain of flame leapt up aft, high above the masthead, to be followed by another explosion which seemed to erupt under the *Graf Spee*, lift her, and drop her back crumpled into the waiting sea. Wreckage showered out in neat parabolas, the main-mast collapsed like a stalk of corn before a scythe, and the great after-turret, which had successfully withstood the shells of the British cruisers, was flung upwards as the magazine beneath exploded.

Now the violent dying spasms were over and self-induced cremation was to follow. Eager, seeking flames swept along the whole length of the ship; and ashore, while excited radio commentators regained their breath, the German Naval Attaché sent a cable to Berlin. It said:

> Pocket battleship *Graf Spee* left Montevideo 18.20 [German time]; blown up by her crew 19.54. Crew at present embarked in *Tacoma*.*

Langsdorff: The End

Three days later, on 20 December, Captain Langsdorff committed suicide, leaving this letter addressed to the German Ambassador and meant for onward transmission to Germany and his Führer.

Your Excellency,

After a long struggle I reached the grave decision to scuttle the pocket battleship *Admiral Graf Spee*, in order to prevent her from falling into enemy hands. I am still convinced that under the circumstances this decision was the only one left, once I had taken my ship into the trap of Montevideo. For with the ammunition remaining, any attempt to fight my way back to open and deep water was bound to fail. And yet only in deep water could I have scuttled the ship, after having used the remaining ammunition, thus avoiding her falling to the enemy.

Sooner than expose my ship to the danger that after a brave fight she would fall partly or completely into enemy hands, I decided not to fight but to destroy the equipment and then scuttle the ship. It was clear to me that this decision might be consciously or unwittingly misconstrued by persons ignorant of my motives, as

* They spent the rest of the war interned in Argentina (Ed.)

being attributable entirely or partly to personal considerations. Therefore I decided from the beginning to bear the consequences involved in this decision. For a Captain with a sense of honour, it goes without saying that his personal fate cannot be separated from that of his ship.

I postponed my intention as long as I still bore responsibility for decisions concerning the welfare of the crew under my command. After to-day's decision of the Argentine Government, I can do no more for my ship's company. Neither will I be able to take an active part in the present struggle of my country. I can now only prove by my death that the fighting services of the Third Reich are ready to die for the honour of the flag.

I alone bear the responsibility for scuttling the pocket battleship *Admiral Graf Spee*. I am happy to pay with my life for any possible reflection on the honour of the flag. I shall face my fate with firm faith in the cause and the future of the nation and of my Führer.

I am writing this letter to Your Excellency in the quiet of the evening, after calm deliberation, in order that you may be able to inform my superior officers, and to counter public rumours if this should become necessary.

Langsdorff

THE MAGNETIC MINE: DEGAUSSING

By the end of October 1939 over fifty thousand tons of Allied and British shipping had been sunk by magnetic mines sown by aircraft, and in November Hitler boasted of this new "secret weapon" as being without counter. On 23 November a magnetic mine was recovered intact off Shoeburyness, and effective counter-measures were devised by the Admiralty.

Hitler's "secret weapon" had yielded its design and powers and manner of operation and the antidote lay in a

belt of energized electrical cable which they were planning
to instal in the ship. As I understood it, the object was to
neutralize the ship's magnetic field by a counter-current
passing through the cable and in this way render the
magnetic needle in the German mine ineffective to
detonate its explosive charge. For operation of the belt, no
special schooling would be needed. The ship's engineer or
electrical officers could attend to it. The only adjustment
the navigator would need to make was in respect of the
compass course that was being steered and, for that, a
fairly simple instrument would be fitted on the bridge. We
were warned to "keep the juice running" at all times when
in port or in shallow waters. An instance of over-confi-
dence was quoted: that of a ship only recently equipped.
Upon arrival at her next port, the master thought he
might safely switch off the protective energy when moored
at his familiar wharf—with the result that the ship's stern
was shattered by the explosion of a magnetic mine that
had been dropped from the air, probably on the night
before. It is not often that one has the key of extinction so
readily at hand. We would need to guard that switch.

During my term of relief duty in the ship I watched the
shipyard workers harness the insulated belt around the
hull on the level of the main-deckline: there seemed to be
miles of it, for she was a sizeable vessel. When the fitting
was completed and the wiring tested by ammeter, she was
said to be immunized and it only remained for the for-
mulae to be approved by the results of the ranging off
Helensburgh Pier before sailing. Certification was important before a programme could be prepared for the se-
quence of that test and I was required to call at Naval
Headquarters to obtain the document. I found the newly
established division in the throes of settling in to what
must speedily have become a major department of the
Admiralty. Despite its newness and understandable con-
gestion and apparent disorder, the experts so recently
gazetted had found a slogan or motto for their "trade".
That they had enrolled a classical scholar in their ranks

was evident from a typewritten slip pinned up above the
desk at which certificates were issued. It was a paraphrase
from Pope's translation of the Odyssey—

> This potent girdle round thy bosom bind
> And sail: throw all thy terrors to the wind.
>
> Sir David W. Bone

4

NORWAY

Early in the war both Britain and Germany were looking anxiously towards Norway, the neutral route from Sweden by which iron ore was transported in large quantities to the Reich. On 19 September 1939 the First Lord of the Admiralty, Winston Churchill, sent a memorandum to the First Sea Lord which began, "I brought to the notice of the Cabinet this morning the importance of stopping the Norwegian transportation of Swedish iron ore from Narvik". Less than two weeks later Admiral Raeder submitted a proposal in which he asked "that the Führer be informed as soon as possible of the opinions of the Naval War Staff on the possibility of extending the operational base to the north. It must be ascertained whether it is possible to gain bases in Norway under the combined pressure of Russia and Germany, with the aim of improving our strategic and operational position."

Both sides watched one another warily. In early 1940 Hitler made active preparations for the occupation of Norway, while the British Cabinet debated whether they should or should not infringe Norwegian neutrality by mining her territorial waters. Although German plans were more deep-laid, it was in fact the British who moved first.

PRELUDE TO INVASION

Quisling

SUPPLEMENTARY to earlier information, I wish to report that Quisling is one of the best-known Norwegian general staff officers. He was Military Attaché in Finland, and from 1927 to 1930, before diplomatic relations between the Soviet Union and Great Britain were broken off, he represented British interests in Moscow. From 1931 to 1933 he was Norwegian War Minister, representing the Norwegian Peasant Party; he then resigned and formed a radical national and socialist party called the National Unity Party. This party had, and still has, anti-semitic views and it recommends closest co-operation with Germany. It has fifteen thousand registered members, and Quisling estimates the number of his direct followers at two to three hundred thousand; this comprises that 10 per cent of the population which is in favour of co-operation with Germany even at the present time, when the general attitude in Norway and Sweden is definitely anti-German. His party also did not participate in voting for the Storthing. . . .

Quisling knows the King very well from the time when he was in office and he believes that the King holds him in esteem, even though the latter is on the whole pro-British.

A plan for possible procedure has been suggested.

According to this plan a number of picked Norwegians will be given training in Germany for this particular task. They will be told exactly what to do, and will be assisted by seasoned National Socialists who are experienced in such matters. These trained men are then to be sent back to Norway as quickly as possible, where details will be discussed. Several focal points in Oslo will have to be occupied with lightning speed, and simultaneously the German Navy with contingents of the German Army will have to put in an appearance at a pre-arranged bay outside Oslo in answer to a special summons from the new Norwegian Government. Quisling has no doubt that such a coup, achieved instantaneously, would at once meet with the approval of those sections of the Army with which he now has connections. Of course, he has never discussed political action with them. As regards the King, he believes that he would accept such a *fait accompli*.

Quisling's estimate of the number of German troops needed for the operation coincides with the German estimates.

> Alfred Rosenberg, Nazi Party foreign affairs expert,
> December 1939

The German plan for the invasion of Norway was christened Operation Weser.

13 March 1940

Führer does not give order yet for "W". He is still looking for an excuse.

14 March

English keep vigil in the North Sea with fifteen to sixteen submarines; doubtful whether reason to safeguard own operations or prevent operations by Germans. Führer has not yet decided what reason to give for Weser Exercise.

> General Jodl, Chief of Hitler's personal staff, diary

General Orders for Operation Weser

The barrage-breaking vessels, *Sperrbrecher,* will penetrate inconspicuously, and with lights on, into Oslo Fjord disguised as merchant steamers.

Challenge from coastal signal stations and look-outs are to be answered by the deceptive use of the names of English steamers. I lay particular stress on the importance of not giving away the operation before zero hour.

Adolf Hitler, 4 April

8 April

His Majesty's Government in the United Kingdom and
the French Government have . . . resolved to deny the
continued use by the enemy of stretches of territorial
waters which are clearly of particular value to him, and
they have therefore decided to prevent unhindered passage
of vessels carrying contraband of war through Norwegian
territorial waters. They accordingly hereby give notice that
. . . areas of Norwegian territorial waters have been rendered dangerous on account of mines. Vessels entering
these areas will do so at their peril.

OPERATION WESER

*The German Minister in Oslo called upon Herr Koht,
the Norwegian Foreign Minister, at 4 a.m. on 9 April and
presented him with a list of demands. Even by Nazi stand-
ards the timing was bad, for at midnight four German
warships had forced an entry into Oslo Fjord, shots had
been exchanged and the invasion had begun. Denmark
was occupied on the same day. The "phoney war" was
over.*

Appeal to his People by the King: 13 April

. . . . In the situation to-day I cannot report to you the
whereabouts in Norway of myself, the Crown Prince, and
the Government. The German forces have in fact engaged
in a violent attack on us, while we were staying in a little
place which was unfortified and undefended. High explosive and incendiary bombs and machine-gun fire were
used against the civilian population and ourselves in the
most unscrupulous and brutal fashion. The attack could
have had but one object—immediately to annihilate all of

us who were assembled to resolve questions in the best interests of Norway. . . . God Save Norway.

Haakon R.

The German Proclamation: 14 April

It is my task to protect Norway against attack by the Western Powers. The Norwegian Government have declined several offers of co-operation. The Norwegian people must now themselves determine the future of their fatherland. If my proclamation meets with the obedience which was very sensibly accorded by the Danish people when faced with similar circumstances, Norway will be spared the horrors of war.

If opposition is offered and the hand of friendship is rejected I shall be forced to employ the severest and most relentless means to crush such opposition.

General von Falkenhorst, C.-in-C., Norway

In response to an appeal from Norway, which previously had been almost belligerently neutral, the British and French Governments decided to send what troops they could to the northern part of the country, the south being considered as already beyond redemption.

The Cabinet heartily approved all possible measures for the rescue and defence of Narvik and Trondheim. The troops . . . lacked aircraft, anti-aircraft guns, anti-tank guns, tanks, transport and training. The whole of Northern Norway was covered with snow to depths which none of our soldiers had ever seen, felt, or imagined. There were neither snow-shoes nor skis—still less skiers. We must do our best. Thus began this ramshackle campaign.

Winston Churchill

The Norwegian Failure

The fact was that, whilst the Germans were disembarking a division each week in Norway, we still had not a man there.

On the 18th,* I wrote to Chamberlain, "It is the pace of enemy reinforcements which should control the pace at which our own troops arrive . . . I am, therefore, asking you to try to make the necessary effort to place at our disposal the tonnage which we need."

On the other hand, the British Fleet gained a great success. During fights which took place up to the 13th, the Navy of the Reich suffered heavy losses. The Vichy Press has scoffed at me for having called the sailing of the German Fleet into the North Sea a strategic error. It is true that the Reich forces established themselves in the port of Narvik on the 9th at 5.15 in the morning and that they held on there until 28 May, the day when the Allied troops finally succeeded in dislodging them. Nevertheless, the fact still remains that the British Fleet, after having destroyed, during engagements between 10 and 13 April, ten of the most modern and speedy destroyers of the Kriegsmarine—which were escorting General Dietl's convoy—blockaded closely all the fjords around Narvik. Not another German boat could, from that date to the end of May, the date of our voluntary evacuation, enter the port. It was therefore . . . a matter of prestige for Hitler to continue holding Narvik. This was why he clung so desperately to it. On 20 April, Mussolini wrote to him: . . . "If you have any means whatever to help you to hold on to Narvik, you must use them. If the evacuation of Narvik took place it would become the subject of noisy exploitation by Allied propaganda."

The future expeditionary force was being organized at this time. If my suggestions were not entirely followed, it was at least decided to form three light divisions (with

* April (Ed.)

two infantry regiments) and the equivalent of a fourth
(Polish and Foreign Legion). Unfortunately each of these
divisions was only to be supplied with very insufficient
equipment: an artillery group, two companies with 22 mm.
guns for attaching low-flying aircraft, but none which had
a ceiling above one thousand metres, a company of out-of-
date tanks (except that of 1 Division), and finally as the
sole "recce" element for all the expeditionary corps, a
squadron of machine-gun carriers, which, however, were
to be dispersed within the different sectors. The Germans
were less parsimonious. It seems probable that they sent a
dozen infantry and two armoured divisions into Norway.

Were these slender resources at least compensated for
by our rapidity in preparing our troops? And, if we had
been forestalled in seizing the ports, was the pace of our
movement going to allow us to reconquer them rapidly?
Unfortunately the timetable laid down was not in the least
inspired by the battle for speed which I had never ceased
to advocate. 1 Light Division (six battalions), the Polish
brigade (four battalions) and the two battalions of the
Foreign Legion were to embark between the 12th and the
23rd. The first echelon of 2 Light Division would in its
turn only embark on the 24th and the second echelon was
not to leave Brest. As regards 3 Light Division, its departure was dependent on the British providing the necessary
ships. In actual fact it was destined never to leave Britan-
ny. Finally, on the 19th, ten days after the first German
landing, the first French troops disembarked in Norway.
The port chosen was Namsos, from which the Wehrmacht
were still some distance, and which was the terminus of
roads leading to Sweden. But, though our troops were able
to disembark there without interference, they were completely incapable of moving off or of offering any action
whatsoever. Their artillery, tanks, anti-aircraft guns, their
mules and even their skis and snowshoes had remained in
the auxiliary cruiser *Ville d'Alger,* which had not been
able to enter harbour because of her length—a detail
which had been forgotten. It was only a week later that
some anti-aircraft guns began to be unloaded. In the

meantime, our forces had suffered violent bombing raids.

The British disembarkations had been carried out on the 13th in the area of Narvik, then at Namsos in the centre, and at Andalsnes, farther south.

The essential problem was to free Trondheim. It was only the road which went from this port which would permit the future support of the Swedish Army and the defence of central Scandinavia, the essential aim which our Supreme Command had allotted itself.

The operation should have been successful. About the 20th, after the major disembarkations had been accomplished, the Germans had in the area only five thousand or six thousand men. Now, the Allied forces comprised in the north (Namsos), eight thousand British and French whom, it was hoped, would finally recover their equipment—and four battalions of Norwegian troops; in the south (Andalsnes), five thousand British and Norwegian troops. The Germans, who had to face simultaneously enemy forces to the north and south and also to defend the sea, were thus at a decided numerical disadvantage. Therefore, at a meeting of the Supreme Council on the 22nd, Chamberlain revealed himself fairly optimistic despite the Germans' aerial superiority.

But three days later the situation had changed. German forces disembarking at Oslo had reinforced those at Trondheim. The Luftwaffe, which occupied the bases, became increasingly stronger and more aggressive. Norwegian troops remained inactive. They had carried out no destruction. Thus the Foreign Office informed M. Corbin on the 26th that the Trondheim expedition was doomed to failure, and that it was necessary to take steps for the withdrawal of troops in this area. Our Ambassador tried in vain to convince the Foreign Office of the contrary. The War Committee, which met on the same day, unanimously declared itself opposed to this withdrawal, which Gamelin considered deplorable. I wrote on the same day to Chamberlain in order to instruct him about our attitude and to advise him to speed up the dispatch of men and material. "One must plan on a big scale," I told him, "or abandon the struggle. One must act quickly or lose the war."

The Supreme Council met on the 27th in London. The results of our delay had become worse, I told the Council; "The expedition into central Scandinavia was based on a technical error. It was impossible to carry it out without first securing both an important port and aerial bases. Even without one of these things, the operation would have been difficult. But, lacking in both, one has cause to wonder if the Allies had the slightest chance of success."

On the other hand the occupation of Narvik was attainable and of the utmost importance since it was the exit door to the mineral iron. Chamberlain stated that the capture of Trondheim was no longer possible, and that he thought this point of view was shared by Gamelin, who, however, insisted upon the importance to the Allies of holding Namsos in order to advance from there on Narvik, occupying different points along the coast. The British Government thought we should continue to fight at Namsos, but it believed that it was scarcely possible to keep a foothold there for long. At Narvik, on the contrary, Chamberlain continued, steps had already been taken to seize the port as quickly as possible when weather conditions would allow, and then to push to the Swedish frontier. But would the Swedish Government, intimidated by German successes, allow us to advance to the iron ore mines? The result, moreover, he added, "would not be as immediate as that resulting from action against the German reserves of oil".

I myself asked in the first place that at least we should save our face by not evacuating central Scandinavia before having attacked Narvik and, subsequently, that we should defend vigorously the road from Namsos to this port. During the night, the only wharf available at Andalsnes was destroyed by an air raid. The War Office ordered evacuation. "Lord Halifax," M. Corbin wrote to me on the 28th, "has assured me that it is only the prospect of not being able to supply the Allied contingents at Andalsnes and Namsos any longer which has brought about the present situation. . . . It is none the less true that the British military leaders have almost completely re-adapted their plan . . . the first step of which has thus been organizing the withdrawal of half of the expedition."

With this inglorious page we must contrast the glorious capture of Narvik on 28 May by our troops and those of our Allies, although they had received the order of evacuation from London on the 26th. On the 30th the Allied forces pinned the enemy on the Swedish frontier. The examinations at the Nuremberg trial have proved that, at this time, Hitler considered the Allies to have won the battle of Narvik, and that the Dietl corps was lost. It was Dunkirk that saved Dietl and his troops.

The disaster of Flanders entailed unfortunately a confirmation of the order for withdrawal. This was done at the request of Churchill, by the Supreme Council, which met in Paris on the 31st. Until our voluntary evacuation, "the permanent road to iron ore supplies", was, I repeat, well and truly cut. The "madcap enterprise" was based, therefore, on a healthy inspiration. It could have been realized, but its execution was defective.

Paul Reynaud, Prime Minister of France

Independent Companies

In order to delay to the utmost the northward advance of the enemy towards Narvik, we were now sending special companies raised in what was afterwards called "Commando" style, under an enterprising officer, Colonel Gubbins, to Mosjoen, a hundred miles farther up the coast. I was most anxious that a small part of the Namsos force should make their way in whatever vehicles were available along the road to Grong. Even a couple of hundred would have sufficed to fight small rearguard actions. From Grong they would have to find their way on foot to Mosjoen. I hoped by this means to gain the time for Gubbins to establish himself so that a stand could be made against the very small numbers which the enemy could as yet send there.

Winston Churchill

Mission to Norway

Shortly after the Germans made their first landing in
Norway, we responded by a gallant failure at Narvik. In
the middle of one night there was a telephone message for
me to report to the War Office. It dawned on me the
reason might be Norway, especially as I had never been
there and knew nothing about it. Norway it was, and I was
ordered to go there immediately to take command of the
Central Norwegian Expeditionary Force. Unfortunately I
was not to take my own division, the 61st, for the Force
was to consist of a brigade and some odd troops sent from
Northern Command, together with a French force composed of Chasseurs Alpins under General Audet. These
troops were to proceed to Namsos.

Having got my orders, I collected my kit and flew up to
Scotland the next day, 13 April. We were to fly across to
Norway the same night but were delayed by a blizzard,
and took off next morning in a Sunderland.

The Norwegian coastline was lovely to look at, with the
majesty of its rough mountains covered in snow, but from
a fighting angle the view had no attraction for me, as obviously in this type of country one would need very specialized troops.

We reached Namsos in the evening and started to
disembark troops at once. It was soon evident that the officers had little experience in handling men, although they
had a first-class commander in Brigadier G. P. Phillips.

In Norway, at that time of the year, there were only
about three hours of darkness, and landing troops with the
whole country under snow, and a vigilant and attentive
enemy, was no easy matter.

The troops were only too anxious to do what they were
told, and to be quick about it, and it says much for them
that not only did they succeed in landing, but they completely obliterated all traces of their landing. The Germans
who flew over next morning suspected nothing.

My orders were to take Trondheim whenever a naval

attack took place. The date was unnamed but I moved my
troops up to Verdael and Steinjaer (both near Trondheim), from where I would lose no time in synchronizing
with the naval attack when it came.

The following night we had to land French troops—the
Chasseurs Alpins under General Audet. Although far better trained than we were, and experienced at looking after
themselves, they did not obliterate the traces of their landings. The next morning the Germans saw that troops had
been put ashore, and the French made themselves still
more noticeable by loosing off their machine-guns at
them, which succeeded in making matters much worse.
The Germans responded by more and more bombs, and in
a matter of hours Namsos was reduced to ashes. The casualties were not heavy, as by that time my troops were all
forward, and the French were bivouacked outside the
town. I went up to the front with Peter Fleming soon after
the bombing started, and by the time we returned there
was little of Namsos left.

The French Chasseurs Alpins were a fine body of
troops and would have been ideal for the job in hand, but
ironically they lacked one or two essentials, which made
them completely useless to us. I had wanted to move them
forward, but General Audet regretted they had no means
of transport, as their mules had not turned up. Then I suggested that his ski-troops might move forward, but it was
found that they were lacking some essential strap for their
skis, without which they were unable to move. Their other
equipment was excellent; each man carried some sixty
pounds and managed his load with the utmost ease. They
would have been invaluable to us if only I could have used
them.

The British troops had been issued with fur coats, special boots and socks to compete with the cold, but if they
wore all these things they were scarcely able to move at all
and looked like paralyzed bears.

As far as planes, guns and cars went, I had no trouble
at all, for we had none, though we commandeered what
cars we could. Landing facilities were conspicuous by

their absence, and to make matters worse we were being supplied by ships larger than the harbour could take. How the sailors got them in and out of these harbours remains a mystery never to be understood by a mere landsman.

The Hun bombers destroyed our small landing-stage. They had the time of their lives with no opposition whatsoever. Some of the ships carried A.A. guns, and a few days before the evacuation I was sent some Bofors guns. The Bofors never actually shot down a Hun plane, but they managed to disconcert them and had a nuisance value, at the same time giving us a fillip at being able to shoot at them.

On one of our more hopeful days an aircraft carrier miraculously cleared the skies of German planes and stayed several hours, but as there were German submarines about it was not able to remain close to the land, and had to go out to sea again where some of the planes could not return to it.

My headquarters in Namsos was one of the few houses to escape destruction, but after the bombardment I moved out to a small farm on the south side of the River Namsen, where we were not bothered much by the enemy, and it was easier for me to get to the front-line troops.

Two or three days after we had occupied Steinjaer and Verdael, about forty or fifty miles south of Namsos, the German Navy gained its one and only victory of the war, for their destroyers came up Trondheim Fjord and shelled my troops out of these two places. We had rifles, a few Bren guns and some 2-inch smoke bombs, but none of them were either comforting or effective against a destroyer.

The troops at Verdael had a particularly bad time. The road ran through the town on the shore of the fjord in full view of the ships, and the troops had to take to the snow-covered hills, ploughing through unknown country in eighteen inches of snow, only to be attacked by German ski-troops. There is no doubt that not many of them would have survived had it not been for the handling of the situation by Brigadier Phillips.

We retired to positions north of Steinjaer and out of reach of the German naval guns, where we were able to hold on. Steinjaer was being heavily bombed and shelled, and it was not surprising that the population in these small towns lived in deadly terror of our arrival. Our intentions were excellent, but our ideas of ultimate deliverance invariably brought the whole concentrated weight of bombing on top of the heads of the population. At the time I felt irritated by their lack of interest in us, but afterwards I realized that, unused as they were to the horror of war, they were stunned by the invasion, and had not had time to come round.

Still I waited for news of our naval attack which was to be my signal to take Trondheim, but still it did not come. Hourly it became more and more obvious to me that with my lack of equipment I was quite incapable of advancing on Trondheim, and could see very little point in remaining in that part of Norway sitting out like rabbits in the snow. I wired the War Office to tell them my conclusions, only to get back the reply that for political reasons they would be glad if I would maintain my positions. I agreed, but said that it was about all I could do. They were so relieved that they actually wired me their thanks.

Now that my chances of taking Trondheim had gone, I sent Peter Fleming to the War Office to find out their future plans. He came back after a couple of days and told me that plans and ideas about Norway were somewhat confused, and adding, "You can really do what you like, for they don't know what they want done."

About this time a complete staff turned up, but I was not very pleased to see them. They took up a lot of unavailable space, there was not much for them to do, and Peter Fleming and Martin Lindsay had more than fulfilled my requirements. We had already been given one most useful addition—Major R. Delacombe—and I felt that soon we would be all staff and no war.

During these last few days I was offered more men. Lack of accommodation and the fact that my only line of communication was a single road and a small railway line functioning spasmodically forced me to refuse them. They were the type of troops that I should have been delighted to have under me, for they were Poles and the French Foreign Legion, but if I had accepted them it would have made evacuation still more difficult.

Several staff officers were sent over in the role of liaison officers, but I don't think they cared much about the job, for they seemed very intent on departing as soon as they could. One of them was particularly amusing: he was so anxious that his plane should not go off without him that he thought he would like to go and sit quite near it in a sloop which was in the fjord. A Hun promptly dropped a bomb on the sloop and sank it, but the gallant officer was not drowned and made a safe return to England, where his report must have been illuminating.

My farmhouse headquarters provided us with some amusement and excitement from the air. My new staff had not seen these air antics played by the Hun, and were startled one day when a German plane came down the road, flying very low and machine-gunning us. It is a most unnerving and unpleasant sensation to be peppered at from a plane bearing straight down on one, and takes a lot of getting used to.

Just as we had settled to an uneventful routine with my troops in their new positions, wires started to flash to and from the War Office. First to evacuate, then to hold on, then to evacuate, then suddenly it was suggested that I should retire on Mosjoen, about a hundred miles to the north of Namsos. I knew the road to be covered in deep snow and impassable for infantry, and I could see no point in the move and wired the War Office to that effect. Meanwhile I sent Peter Fleming and Martin Lindsay to reconnoitre the route in a car, and they took twelve hours to cover forty miles.

I believe the War Office considered me very unenterprising for opposing their suggestion, but I felt at that moment the move only looked feasible on a map.

More orders came to evacuate, and this time I started to set about it. General Audet came to see me and begged

me not to leave his troops until the last when the hour
came to embark. He seemed much moved, and on my
assuring him that not a single British soldier would be embarked until every Frenchman was on board ship, I had a
narrow escape from being embraced and was told that I
was *un vrai gentleman*.

Gradually we retired towards Namsos, where we were
to embark. The evacuation was to take place on two consecutive nights. I intended sending the French troops off
the first night, and they had all gone down at dusk to be
ready to embark. We waited—no ships turned up. There
was no word from the Navy, and I must admit to feeling
anxious. Just before dawn I had to move the troops up into their positions again, leaving them, depressed and
disappointed, to await another night.

I was getting more and more anxious as Mr. Neville
Chamberlain had told the House of Commons that
General Paget's force had been evacuated from Andalsnes, which left me the only unenvied pebble on the
beach. Alone against the might of Germany.

In the course of that last endless day I got a message
from the Navy to say that they would evacuate the whole
of my force that night. I thought it was impossible, but
learned a few hours later that the Navy do not know the
word.

Apparently there was a dense sea mist quite un-
suspected by us on shore, and this had prevented their
coming in the night before, but- Lord Mountbatten
managed to feel his way into the harbour, and the other
ships followed him in. It was a tremendous undertaking to
embark that whole force in a night of three short hours,
but the Navy did it and earned my undying gratitude.

As day was breaking the Germans spotted us leaving
the fjord and bombed us heavily. We lost the *Afridi* and a
French destroyer and I lost my chance of being sunk.
Having known the *Afridi* so well I asked to go on board,
but had been told she was not coming in that night. When
I found that she had come in after all I asked again to go in
her, only to be told that my kit had been put on the *York*

and it would be best for me to go in her instead. I did, and missed a very great experience. Unfortunately the wounded from the French destroyer had been put on board the *Afridi* and nearly all of them were drowned.

On my sixtieth brithday, 5 May, we arrived back at Scapa Flow exactly eighteen days after we had set forth. Captain Portal, who commanded the *York,* thought it was a most fitting occasion for a bottle of champagne. He must have known that to me the taste is extra good after a surgical operation or a major disaster.

General Sir Adrian Carton de Wiart

The King and the Government have at this moment seen themselves compelled to remove their abode and their activities outside the frontiers of the country. . . . The hard necessity of war has compelled the Allied Governments to muster all their strength to fight upon other fronts, and they have full scope for all their men and material on those fronts.

Under these conditions it is impossible to maintain the struggle in this country against a preponderance like that of Germany.

. . . . The Higher Command of our defence has therefore advised the King and the Government for the present to give up the struggle within the country, and the King and Government have considered it their duty to follow that advice. They are, therefore, now leaving the country.

Haakon R.
Johan Nygaardsvold*
7 June

* Norwegian Prime Minister (Ed.)

5

THE BATTLE IN THE WEST: TO DUNKIRK

On the traditional battlefields of the West, the "phoney war" came to an end on 10 May, when Germany invaded Holland, Belgium and Luxembourg, having prepared the way with Fifth-Columnists and soldiers infiltrated in plain clothes.

HITLER TURNS WEST

FOR the first time in history we have to fight on only one front, the other front is at present free. But no one can know how long that will remain so. I have doubted for a long time whether I should strike in the East and then in the West. Basically I did not organize the Armed Forces in order not to strike. The decision to strike was always in me. Earlier or later, I wanted to solve the problem. Under pressure it was decided that the East was to be attacked first. If the Polish war was won so quickly, it was due to the superiority of our Armed Forces. The most glorious appearance in history. Unexpectedly small expenditures of men and material. Now the Eastern front is held by only a few divisions. It is a situation which we viewed previously as unachievable. Now the situation is as follows: The opponent in the West lies behind his fortification. There is no possibility of coming to grips with him. The decisive question is: How long can we endure this situation?

England cannot live without her imports. We can feed ourselves. The permanent sowing of mines on the English

coasts will bring England to her knees. However, this can
occur only if we have occupied Belgium and Holland. It is
a difficult decision for me. None has ever achieved what I
have achieved. My life is of no importance in all this. I
have led the German people to a great height, even if the
world does hate us now. I risk the loss of this achieve-
ment. I have to choose between victory or destruction. I
choose victory. . . . My decision is unchangeable. I shall
attack France and England at the most favourable and
earliest moment. Breach of the neutrality of Belgium and
Holland is meaningless. No one will question that when
we have won. We shall not bring about the breach of
neutrality as idiotically as it was done in 1914. If we do
not break the neutrality, then England and France will.
Without attack the war cannot be ended victoriously.

Adolf Hitler to the German High Command
3 November 1939

France: The Storm Breaks

Back in the line, as the weather gradually improved,
there was a sense of heightening tension and a speeding-up
of the tempo of training; fire programmes of enormous
size and marvellous intricacy poured out of Corps H.Q.,
to be worked out in record time as the battery teams became more expert; short courses were held for adjutants,
staff officers and even budding C.R.A.s, while many officers and other ranks attended a practice camp down in
the French area.

There was, even so, time for some relaxation, and there
were many cheerful dinners in Lille or in unit messes and
visits to old friends of 1916-17.

But thoughts inevitably turned to the end of this phase
of "phoney" war and the famous Plan D began to be
made known. It was unfortunate that the French slang for
what the Navy so aptly called a "shambles" should have
been *système D,* for nothing could have been more fool-
proof or more carefully worked out than that famous
march table. More and more the C.O. wondered how long

this calm could last, but he was less worried now; batteries had knit into efficient units, the unfit had been weeded out and he had a firm confidence in the sturdy common sense of these north-countrymen. They were fit, they were trained and he felt they would play a worthy part if only he could give them a fair chance.

But April drew into May and it was almost with a feeling of relief that at last the C.O. woke one morning to the sound of bombs dropping on the nearby aerodrome.

He realized that at long last the "phoney" war was over and the hunt was up.

British gunner officer

Parachutists and Fifth Column

In the planning for the surprise invasion of Holland, Belgium and Luxembourg, a major preoccupation was whether it would be possible to seize the bridges over the Maas and the Albert Canal intact. Only if that could be done would the army be able swiftly to reach the Peel position in Holland and thereafter quickly relieve the paratroops dropped in the vicinity of Rotterdam.

In November 1939 a conference on the subject was held in the Reich Chancellery with Hitler presiding. As a result the Abwehr was ordered to prepare a plan for the seizure by means of a *ruse de guerre*—by troops, that is, dressed in Dutch and Belgian uniforms—of the most important bridges over the Maas, the two road and one railway bridge at Maastricht and the one road and one railway bridge at Gennep.

Early in the preparations a most annoying setback was experienced. The agent who had been detailed to procure pattern uniforms was captured by the Belgians with the uniforms in his possession. In connection with this mysterious theft of uniforms a Flemish newspaper published a caricature of Goering, wearing the uniform of a Brussels tram conductor and admiring himself in a mirror, with the caption, "This *does* suit me well!"

It is quite astonishing that this episode aroused no

suspicions either in Holland or Belgium, and that no additional precautionary instructions were as a result issued to
the frontier guards. Had the Dutch realized, for instance,
what the significance of this abuse of their uniforms was
to have been, they would have been spared the surprise
overthrow they suffered at Gennep and might have caused
a delay in the German advance, which, while it would
probably not have affected the fate of the Western campaign, might well have led to the cutting off of the airborne
troops landed behind the Dutch lines.

The operations against the Maastricht bridges were carried out by . . . a volunteer unit of Sub-station Breslau
(Special Duty Battalion 100). An advance guard, dressed
in uniforms surrendered by Dutchmen, drove in the early
hours of 10 May 1940 via Raedern and Sittart to
Maastricht. What happened next is not generally known.
The only certainty appears to be that one of the road
bridges leading to Maastricht was seized, but the detonat-
ing charge could not be removed. After a wild shooting af-
fray, in which the commander of the bogus Dutchmen,
Lieutenant Hocke, lost his life, all three bridges blew up.
The Maastricht enterprise had ended in complete failure,
and it was a depressing sight for the Abwehr chief when
on his arrival a few hours later he found whole columns of
tanks and lorries jammed on the roads leading to
Maastricht and waiting impatiently until the Engineer
Corps had thrown a field-service bridge across the river.
For it was precisely to avoid this loss of time in the blitz
attack that the Maastricht operation had been devised.

The success of the operation at Gennep, carried out by
a unit of the Brandenburg Special Duty Battalion 800 under the command of Lieutenant Walther, however, more
or less counterbalanced the failure at Maastricht; and as
soon as he heard that the Gennep bridges had been
secured intact, General von Reichenau, the Commander-
in-Chief of 6 Army, forcing its way through the narrow
gap between Roermond and Liège, was able immediately
to divert some of the units stuck fast at Maastricht to the
Gennep route.

This Gennep enterprise was most carefully planned and was executed in partial camouflage. A reconnaissance platoon, disguised as German prisoners under Dutch escort, seized the bridge well before zero hour, and, before the Dutch could recover from their surprise, a column of German tanks was rolling across this important Meuse crossing. The "prisoners" were men of the Brandenburg Regiment, with hand-grenades and automatic pistols concealed under their greatcoats. And the "escort" were agents from the Flemish nationalist Mussert movement, disguised as men of the Dutch frontier guards. The gaining of a purely military objective by Secret Service methods—in other words, the tactical co-ordination of the action of regular troops and agents—was successfully employed for the first time in this Gennep affair.

Paul Leverkuehn, German intelligence officer

HOLLAND

Rotterdam: Friday, 10 May

Something terrible happened last night. War began!!! Uncle Pieter was *right*. The city has been *bombed* all day. Am writing this in the Baron's air-raid shelter. There are not many air-raid shelters here but the Baron and Father and Mevrouw Klaes had this one built for us, and all our neighbours said it was a waste of money. This has been a terrible day and everything is upset and people are very sad and excited. This is what happened. Before daylight I woke up and for several minutes did not know what had happened. I could hear explosions and people were shouting under our windows. Mother came running in in her nightie and dressing gown and told me to get my coat on and come quickly. On the way downstairs she told me there was bombing going on but no one knew yet what it meant but she supposed it was war all right. The noise seemed very near. Father had Keetje in his arms and we hurried across the street to the Baron's and went down into his air-raid shelter. Betje and Brenda and Grietje, Mother said, were already gone to the Baron's. Father pointed toward the city and Mother nodded. There were great flames shooting up into the sky and beams of light from the searchlights and the sirens were going very loud. They are on the tops of buildings and have things on them to make them very loud. We could see bullets going up from our guns. The Baron's air-raid shelter was full of people, all our neighbours and some people I didn't know. They were all talking loudly and no one was dressed, just coats over their nightclothes. Keetje began to cry and Father whispered something to her and kissed her and she stopped. Finally she went to sleep in his arms. We waited about two hours. At first most people thought the noise was only practice. All the time people kept running outside and coming back with news. It was war all right and the radio was giving the alarm and calling all the time for all men in the reserves to report for duty at the nearest place. The radio said this over and over. It was very exciting. The bombing kept on all the time, boom-boom-boom, and everyone said they were falling on Waalhaven, the airport, which is only about five miles away. The Baron went upstairs and began telephoning. The voices on the radio sounded strange and terribly excited. Father put Keetje into Mother's arms and went away. A few minutes later he came back dressed and carrying a gas mask and a knapsack. He kissed Mother and Keetje and me very hard and then hurried out. He shouted back something about taking care of his animals and Mother nodded and told him to be careful, *please*.

After the radio called for the men they all left the shelter and there was no one but the old men and the women and children. At 6.30 the radio said the bombing was over. We all went outside and were glad to get out.

Saturday, 11 May

This was another bad day. The war didn't stop but got worse everywhere. Mother says the Germans have taken all of North Holland and she tried to telephone

Grandfather and Grandmother Huyn but the telephone connections are gone now for good to that part of Friesland. To-day was not like yesterday although the bombing and trouble are the same. It is now night and I am going to write what happened all day. We are in the air-shelter again. People are not talking as much as yesterday. Everyone is very tired from working. Yesterday no one knew what to do because the war had come so quickly but to-day we all worked, even the Baron and Uncle Pieter. The radio told citizens what to do to protect themselves. We have been piling sandbags around the houses and digging trenches away from cellars and laying in lots of food. Mother went to the bank this morning to get some money in case we had to leave but there was a long line and no one could take out more than two thousand guilders. There have been many air raids but we worked on outside during some of them. Soldiers are patrolling our little street, just going up and down which is patrolling. There are some soldiers on the housetops farther away. They are looking for parachutists and Dutch Nazis. A few people have tin or steel helmets like the soldiers but I wore a kettle over my head and so did many other people. We do this to keep from getting hit by shrapnel from the anti-aircraft guns and machine-guns. People look very funny going around wearing kettles and pots over their heads and Keetje's keeps falling off all the time. The trolley cars have stopped running, to save electricity, the Baron says, and there is no drinking water in any of the houses in our section because the Germans blew up some of the water pipes yesterday. The telephone is not working either and all letters and telegrams have stopped coming. This is because of the traitors and parachutists. The radio says that no one is to go on the streets after 8.30 to-night unless he had the proper papers and not to go anyway unless it's absolutely necessary. There were seven air raid alarms between nine this morning and supper. The radio says not to depend on sirens for warning because some of the traitors are giving false alarms. Uncle Pieter is furious about this and says he will shoot all traitors on sight and he has an army pistol to do it with too. He carries it inside his coat. There are not so many people here to-night because some of them were called out to fight fires and stand guard and help rescue and dig for people in fallen buildings. I wish I could do more.

This afternoon we saw our first parachutist. We were pasting strips of paper across the Baron's windows—the ones not broken—and across the windows of our own house so they won't break any more when the bombs come. About half of them were broken in all the houses around here yesterday. The parachutist came down at three o'clock. About fifty came down at once. This one was separated from the others. We saw the planes drop them but they seemed far away at first. Keetje was the first to see him because she was not doing much work. Mijnheer van Helst was near Keetje and when he saw the parachutist he called out to the women to go inside and then ran toward the man. The man came down behind the Baron's barn. We saw Mijnheer van Helst take out his pistol and aim and then he fired three times. He came back a moment later looking very sad and said the German was shot. The Baron and several others ran forward to see the German but Brenda kept me from going. Heintje Klaes went and came back and said the German was really dead and he was glad. Mijnheer van Helst didn't look glad and his hands were trembling. He is an old and very kind man and not used to shooting people the way regular soldiers do.

The parachutist, Heintje said, wore a one-piece green suit like overalls and his uniform was like a pair of ski pants. He had a flying eagle on his helmet which was of metal. The Baron brought back the helmet and he said someone could use this but no one wanted to put it on. Heintje got it later and is wearing it now. It is too big for him and he looks silly in it. Heintje is pretty silly-looking anyway and his eyes stick out like tulip bulbs most of the time. Mevrouw Klaes went out to see the dead parachutist and came back very excited. She swore she knew him and that he was named Friedrich Buehler and had grown up in

Holland after the other war. This caused a great deal of talk and excitement and Uncle Pieter said, "The damned ungrateful swine. We took their war babies and fed them and this is what we get back." Some soldiers came and took the dead parachutist away.

Some of the German planes dropped pieces of paper to-day and Max Blok brought one of the papers into our air-shelter. It said many things in Dutch and was written by the Germans. It said the Germans came as friends and they were sorry to be doing what they were doing but they had to protect us from the English and the French. This made everyone laugh at first and made them angry too. The paper also said that we should stop fighting for it was foolish and crazy for us to go on fighting when our country was almost completely beaten. Why did we want to fight against our friends the Germans?, the paper asked. Our friends the Germans, Mijnheer van Helst said, spitting. He stuck the paper on the wall and ran his pencil through it.

The worst air-raid of all has just come. About half the houses on our street are gone. One bomb landed on the lawn by our air-shelter and one side of the shelter is caved in but the Baron and the others are repairing it now. Mevrouw Hartog broke down and cried during the air-raid and got everyone very nervous when she yelled. I think she almost went crazy.

Heintje Klaes was killed! He went outside to see the light from the big flares and incendiary bombs and didn't come back. He slipped out. Heintje was not afraid of anything but the bombs got him. The whole house rocked when the bombs came close. We put our fingers in our ears but it didn't help much. The fire engines are working outside now and half the people in the air-shelter including Uncle Pieter have gone out. I went out for a while and they were taking dead people out of the bombed houses. Uncle Pieter sent me back to stay with Keetje. There is a funny smell in the air like burnt meat and a funny yellow light all over the country from the incendiary bombs. Three men were killed trying to get a bomb away that hadn't gone off yet. One of the men was our postmaster and I loved him very much. He gave me my first bicycle ride. It is awful to watch the people standing by their bombed houses. They don't do much. They just walk around and look at them and look sad and tired. I guess there isn't anything else they can do, but it seems awful.

Our house wasn't hit but the street in front of it between our house and the Baron's is just a great big hole and all the cobblestones are thrown up on our lawn and the Baron's until it doesn't look as if there ever was a street there. Mother is going to be surprised when she sees it. The street was just made over last year and was very smooth and nice.

At the end of our street the water is coming in where the canal locks were hit and I guess it will just keep running over the land until it is fixed. No one does anything about it because there are too many people to be helped and fires to fight. Twelve people on our street were killed and I knew every one of them but I knew Heintje best. Mevrouw Klaes has been crying ever since the bombing. Some people prayed all the time and some sang the national anthem and some just sat and stared. A woman who is very sick with a bad heart looked as if she might die. She was very pale when she came and still is. Jan Klaes is Mevrouw Klaes' other son and he is fighting somewhere like my father is. I said a prayer to myself for Father and I hope God heard it in spite of all the noise. I told Uncle Pieter I had prayed but he didn't say anything, just laid his hand on my shoulder. Uncle Pieter has gone off to the hospital to try to find Mother. It is getting late and he is worried, I think. I know he will find her. Keetje has gone to sleep again but she talks in her sleep and wakes up all the time asking if the war is over and things like that. Poor Keetje, she is so little and doesn't know what is happening. I think I do and it is worse than anything I ever heard about and worse than the worst fight in the cinema. The ambulances coming and going and so many dead people make it hard for me not to cry. I did cry some while the bombing was going on but so many other little chil-

dren were that no one noticed me, I think. I just got into
bed with Keetje and hid my face. I was really frightened
this time.

Later

Uncle Pieter came back. He didn't find Mother because
she is dead. I can't believe it but Uncle Pieter wouldn't lie.
We aren't going to tell Keetje yet. The ambulances are still
screaming. I can't sleep or write any more now or anything.

"Dirk van der Heide", aged twelve

The Conquerors

A few days after the start of the offensive Velten was
ordered to go as the messing officer's interpreter on a trip
into newly-occupied territory. Just as Quickloot and Grab-
ber in Goethe's *Faust* follows in the footsteps of the war-
lord to get their greedy claws on enemy possessions, so
now did a corps of administrative units, foragers and
"procurement men" move in behind the German armies.
The troop began to live from the land even before the
country was fully occupied. The headquarters paymaster
had a copious supply of the newly printed scrip on a par
with the currency of the conquered country. So when
Second Lieutenant Schloyka, the messing officer, drew out
sufficient to cover his purchases, Velten, too, converted a
portion of his cash.

When their open tourer drew up at the Dutch-German
frontier, somewhere near Venlo, they found the road
barred by a turnpike just as in the most balmy days of
peace. But German soldiers and customs officials watched
over it; and on the other side the Dutch frontier guards
were missing. The countryside lay at peace in the sunlight,
the lush green of the meadows alternating with the silvery
grey of the cornfields. The houses in the villages and
hamlets through which they passed shone prosperously in
the cleanliness of their neat red bricks and white win-

dowframes. Except for an occasional road-block one could drive unimpeded along the smooth well-kept highways of this rich little country. Only columns of prisoners slowed them down from time to time—tired, listless men in Belgian and French uniforms. Dutch prisoners were less frequently encountered, having already been marshalled on municipal sports grounds behind hastily erected barbed-wire entanglements. In the first flush of victory they were being magnanimously treated. Before long they were to regain full liberty.

Schloyka, who had already been in Holland the day before, was telling Velten of the treats to come at a café in the town where he had to make purchases for the mess kitchen.

They were not disappointed. If one ignored the slight restlessness of a people usually so stolid, there was an entirely peace-time atmosphere about the little place. All the businesses and shops were open and German soldiers and Dutch civilians mingled indiscriminately. When they sat down on the sunny terrace of the café and Schloyka ordered *Bohnenkaffee,* the waiter grinned and inquired what other kind of coffee they imagined there was. During the first months of the war it was not easy to make the citizens of this prosperous colonial power understand that in a country where the slogan "Guns instead of Butter" was a mark of heroism rather than an imposition, the word coffee could signify a brew of malt and dried turnips.

As they walked through the town after their sumptuous repast, Velten noticed how Dutch women watched the German soldiers buying half a dozen pairs of artificial silk stockings at a time, as well as shirts, neckties and underclothing. "They're hoarding, you know, hoarding!" he heard them whisper to each other excitedly.

Shortly afterwards Velten found himself in the narrow office of the wholesale dealer on whom they had called to buy coffee and cocoa at eighty cents per kilo. The sacks and cartons were already being loaded into the car outside. The dealer was a well-fed man with a thick gold watch-chain across his comfortable paunch. When Velten, having calculated what he owed in marks at the official rate of exchange, laid a roll of German scrip on the table, the Dutchman gazed at the notes in astonishment and suspicion.

"Come along with you," said Velten, "that's good money. If we win the war, you'll be glad to have it. And," he added hesitatingly, "if we lose, we shall still have to pay up." At that a broad smile spread over the man's round face. "If you poor devils lose this war," he said good-naturedly in his heavy Limburg dialect, "I don't believe you'll be able to pay a single *pfennig*." Then he pocketed the notes without counting them and gave Velten the change in clinking silver guilders and those dainty little ten-cent pieces called *dubbeltjes* which are also made of silver.

Velten lost no time in leaving.

Gerhard Kramer

BELGIUM

10 May

At 8.30 a.m. the German Ambassador came to the Ministry of Foreign Affairs. When he entered the Minister's room, he began to take a paper from his pocket. M. Spaak—that is the Belgian Minister—stopped him: "I beg your pardon, Mr. Ambassador, I will speak first." And in an indignant voice, he read the Belgian Government's protest: "Mr. Ambassador, the German Army has just attacked our country. This is the second time in twenty-five years that Germany has committed a criminal aggression against a neutral and loyal Belgium. What has just happened is perhaps even more odious than the aggression of 1914. No ultimatum, no note, no protest of any kind has ever been placed before the Belgian Government. It is through the attack itself that Belgium has learned that Germany has violated the undertakings given by her on 13 October, 1937, and renewed spontaneously at the beginning of the war. . . ."

An Invasion is Organized

We began to have some idea of the scope and importance of the German parachutists' activities when the police came around, about the third day, to remove from the hotel all advertising signs for "Pacha" Chicory, a step being taken all over Belgium at that moment. As the police officer explained, it had been discovered that the "Pacha" signs bore on the back information for the use of German parachutists; this was later confirmed by repeated radio warnings.

Chicory is widely used on the Continent, as a coffee substitute, or as a mixture with it, and "Pacha" was the most widely used brand of chicory in Belgium. In consequence, every little food shop in the country had signs advertising "Pacha". These signs had been printed in Belgium, but complicity on someone's part had permitted the Germans to put on the back of them indications useful to parachutists landing in the locality where that particular sign was to be used. Thanks to this arrangement, a German parachutist needed to carry on his person no incriminating maps and addresses; wherever he might land, he needed only to find the nearest "Pacha" chicory sign, which might be in a grocery shop or along a public highway, and on its back he would find cryptic indications giving him the location of the nearest German agent and how to find him.

Lars Moen, research worker

The B.E.F. Advances Into Belgium: 12 May

Yesterday, so overjoyed were the Belgian people to see our troops that the B.B.C. car was partly filled with tulips and narcissi, our drivers were taken to lunch and loaded with cigarettes. A Lancashire lad said, "Ee, I'm havin' a terrible time"—he'd been kissed by half-a-dozen girls.

The bombing, so far as my colleagues have been able to judge at the moment, appears to be directed for the most part at military objectives—aerodromes, railway stations, level crossings and so forth. But on this, indeed, it is extremely difficult to form an opinion. The pilot tries to bomb a level crossing—he misses the crossing and demolishes a couple of villas two hundred yards away. Or a pilot is attacked by a fighter and, in making his escape, lightens his machine by dropping his bombs indiscriminately. That action kills half-a-dozen civilians. It seems to their friends deliberate murder; to the pilot no more than the chance of war.

I'm told four British airmen interned in Belgium through a forced landing have now been able to go to England, that they were not on parole, but found the life lonely because few besides members of the British Embassy could visit them.

This is a day of great beauty, and if the occasion were not so grave, one could enjoy it thoroughly. Even so, it is difficult not to enjoy it. The sun is always the sun, and flowers are no less lovely because bombers zoom overhead. Indeed, war puts an edge on beauty—it is as though beauty said, "Take a long look at me, enjoy me while you may. Who knows for how long it will be?" It may seem incongruous that spring's foliage should be used to camouflage motorcycles and that steel helmets should be adorned with green leaves, but so it is.

The procession on the roads has drawn villagers to their doors. They sit on chairs on the pavement watching the cavalcade go by: British guns (medium and light) draped in dust-sheets, Bren carriers, motor lorries—all the impedimenta of war; and on the other side of the road, speeding towards us, those fleeing from war as from the plague—thousands upon thousands of refugees. I don't know how many passed this way yesterday but the numbers to-day are colossal. Somebody said last night to me, "It is Poland over again." But, I thought, hardly that, for these can, at least, put British troops between themselves and the German horde. These seem to be the richer folk with cars—some are large cars, and they go by at a great pace; others are ramshackle affairs—one with two people clinging to the running-board. A host of them carry a mattress on top, partly to guard against machine-gun bullets, partly because this is the most convenient way of carrying it.

And yet even this pitiful sight—and you cannot see it unmoved—bears from time to time, and for a swift instant or two, an air of holiday, a touch of Derby Day. For a lorry will come along holding a large family—grandfather driving the old horse, mother and grandmother sitting aloft surrounded by young children, and all of them raising a hand or waving a greeting. A moment later that impression is blotted out by the sight of a sick woman lying back on her pillows open to the sky.

The route by which we go is marked by sticks on which is painted a black upright arrow rather resembling a plane in flight. Within two or three hours of our entry into Belgium, roads were marked as clearly and traffic guided as efficiently as to the Aldershot Tattoo.

We drive along in the direction of Brussels. Here we pass a motor-lorry on which our lads have chalked: *Berlin or Bust.* My French colleague asks what it means, and is tickled when he learns. We pull up alongside a refugee motor-car broken down—a back wheel is off. They have come from near Liège—the grandmother, whose face wears that numbed, stricken look which is worst of all, was a refugee in the last war also. That is what one finds so repeatedly—people are enduring again what they suffered twenty-odd years ago. They've had no sleep for two nights; they have no food.

Here are two cottages half-obliterated by a bomb. That bomb killed people yesterday. But the hole it made in the road is mended—it almost seems a long time ago since the bomb fell.

Occasional gunfire thuds heavily, like someone beating a carpet a long way off; from time to time a shrill air-raid siren blows; but the procession does not stop. Refugees, exhausted, lie asleep in the fields beside their bicycles.

I talk to an old man leaning over his garden gate, brown eyes deep-sunken. He says, "It is the Boche, monsieur. He does not change. I saw it coming—like a cloud of dust in the road concealing you know not what. And then, from the dust emerges a shape—a shape we knew before—the Boche, monsieur. Yes, I have seen it before." He stops. Presently his face lightens. "It is spring," he says slowly, "and in spring there is hope. Your men bring us hope; and since it is spring, we give them our flowers—lilac, tulips, narcissus." He looks at our stolid lads with their brick-red faces, sweaty, dusty, rolling by in their lorries, some of them asleep in the sun, and for a moment there is a light in his old eyes. . . .

J. L. Hodson

On 13 May, Winston Churchill made his first speech to the House of Commons as Prime Minister.

I would say to the House, as I said to those who have joined this Government, "I have nothing to offer but blood, toil, tears and sweat."

We have before us an ordeal of the most grievous kind. We have before us many, many long months of struggle and of suffering. You ask what is our policy? I will say: it is to wage war, by sea, land and air, with all our might and with all the strength that God can give us: to wage war against a monstrous tyranny never surpassed in the dark, lamentable catalogue of human crime. That is our policy. You ask, what is our aim? I can answer in one word: victory—victory at all costs, victory in spite of all terror, victory, however long and hard the road may be; for without victory, there is no survival. Let that be realized; no survival for the British Empire; no survival for all that the British Empire has stood for, no survival for the urge and impulse of the ages, that mankind will move forward towards its goal. But I take up my task with buoyancy and hope. I feel sure that our cause will not be suffered to fail among men. At this time I feel entitled to claim the aid of all, and I say, "Come, then, let us go forward together with our united strength."

Winston Churchill

The Formation of the Home Guard: 14 May

I want to speak to you to-night about the form of warfare which the Germans have been employing so extensively against Holland and Belgium, namely, the dropping of troops by parachute behind the main defensive lines.

The success of such an attack depends on speed. Consequently, the measures to defeat such an attack must be prompt and rapid. It is upon this basis that our plans have been laid. You will not expect me to tell you, or the enemy, what our plans are, but we are confident that they will be effective. However, in order to leave nothing to chance, and to supplement, from sources as yet untapped, the means of defence already arranged, we are going to ask you to help us in a manner which I know will be welcome to thousands of you. Since the war began the Government have received countless inquiries from all over the Kingdom from men of all ages who are for one reason or another not at present engaged in military service and who wish to do something for the defence of the country.

Now is your opportunity. We want large numbers of such men in Great Britain who are British subjects between the ages of seventeen and sixty-five to come forward now and offer their service in order to make assurance doubly sure. . . .

Anthony Eden, Secretary of State for War

BLITZKRIEG

On 13 May the Germans broke through the line of the Meuse, and two days later had shattered the French 9 Army of General Corap. In the next seven days the Panzers swept west and north-west, cutting off the French, British and Belgian armies to the north, which soon had their backs to the sea.

The Master Plan

. . . . Each of us generals outlined what his task was and how he intended to carry it out. I was the last to speak. My task was as follows: On the day ordered I would cross the Luxembourg frontier, drive through southern Belgium towards Sedan, cross the Meuse and establish a bridgehead on the far side so that the infantry corps following behind could get across. I explained briefly that my corps would advance through Luxembourg and southern Belgium in three columns; I reckoned on reaching the Belgian frontier posts on the first day and I hoped to break through them on that same day; on the second day I would advance as far as Neufchâteau; on the third day I would reach Bouillon and cross the Semois; on the fourth day I would arrive at the Meuse; on the fifth day I would cross it. By the evening of the fifth day I hoped to have established a bridgehead on the far bank. Hitler asked, "And then what are you going to do?" He was the first person who had thought to ask me this vital question. I replied, "Unless I receive orders to the contrary, I intend on the next day to continue my advance westwards. The supreme leadership must decide whether my objective is to be Amiens or Paris. In my opinion the correct course is to drive past Amiens to the English Channel." Hitler nodded and said nothing more. Only General Busch, who commanded 16 Army on my left, cried out, "Well, I don't think you'll cross the river in the first place!" Hitler, the tension visible in his face, looked at me to see what I would reply. I said, "There's no need for you to do so, in any case." Hitler made no comment.

General Heinz Guderian, G.O.C. Panzer Corps

Crossing the Meuse

On 13 May I drove off to Dinant at about 04.00 hours
with Captain Schraepler. The whole of the divisional artillery was already in position as ordered, with its forward
observers stationed at the crossing points. In Dinant I
found only a few men of the 7th Rifle Regiment. Shells
were dropping in the town from French artillery west of
the Meuse, and there were a number of knocked-out tanks
in the streets leading down to the river. The noise of battle
could be heard from the Meuse valley.

The situation when I arrived was none too pleasant.
Our boats were being destroyed one after the other by the
French flanking fire, and the crossing eventually came to a
standstill. The enemy infantry were so well concealed that
they were impossible to locate even after a long search
through glasses. Again and again they directed their fire
into the area in which I and my companions—the commanders of the Rifle Brigade and the Engineer Battalion—were lying. A smoke screen in the Meuse valley
would have prevented these infantry doing much harm.
But we had no smoke unit. So I now gave orders for a
number of houses in the valley to be set alight in order to
supply the smoke we lacked.

Minute by minute the enemy fire grew more unpleasant.
From up river a damaged rubber boat came drifting down
to us with a badly wounded man clinging to it, shouting
and screaming for help—the poor fellow was near to
drowning. But there was no help for him here, the enemy
fire was too heavy.

With Captain Schraepler, I now drove south down the
Meuse valley road in a Panzer IV to see how things were
going with the 7th Rifle Regiment. On the way we came
under fire several times from the western bank and
Schraepler was wounded in the arm from a number of
shell splinters. Single French infantrymen surrendered as
we approached.

By the time we arrived the 7th Rifle Regiment had

already succeeded in getting a company across to the west bank, but the enemy fire had then become so heavy that their crossing equipment had been shot to pieces and the crossing had had to be halted. Large numbers of wounded were receiving treatment in a house close beside the demolished bridge. As at the northern crossing point, there was nothing to be seen of the enemy who were preventing the crossing. As there was clearly no hope of getting any more men across at this point without powerful artillery and tank support to deal with the enemy nests, I drove back to Division Headquarters, where I met the Army commander, Colonel-General von Kluge and the Corps commander, General Hoth.

After taking over the situation with Major Heidkaemper and making the necessary arrangements, I drove back along the Meuse to Leffé [a village on the outskirts of Dinant] to get the crossing moving there.

At Leffé weir we took a quick look at the footbridge, which had been barred by the enemy with a spiked steel plate. The firing in the Meuse valley had ceased for the moment and we moved off to the right through some houses to the crossing point proper. The crossing had now come to a complete standstill, with the officers badly shaken by the casualties which their men had suffered. On the opposite bank we could see several men of the company which was already across, among them many wounded. Numerous damaged boats and rubber dinghies lay on the opposite bank. The officers reported that nobody dared show himself outside cover, as the enemy opened fire immediately on anyone they spotted.

Several of our tanks and heavy weapons were in position on the embankment east of the houses, but had seemingly already fired off almost all their ammunition. However, the tanks I had ordered to the crossing point soon arrived, to be followed shortly afterwards by two field howitzers from the Battalion Grasemann.

All points on the western bank likely to hold enemy riflemen were now brought under fire, and soon the aimed fire of all weapons was pouring into rocks and buildings.

Lieutenant Hanke knocked out a pill-box on the bridge ramp with several rounds. The tanks, with turrets traversed left, drove slowly north at fifty yards' spacing along the Meuse valley, closely watching the opposite slopes.

Under cover of this fire the crossing slowly got going again, and a cable ferry using several large pontoons was started. Rubber boats paddled backwards and forwards and brought back the wounded from the west bank. One man who fell out of his boat on the way grabbed hold of the ferry rope and was dragged underwater through the Meuse. He was rescued by Private Heidenreich, who dived in and brought him to the bank.

I now took over personal command of the 2nd Battalion of the 7th Rifle Regiment and for some time directed operations myself.

With Lieutenant Most I crossed the Meuse in one of the first boats and at once joined the company which had been across since early morning. From the company command post we could see Companies Enkefort and Lichter were making rapid progress.

I then moved up north along a deep gully to the Company Enkefort. As we arrived an alarm came in: "Enemy tanks in front." The company had no anti-tank weapons, and I therefore gave orders for small arms fire to be opened on the tanks as quickly as possible, whereupon we saw them pull back into a hollow about a thousand yards north-west of Leffé. Large numbers of French stragglers came through the bushes and slowly laid down their arms.

On arrival at Brigade Headquarters on the west bank I found the situation looking decidedly unhealthy. The commander of the 7th Motor-cycle Battalion had been wounded, his adjutant killed, and a powerful French counter-attack had severely mauled our men in Grange. There was a danger that enemy tanks might penetrate into the Meuse valley itself.

Leaving my signals truck on the west bank, I crossed the river again and gave orders for first the Panzer Company, and then the Panzer Regiment, to be ferried across during the night. However, ferrying tanks across the 120-yards-wide river by night was a slow job, and by morning there were still only fifteen tanks on the west bank, an alarmingly small number.

At daybreak [14 May] we heard that Colonel von Bismarck had pressed through his attack to close on Onhaye [three miles west of Dinant], where he was now engaged with a powerful enemy. Shortly afterwards a wireless message came in saying that his regiment was encircled, and I therefore decided to go to his assistance immediately with every available tank.

At about 09.00 hours the 25th Panzer Regiment, under the command of Colonel Rothenburg, moved off along the Meuse valley with the thirty tanks which had so far arrived on the west bank and penetrated as far as a hollow five hundred yards north-east of Onhaye without meeting any resistance. It transpired that von Bismarck had actually radioed "arrived" instead of "encircled"* and that he was now on the point of sending an assault company round the northern side of Onhaye to secure its western exit. This move, as had been shown by an exercise we had carried out earlier in Godesberg, was of the greatest importance for the next stages of the operation. Accordingly, five tanks were placed under von Bismarck's command for this purpose—not to make a tank attack in the usual sense, but to provide mobile covering fire for the infantry attack on the defile west of Onhaye. It was my intention to place the Panzer Regiment itself in a wood a thousand yards north of Onhaye and then to bring all other units up to that point, from where they could be employed to the north, north-west or west, according to how the situation developed.

I gave orders to Rothenburg to move round both sides of the wood into this assembly area, and placed myself in a Panzer III which was to follow close behind him.

Rothenburg now drove off through a hollow to the left with the five tanks which were to accompany the infantry,

* Translator's note: *eingetroffen* instead of *eingeschlossen*.

thus giving these tanks a lead of a hundred to a hundred
and fifty yards. There was no sound of enemy fire. Some
twenty to thirty tanks followed up behind. When the commander of the five tanks reached the rifle company on the
southern edge of Onhaye wood, Colonel Rothenburg
moved off with his leading tanks along the edge of the
wood going west: we had just reached the south-west corner of the wood and were about to cross a low plantation,
from which we could see the five tanks escorting the infantry below us to our left front, when suddenly we came under heavy artillery and anti-tank gunfire from the west.
Shells landed all round us and my tank received two hits,
one after the other, the first on the upper edge of the turret
and the second in the periscope.

The driver promptly opened the throttle wide and drove
straight into the nearest bushes. He had only gone a few
yards, however, when the tank slid down a steep slope on
the western edge of the wood and finally stopped, canted
over on its side, in such a position that the enemy whose
guns were in position about five hundred yards away on
the edge of the next wood could not fail to see it. I had
been wounded in the right cheek by a small splinter from
the shell which had landed in the periscope. It was not
serious though it bled a great deal.

I tried to swing the turret round so as to bring our 37
mm. gun to bear on the enemy in the opposite wood, but
with the heavy slant of the tank it was immovable.

The French battery now opened rapid fire on our wood
and at any moment we could expect their fire to be aimed
at our tank, which was in full view. I therefore decided to
abandon it as fast as I could, taking the crew with me. At
that moment the subaltern in command of the tanks
escorting the infantry reported himself seriously wounded,
with the words, "Herr General, my left arm has been shot
off." We clambered up through the sandy pit, shells
crashing and splintering all round. Close in front of us
trundled Rothenburg's tank with flames pouring out of the
rear. The adjutant of the Panzer Regiment had also left
his tank. I thought at first that the command tank had

been set alight by a hit in the petrol tank and was extremely worried for Colonel Rothenburg's safety. However, it turned out to be only the smoke candles that had caught light, the smoke from which now served us very well. In the meantime Lieutenant Most had driven my armoured signals vehicle into the wood, where it had been hit in the engine and now stood immobilized. The crew was unhurt.

I now gave orders for the tanks to drive through the wood in a general easterly direction, a move which the armoured cars, which stood at my disposal, were of course unable to follow. Slowly Rothenburg's command tank forced its way through the trees, many of them tall and well grown. It was only the involuntary smoke-screen laid by this tank that prevented the enemy from shooting up any more of our vehicles. If only the tanks had sprayed the wood which the enemy was believed to be holding with machine-gun and 37 mm. gunfire during their advance, the French would probably have immediately abandoned their guns, which were standing in exposed positions at the edge of the wood, and our losses would almost certainly have been smaller. An attack launched in the evening by the 25th Panzer Regiment was successful, and we were able to occupy our assembly area.

General Erwin Rommel, G.O.C. 7 Panzer Division

Break-through: 15 May

The way to the west was now open. The moon was up and for the time being we could expect no real darkness. I had already given orders, in the plan for the break-through, for the leading tanks to scatter the road and verges with machine and anti-tank gunfire at intervals during the drive to Avesnes, which I hoped would prevent the enemy from laying mines. The rest of the Panzer Regiment was to follow close behind the leading tanks and be ready at any time to fire salvoes to either flank. The mass of the division had instructions to follow up the Panzer Regiment lorry-borne.

The tanks now rolled in a long column through the line
of fortifications and on towards the first houses, which
had been set alight by our fire. In the moonlight we could
see the men of 7th Motor-cycle Battalion moving forward
on foot beside us. Occasionally an enemy machine-gun or
anti-tank gun fired, but none of their shots came anywhere
near us. Our artillery was dropping heavy harassing fire
on villages and the road far ahead of the regiment. Gradually the speed increased. Before long we were five hundred—a thousand—two thousand—three thousand yards
into the fortified zone. Engines roared, tank tracks
clanked and clattered. Whether or not the enemy was firing was impossible to tell in the ear-splitting noise. We
crossed the railway line a mile or so south-west of Solre
le Château, and then swung north to the main road which
was soon reached. Then off along the road and past the
first houses.

The people in the houses were rudely awoken by the
din of our tanks, the clatter and roar of tracks and
engines. Troops lay bivouacked beside the road, military
vehicles stood parked in farmyards and in some places on
the road itself. Civilians and French troops, their faces
distorted with terror, lay huddled in the ditches, alongside
hedges and in every hollow beside the road. We passed
refugee columns, the carts abandoned by their owners,
who had fled in panic into the fields. On we went, at a
steady speed, towards our objective. Every so often a
quick glance at the map by a shaded light and a short
wireless message to Divisional H.Q. to report the position
and thus the success of the 25th Panzer Regiment. Every
so often to look out of the hatch to assure myself that
there was still no resistance and that contact was being
maintained to the rear. The flat countryside lay spread out
around us under the cold light of the moon. We were
through the Maginot Line!* It was hardly conceivable.
Twenty-two years before we had stood for four and a half

* In fact, this was the recently-built northward extension of the
Maginot Line proper, which lay farther to the south (Ed.)

long years before this self-same enemy and had won victory after victory and yet finally lost the war. And now we had broken through the renowned Maginot Line and were driving deep into enemy territory. It was not just a beautiful dream. It was reality.

Suddenly there was a flash from a mound about three hundred yards away to the right of the road. There could be no doubt what it was, an enemy gun well concealed in a concrete pill-box, firing on the 25th Panzer Regiment from the flank. More flashes came from other points. Shell bursts could not be seen. Quickly informing Rothenburg of the danger—he was standing close beside me—I gave orders through him for the regiment to increase speed and burst through this second fortified line with broadsides to right and left.

Fire was opened quickly, the tank crews having been instructed in the method of fire before the attack. Much of our ammunition was tracer and the regiment drove on through the new defence line spraying an immense rain of fire into the country on either side. Soon we were through the danger area, without casualties. But it was not now easy to get the fire stopped and we drove through the villages of Sars Poteries and Beugnies with guns blazing. Enemy confusion was complete. Military vehicles, tanks, artillery and refugee carts packed high with belongings blocked part of the road and had to be pushed unceremoniously to the side. All around were French troops lying flat on the ground, and farms everywhere were jammed tight with guns, tanks and other military vehicles. Progress towards Avesnes now became slow. At last we succeeded in getting the firing stopped. We drove through Semousies. Always the same picture, troops and civilians in wild flight down both sides of the road.

Rommel

Amiens

1 Panzer Division's attack went well, and by about noon we had taken the city and forced a bridgehead to a

depth of some four miles. I had a quick look over the
ground we had seized and also the city with its beautiful
cathedral, before hurrying back to Albert where I expected to find 2 Panzer Division. I met the colums of my
advancing troops and had to drive through crowds of
fleeing refugees. I also ran into a number of enemy vehicles which, thick with dust, had joined the German columns and hoped in this fashion to reach Paris and avoid
being taken prisoner. I thus quickly captured some fifteen
Englishmen.

In Albert I found General Veiel. 2 Panzer Division had
captured an English artillery battery, drawn up on the bar-
rack square and equipped only with training ammunition,
since nobody had reckoned on our appearance that day.
Prisoners of all nationalities filled the market-place and
the adjoining streets. 2 Panzer Division were almost out of
fuel and were therefore proposing to stop where they
were, but they were soon disillusioned. I ordered them to
advance at once to Abbeville and by 19.00 hours they had
reached this objective, passing through Doullens-
Beaumetz-Saint Riquier.

The divisional commander was mistaken in thinking
that his troops were out of fuel. After regulating the fuel
stocks in the hands of the troops it proved possible to continue the advance. One must always distrust the report of
troop commanders, "We have no fuel." Generally they
have. But if they become tired they lack fuel. That is a
common experience of war with the forward troops. During the campaign in France there was no lack of fuel—
good staff work can avoid this calamity. Later in the war
we often had a real scarcity of fuel because of the destruction of our industry. But in 1940 it was only a question of
transport and easy to solve.

                                    General Heinz Guderian

A Postcard

I received a postcard at my address, found on the body
of an officer of Corap's army, who had just committed

suicide in Le Mans station. He wrote, "I am killing myself, Mr. President, to let you know that all my men were brave, but one cannot send men to fight tanks with rifles."

Paul Reynaud

Sauve Qui Peut

For twenty-one hours Captain Billerot was cut off from the colonel's headquarters. Then he decided to send out three men in search of the Ferme Saint-Denis. Adjudant Lesfauries, Sergeant Keruran, and I volunteered. We all had our bellyful of that wood. Sergeant-Major Gerber joined us at the last moment.

After four hours we found the Ferme and our colonel, but we had lost Gerber on our way. The colonel told us he had taken up position with his three battalions without knowing the whereabouts of the regiment we were supposed to relieve. This regiment, the 48th Infantry, had vanished, he said. A battalion of anti-tank guns that happened to be nearby had rushed to his assistance and for the moment was holding back the Germans. Captain Duvivier had gone off to find the divisional commander—his exact whereabouts were not known. Infuriated that the two companies had not yet arrived, Colonel de Buissy asked me if I could show him the exact location of the woods in which Captains Billerot and Berley were entrenched. I could not, because the colonel owned only a Michelin automobile map: the only military map in the regiment had been taken by Captain Duvivier.

The colonel asked me whether I would undertake to find my way back to the wood and guide both companies to the Ferme. I set out. Considering that the Germans seemed to be asleep and that the *Mouchard** had gone home, I decided to avoid the woods and follow the main road straight through Châtillon. This road offered an amazing spectacle. Everywhere I saw guns, knapsacks,

* German reconnaissance plane.

tins of food, cartridge-cases in the ditch. Equipment worth hundreds of thousands of francs was strewn along the road: no one thought of picking it up. All these things had become too heavy for the infantrymen.

A short distance beyond Châtillon I met a soldier sitting on his knapsack and devouring a tin of meat.

"What regiment?" I asked him.

"48th Infantry."

"Where's your regiment?"

"Don't know."

He quietly went on eating.

"Where are you going now?"

He looked sullenly ahead. He was a square-built, dark-haired fellow. His dark eyes had so dull a look that I thought: he wouldn't notice if a bullet hit him.

"Don't know," he said at last. "I'm looking for my regiment."

I asked him whether they had been ordered to retreat.

"How do I know?" said the soldier. He rubbed his knee, adding, "All of a sudden someone began to yell, *"Sauve qui peut!"*—and then we ran for it."

"Were the Germans there?"

He reflected a while.

"No, we didn't see any."

He rose, looking at me with distrust.

"Let's go!"

He took his field flask and made ready to follow me.

"What about your gun?" I asked.

He cast a glance at his gun lying in the ditch—a farewell glance.

"Much too heavy," he said. "And rusty. Can't get it open. There's plenty of guns all over the place."

He thrust his hands into his trouser pockets and limped along by my side. But there was nothing unusual in his limp. All of us limped.

We came to a house where two shell-stricken negroes sat smoking. They belonged to the 24th Colonials. They joined us. They, too, were "looking for" their regiment. One of them was a corporal and understood French. He asked me whether it would soon be "over". He too, thought Germany hadn't done anything to him. I tried to explain that France was in danger. He didn't seem to understand.

"Hitler no come Senegal", he kept repeating. He smiled, showing his teeth, and spoke at quick intervals to his comrade. "Hitler no come Senegal. I no come Germany. I and Hitler no enemy."

A stray German shell exploded a few yards ahead of us. We threw ourselves on the ground. The Senegal negro—the one who did not speak French—shouted, "*Sauve qui peut!*" It sounded like "*shof ki po*". He probably did not understand the meaning of his cry. He had heard it at a moment of great peril, and from that time on he repeated it whenever he thought himself in danger.

The Frenchman lay in the ditch beside me, the two negroes about five steps from us. The sound of bursting shrapnel grew clearer and clearer, closer and closer. I lay on an abandoned knapsack. At every explosion the Senegalese yelled, "*Shof ki po! Shof ki po!*"

Soon it began to sound like an Oriental prayer.

The Germans shortened their range. Now the shrapnel burst on the field to the right of us. Suddenly I heard an inhuman cry. It was one of the negroes. The other, the black corporal, threw himself sobbing and lamenting over his comrade. I crawled as close to them as I could. The negro's whole back had been torn open by a shrapnel splinter.

He was the first dying man I saw at the front. His eyes were wide open, his mouth was foaming. His tongue, a thick black tongue, moved between his lips. And, like a last wish or the name of someone he loved, he mumbled the words, "*Shof ki po! Shof ki po!*"

Run for your lives! This was the slogan of the French Army.

Run for your lives. *Shof ki po.*

Hans Habe

The Battle of Sainte-Menehould

When I went out of the church with Kohn Gabriel I heard the first German tanks entering the town.

The panic had started while we were inside. Soldiers ran up and down in the square looking for cover. There were practically no officers left; at least none appeared in the square. Even to-day I believe that some of the men lost their minds at this moment. I still can see Sergeant Rupin dashing madly about the square on his bicycle, round and round, like a participant in a six-day cycle race. Again and again he flitted by my nose, and I couldn't stop him. Adjutant Lesfauries stumbled by me asking, with an infinitely stupid look, whether there was anything new. He did not wait for my answer. Some lay flat on the pavement, pressing their guns to their shoulders. This gesture—only natural on the battlefield—here seemed grotesque. Men with rifles, with knapsacks on their backs, lay on the pavement of the main square like toy soldiers on the carpet of a nursery. The first planes appeared. We could no longer distinguish between the sound of the planes and the tanks. A bomb fell in the middle of the square. Stones hurled through the air. You could hardly tell whether it was day or night. Each bomb that fell spread light and then darkness.

I lay in front of the church. Suddenly I heard a voice, "Take cover, in the houses! Stop the tanks!"

No one knew who had cried out. We obeyed mechanically. I slipped under a gate at the corner of the square and the Rue Margraine. At the same moment the German tanks turned into the narrow street. They didn't seem to be moving down the street—the whole street seemed to be moving—moving with the armoured cars. They filled the street. They took it with them. The red maws of the tanks drilled their flaming tongues into the walls of the houses. It looked as though nothing could remain in their wake. It was as though each tank peeled a piece off the crust of the earth. But for this very reason we were not frightened. The whole thing seemed unreal. It was more like a bad film of the future, with warriors from Mars and synthetic men popping out of bottles. Everything moved as on a screen. We felt that it couldn't go on much longer.

Suddenly, in the midst of the deafening noise of the circling bombers and the slowly advancing tanks, I heard a familiar sound—the rattle of a machine-gun not far from me. The sound was almost friendly, almost musical. I looked up. From the second or third floor of the adjoining house a machine-gun was firing—firing at the approaching tanks. And the same thing happened that always happens when a man turns up in a faint-hearted crowd. Suddenly firing started from all sides. It was a childish effort. Our experience had taught us that even the anti-tank guns were powerless against the heavy German units. Only the seventy-fives obtained some success. And now we were firing our machine-guns and old carbines. But what did that matter? There was a sudden patter from all the houses. I quickly ran to the other side of the street. Bullets whistled past me on both sides. Our soldiers had made up their minds to lay a barrage across the street.

I ran up the steps. It was a little old house with wooden stairs. Half-way to the first floor a door was open—the door to the W.C. Nothing on earth is funnier than a W.C. when the whole world is collapsing.

I did not know the machine-gunners. But at the window of the adjoining room stood a man whom I immediately recognized, even from behind. It gave me a feeling of indescribable joy. I say "indescribable", because a normal human being in his daily routine rises to the joys of his existence from a settled level of mediocrity. One must fall to the depths to understand what it means to find a friend. At the window stood Saint-Brice.

For some unknown reason the tank, followed by innumerable others—the street was so narrow that they could move only in single file—halted. At the same time the roar of the aeroplane engines redoubled in intensity. The tank stood at the northern end of the Rue Camille

Margraine. The machine-guns stopped rattling. Half-hidden in our room, we looked down into the street. Fallen soldiers lay on the asphalt. Blood ran down the gutter. It is so easy to write these words, forgetting what they mean: blood running down the gutter. In writing, everything seems two-dimensional in effect, without background. Blood in the gutter: nothing behind it. No suffering, no pain, no meaning. Red water in the drain. Gurgling red water. You move as in a film, watching yourself. And that is what makes it all bearable.

A few steps from our house a wounded soldier was screaming. From time to time the upper part of his body rose. Each time he fell down again he stopped crying. Again and again we believed that he was dead. But at regular intervals he sat up. At regular intervals the dead man screamed.

Behind the tank German motor-cycles appeared. As the street was too narrow they formed on the pavement. Each cycle had a sidecar with two men in it. Each of them was armed with an automatic rifle. But they had not yet started to move. My brain throbbed with the tension. Something seemed to be flying through my temples. Behind street corners and windows a group of desperate men was waiting. How many were they? Were we not alone? Alone with a few dead and the half-dead whose cries rent the air. We did not know. Any sound would have been more bearable than this silence in which you couldn't tell where your comrades were. Even the machine-gunners in the next room did not stir.

At last the motor-cyclists started. They emerged at the right and left of the armoured car. One of the two men on each motor-cycle held his automatic rifle upward, the other horizontally down the street. They fired without interruption. In less than a fraction of a minute they were in front of our house. At least fifteen of them arrived at the same time. I was half-crouching under a window. Saint-Brice bent forward. I saw that he was taking aim. I made ready to shoot. Saint-Brice pulled the trigger. I followed him immediately. The miracle occurred—my Remington went off! I reloaded in feverish haste. Despite the infernal noise that was suddenly unleashed—motor-cycles, armoured cars, aeroplanes, bombs, machine-gun fire, rifles—I distinctly heard orders shouted in German. Somebody cried, *"Rein ins Haus!"* ("Into the house!") Simultaneously the pane splintered. They were firing at our window.

I crawled into the adjoining room for ammunition. A bullet whistled by me. Curious, I thought unconsciously, this shot cannot come from the street. Then I heard somebody saying beside me, *"Oh, les salauds!"*

I crawled to the three men at the machine-gun. And then I saw what, for the first time, struck me with horror. In a window of one of the few undamaged houses on the opposite side of the street—the same house under the gate of which I had been hidden a short time before—a machine-gun had been set in place. Behind the machine-gun a German steel helmet emerged and quickly disappeared. But the man could not disappear quickly enough; I saw his face. His eyes stared at me. It was probably only my imagination, but it seemed to me that I had never before seen more evil eyes. And though I had never feared all the terrifying things invented by man, I was afraid of this man. Cannon, shells, and bombs are not terrifying. Only man is terrifying.

Suddenly I realized that Saint-Brice had seized me by the arm. . . .

"We've got to get out of here!" Saint-Brice whispered into my ear. I followed him. He pushed me forward and covered our retreat with his unloaded revolver. He must have explored the premises in advance; he took me through a narrow corridor, through a half-demolished room, down a wooden staircase, and finally through a store-room. And then we were outside.

We must have left the house by the back door. We stood in a little vegetable garden, bordered by an old stone wall. Suddenly we found ourselves in the midst of a summer morning. I stood still, breathing deeply. The din of the battle was muffled.

"Come on," said Saint-Brice.

We ran across a field. What did we care whether planes spotted us? We breathed. We were alive.

And we knew what it meant to be alive.

But there was no time to pause. To reach the bridge we had to go back through the town. Meanwhile the Germans had moved in everywhere. But our regiments were resisting desperately. I saw soldiers firing from behind corpses, resting their guns on the bodies of their dead comrades. The town stank of corpses, smoke, and sugar. I had a glimpse of Colonel de Buissy trying with a few men to erect a tank barricade. The whole scene had a toylike effect, comic and tragic at once: on one side a few riflemen, the lieutenant with the revolver, the meagre fabric of barbed wire, the forlorn machine-gun; the other side, tanks, armoured cars that reached nearly to the second storey, motor-cycles, machine-guns on wheels.

A single machine-gun was holding the south bridge. A young Frenchman of the 11th Regiment whom I knew and a negro of the same regiment were firing the gun. Suddenly the negro clutched his chest and collapsed. From the bridge I saw Mayer-Mayerescu of Bucharest throw himself on the dead man. He lay on the negro's body and guided the machine-gun belt.

Soldiers of the engineering corps ran across the bridge with me. Quicker than I could think, with the town still full of our men, they carried out their orders. I had scarcely passed when the bridge blew up. It was the only avenue of retreat.

France had men. One of them was Pierre Saint-Brice.

We had separated when we saw the colonel. We agreed that I should wait on the other side of the bridge. Unseen to one another, we had crossed it at about the same time. Then suddenly we found ourselves side by side. I told him about little Mayer's exploit. He thought for a while. Then he said, "Come on! Quick!"

We ran along the river bank. At one place the river was particularly narrow. Saint-Brice sat down on the grass and began silently to pull off his boots.

"What are you doing?" I asked.

"I'm going to get little Mayer!"

I said nothing. I sat beside him and tried to unbuckle my puttees.

"What are you doing?" Saint-Brice asked with annoyance.

"I'm going with you."

"What for?"

"So that you won't be alone."

He looked at me, smiling behind his glasses.

"All right," he said. "Let's take a bath."

We both cursed as we pulled off our shoes. It was a real operation to take them off our swollen, bleeding feet.

"I am not tired any more," said the lieutenant.

"Neither am I. I've forgotten all about it."

He jumped into the water first.

When I left my watch—a gift from my father, to which I was particularly attached—in my shoes the time was two o'clock in the afternoon. When I came back with the soldiers whom I had found in the place indicated by Saint-Brice it was three o'clock. Little Mayer was sitting on the grass. But in the meantime Saint-Brice had returned to the burning town. He had "delivered" Mayer only a short while before, and had immediately gone for another bath. Between two and seven in the evening he made three trips to the town, which had meanwhile been completely occupied by the enemy. Each time he saved seven or eight soldiers from certain death.

Hans Habe

Colonel de Buissy

Colonel de Buissey, at the head of his regiment, had defended Sainte-Menehould with heroism. De Buissy was nearly sixty years old. He had been wounded seven times in the Great War. He had spent eighteen years in Africa, commanding the 4th Foreign Legion, the most famous of all the famous regiments of the Foreign Legion. He had distinguished himself in the great Moroccan battles. At the

outbreak of the present war the colonel, who had been
pensioned shortly before, left his home in Lille and offered his services to France. In consideration of his particular abilities and merits, he was immediately appointed
commander of the 1st Foreign Volunteer Regiment, which
was later renamed the 21st. He was an officer of the
Legion of Honour and bearer of almost every high distinction that a French officer can achieve.

Colonel de Buissy was ordered to appear at Passavant
at nine o'clock on the night before Saint-Brice and myself
reached that village. The general commanding our brigade
waited for the colonel in the notary's house. It proved impossible, however, to interrupt the battle of Sainte-
Menehould according to a pre-arranged schedule. If the
retreat of the innumerable regiments streaming southward
was to be even partly covered we had to hold the enemy in
and around Sainte-Menehould. Colonel de Buissy reached
Passavant at five in the morning, on foot, totally exhausted, having escaped death by a miracle. Lieutenant
Costa, a brave Corsican who commanded our motor-
cyclists—motor-cyclists without motor-cycles, mind you—
had fallen on the battlefield only a few steps from the
colonel.

The following conversation took place between the
General and the Colonel:

The General: "Why are you so late, Colonel de
Buissy?"

The Colonel: "We held Sainte-Menehould as long as we
could."

The General: "You could have retreated long ago. I
have been waiting here for twenty-one hours."

The Colonel: "I am sorry. We tried to resist. Unfortunately, *mon général,* our arms were more than defi-
cient, as you well know."

The General: "How many men were killed?"

The Colonel: "At least five hundred. With normal
equipment we should have had four hundred less casualties."

The General: "Five hundred Jews the less."

The Colonel: "The Jews fought like the rest. Moreover, there were at least as many Christians as Jews."

The General: "You don't look well, Colonel."

The Colonel: "I am somewhat tired."

The General: "Excellent! Madame de Buissy will be very glad to have you back."

The Colonel: "Do you mean that I am relieved of my command?"

The General: "I mean that within one hour you will be taken to the peaceful south in an ambulance."

The Colonel: "Thank you! But I am neither sick nor injured. I have been with this regiment from the first minute of its existence, and I intend to remain at the head of my men to my last breath. My regiment has fought heroically. I deserve——"

The General: "How old are you, Colonel de Buissy?"

The Colonel: "Fifty-eight."

The General: "You deserve a rest, my dear de Buissy. Your nerves are frayed. You'll be taken to the rear in one hour. At the same time Lieutenant-Colonel Landry will arrive here."

The Colonel: "You mean that my successor has already been appointed?"

The General: "Yes! And I hope you enjoy your well-deserved rest."

The Colonel: "Is that an order?"

The General: "Yes."

The Colonel: "I accept under protest."

The General: "I am convinced that Madame de Buissy will not protest against having you back with her."

One hour later our colonel was loaded on an ambulance sent by the High Command and taken to the divisional headquarters at Commercy. The colonel on his stretcher was brought to a hall where two generals—the commanders of the brigade and the division—were engaged in a conversation. The hall was large, and the two generals apparently thought that the colonel would not hear their whispering. Besides, Colonel de Buissy pretended to be asleep.

This is what he heard:

The Brigade Commander: "Colonel Landry has taken over his post."

The Divisional Commander: "This de Buissy has given me enough trouble."

The Brigade Commaner: "He wanted to resist at any cost."

The Divisional Commander: "These *Légionnaires* are intriguing politicians, all of them."

The Brigade Commander: "What shall I write in my report?"

The Divisional Commander: "I don't know."

The Brigade Commander: "He told me he would protest against his dismissal on the ground of sickness."

The Divisional Commander: "I'm telling you, the man has caused us nothing but trouble. He has completely adapted himself to the rabble he commanded. Can't you find something? Something incriminating in his record?"

The Brigade Commander: "No. I went through all his belongings. But there was nothing, except——"

The Divisional Commander: "Except——?"

The Brigade Commander: "Except an empty bottle."

The Divisional Commander: "Was there liquor in it?"

The Brigade Commander: "Perhaps."

The Divisional Commander: "Excellent! Report that his alcoholic excesses necessitated his sudden dismissal."

Colonel de Buissy had overheard this whole conversation. He opened his eyes. The Brigade Commander approached the stretcher. He assured de Buissy that he was happy to have been able to put through his well-deserved retirement. He asked whether Madame de Buissy had succeeded in reaching Perpignan. He whispered that he intended to propose the colonel for a high distinction on account of his regiment's magnificent bravery. The colonel did not answer. When the General had finished, de Buissy inquired, "Has a bottle been found among my belongings: a bottle of iodine? It's a habit I acquired in Africa. I always carry a bottle of iodine."

The general said with embarrassment that the colonel

would have no further need for iodine.

The same day Colonel Paul de Buissy was sent south. We were given a new commander. Subsequent events demonstrated that the new chief was a man of his word, and that his superiors had no reason to regret his appointment. He offered the Germans no resistance.

Hans Habe

The Germans Enter Antwerp: 18 May

On Thursday afternoon, the police came around to notify us that for a period of forty-eight hours, no one might go out into the streets for any reason whatsoever. It was even forbidden to look out of a window. Newspapers had ceased publication, there was little news on the radio, and we had almost no idea of what was happening. It should be remembered that Antwerp was so near the border of Holland that some of the Antwerp tramway lines actually went to the Dutch frontier, so it was clear to us that, now that Holland had fallen, we should not have long to wait for the arrival of the Germans in Antwerp. Rumours had been rife for several days that Antwerp would not be defended, but would be handed over to the Germans in order to spare the civilian population, if it became clear that the Allies must fall back.

When the police told us that no one might go out for forty-eight hours, I had an intuitive feeling that this meant that Antwerp was being handed over—that twenty-four hours were for the retreat of the Allied armies, and twenty-four hours for the Germans to take over. The prohibition even to look out of windows sounded much more like a condition dictated by the Germans than anything emanating from the Allied command, which had shown no such nervousness when advancing to the front through Antwerp.

Friday, the first day indoors, passed without incident. Forbidden though it was, we peered out of the windows from time to time, but the streets were practically deserted. No movements of troops were visible, but occa-

sionally a motor-cycle courier or an army truck sped
through the town. Such movement as there was was always away from the front, never towards it. The most dis-
quieting sign was the departure of groups of firemen and
police officers, still in uniform, some with bicycles and all
with parcels and valises.

On the second night of our confinement the bombardment became terrific, and to it was added a new note: for
hours we heard the sound of big guns firing, not far from
Antwerp; the battle had reached our doorstep. If, as I
believed, the Allied armies were going to pass through
Antwerp that night, they would have to go through the tunnel under the river, which would take them past our door.

Presently I heard the whine of falling shells, followed
by shattering explosions, very near, which shook the base-
ment. With the monotonous regularity of metronome
beats, one shell followed another, and the blasts became
more violent as the shells fell closer and closer to the near-
by tunnel. First I heard the sound of the distant gun, then
the whine of the shell overhead, and finally, the crash as it
burst; each time the explosion seemed nearer, which may
well have been the effect of my own imagination. As I lay
there in the darkness, I knew that the others were awake as
well, but no one spoke. There was little that could be said
to comfort one another, and none of us, I suppose, wanted
to say anything that would further depress the others. For
that matter, I cannot remember that we ever spoke of that
night in the months that followed; it was not something
that we wanted to remember. For the first time since the
beginning of the invasion I felt deep, panic-stricken fear.
The cellar seemed like a rat-trap. My imagination pictured
what it would feel like if a shell came crashing and tearing
through the floors above, to burst over our heads and bury
us beneath the masonry which was our only bulwark
against the battle going on above us. Worst of all was the
feeling of total helplessness; I did not want to die,
there—and if I went somewhere else, that might be the
very place a shell was fated to fall.

Still the shells continued to fall near us, until finally the earth seemed split as a mighty explosion, which made the shell bursts insignificant and puny, rocked the hotel. The artillery fire ceased and the rest was a dead silence.

Finally, unutterably weary from the hours of strain, I fell into an uneasy sleep.

Towards morning, as a little daylight began to filter down into the forward part of the cellar, which lay beneath the pavement, I was awakened by the sound of steel-shod boots running along the street. Belgian or French boots did not make that angry, metallic noise; I was not so sure about British Army footwear, but intuition told me that it was the Germans who were there. Bursts of automatic rifle and machine-gun fire became more frequent, and from time to time a heavier explosion suggested that hand grenades were being thrown.

The three women were now also awake, and we discussed in a low voice what the significance of these noises might be. Perhaps what we were hearing was the sound of Allied patrols left behind to delay the German advance—or had the Germans already arrived?

Shortly after eight o'clock I decided to end the uncertainty, and despite the protests of the others, I went upstairs to try to see what was happening. I passed through the kitchen and into the restaurant, half expecting to find it already filled with German soldiers. I could see nothing from there, for at the beginning of the forty-eight-hour quarantine period we had hastily boarded up the street windows and the front door. I went up to my room on the third floor, and cautiously advanced towards the window. There, below, just in front of the cathedral, was what I had dreaded to see—a German soldier. The moment was a bitter one, but its grimness was relieved by a ludicrous touch. The German soldier mounting guard over the great cathedral was short, squat and bow-legged, and his mushroom-like helmet suggested a man who had been flattened out by heavy pressure from above. As I peered down at his ludicrous figure, an automobile drove up and a flag officer in blue uniform with gold braid stepped smartly out. The sentry saluted, and the officer entered the door leading to the stairway which mounted to the top of the cathedral tower.

I had seen all I wanted. I returned to the cellar, and announced to the others, "The Germans are here!"

Lars Moen

DESIGN FOR PANIC

I was given a special assignment. Working with experts of the Propaganda Ministry, I devised radio broadcasts and propaganda for other media designed to create the greatest possible confusion among our enemies, especially the French. Dr. Adolf Raskin, then Director of Radio Saarbrücken, and a close friend of mine, was the man chiefly responsible for the great successes we achieved. Working with three transmitters specially equipped with a very powerful signal, he sent a continual stream of news reports in French, purporting to be of official French origin but which were in fact his own imaginative inventions. These false news items were the chief cause of the fatal panic and confusion among the French civil population. Streams of refugees blocked all the highways of France and made troop movements behind the French lines almost impossible. Meanwhile, in spite of the difficulties created by the military situation, our agents in France continued to collect information, which was transmitted to us by a special network of frontier-crossing couriers and by telephone, a cable having been laid across the Maginot Line to Saaralben.

Another device which did great damage was a small and apparently innocuous pamphlet which was distributed in great numbers by our agents and also dropped from aircraft. Printed in French and described as being the prophecies of Nostradamus—many of whose prophecies were actually included—the pamphlet predicted terrifying destruction from "flying fire-machines", stressing all the time that south-eastern France would be preserved from this horror. While preparing these brochures, I had never imagined that they would have such a tremendous effect. All the effort of the civilian and military authorities to divert the great streams of refugees from attempting to reach south-eastern France proved useless.

Walter Schellenberg

Panic

It was six in the morning, and Dutertre and I, coming out of our billet, found ourselves in the midst of chaos. All the stables, all the sheds, all the barns and garages had vomited into the narrow streets a most extraordinary collection of contrivances. There were new motor cars, and there were ancient farm carts that for half a century had stood untouched under layers of dust. There were hay wains and lorries, carry-alls and tumbrils. Had we seen a mail-coach in this maze it would not have astonished us. Every box on wheels had been dug up and was now laden with the treasures of the home. From door to vehicle, wrapped in bedsheets sagging with hernias, the treasures were being piled in.

Together, these treasures had made up that greater treasure—a home. By itself each was valueless; yet they were the objects of a private religion, a family's worship. Each filling its place, they had been made indispensable by habit and beautiful by memory, had been lent price by the sort of fatherland which, together, they constituted. But those who owned them thought each precious in itself and for itself. These treasures had been wrenched from their fireside, their table, their wall; and now that they were heaped up in disorder, they showed themselves to be the worn and torn stock of a junk-shop that they were. Fling sacred relics into a heap, and they can turn your stomach.

"What's going on here? Are you mad?"

The café-owner's wife shrugged her shoulders.

"We're evacuating."

"But why, in God's name!"

"Nobody knows. Mayor's orders."

She was too busy to talk, and vanished up her staircase. Dutertre and I stood in the doorway and looked on. Every motor car, every lorry, every cart and charabanc was piled high with children, mattresses, kitchen utensils.

Of all these objects the most pitiful were the old motor cars. A horse standing upright in the shafts of a farm-cart gives off a sensation of solidity. A horse does not call for spare parts. A farm-cart can be put into shape with three nails. But all these vestiges of the mechanical age! This assemblage of pistons, valves, magnetos, and gear-wheels! How long would it run before it broke down?

"Please, captain. Could you give me a hand?"

"Of course. What is it?"

"I want to get my car out of the garage."

I looked at the woman in amazement.

"Are you sure you know how to drive?"

"Oh, it will be all right. The road is so jammed, it won't be hard."

There was herself, and her sister-in-law, and their children—seven children in all.

That road easy to drive? A road over which you made two or ten miles a day, stopping dead every two hundred yards? Braking, stopping, shifting gears, changing from low into second and back again every fifty yards in the confusion of an inextricable jam. Easy driving? The woman would break down before she had gone half a mile! And fuel! And oil! And water, which she was sure to forget!

"Better watch your water. Your radiator is leaking like a sieve."

"Well, it's not a new car."

"You'll be on the road a week, you know. How are you going to make it?"

"I don't know."

She won't have gone three miles before running into half a dozen cars, stripping her gears and blowing out her tyres. Then she and her sister-in-law and the seven children will start to cry. And she and her sister-in-law and the seven children, faced by problems out of their ken, will give up. They will abandon the car, sit down by the side of the road, and wait for the coming of a shepherd.

"Why don't you stay home?"

"God knows, we'd rather stay."

"Then why do you leave?"

"They said we had to."

"Who said so?"

"The mayor."

Always the mayor.

"Of course we'd rather stay home."

It is a fact that these people are not panicky; they are people doing a blind chore. Dutertre and I tried to shake some of them out of it.

"Look here, why don't you unload and put that stuff back into your house. At least you'll have your pump-water to drink."

"Of course that would be the best thing."

"But you are free to do it. Why don't you?"

Dutertre and I are winning. A cluster of villagers has collected round us. They listen to us. They nod their heads approvingly.

"He's right, he is, the captain."

Others come to our support. A roadmender, converted, is hotter about it than I am.

"Always said so. Get out on that road and there's nothing but asphalt to eat."

They argue. They agree. They will stay. Some go off to preach to others. And they come back discouraged.

"Won't do. Have to go."

"Why?"

"Baker's already left. Who will bake our bread?"

The village has already broken down. At one point or another it has burst; and through that hole its contents are running out. Hopeless.

Farther on, in the open country, the enemy fighters would be flying low and spitting forth their bursts of ma-chine-gun fire upon this lamentable flock. But it was astonishing how on the whole the enemy refrained from total annihilation. Here and there stood a car in flames,

but very few. And there were few dead. Death was a sort
of luxury, something like a bit of advice. It was the nip in
the hock by which the shepherd dog hurried the flock
along.

                                        Antoine de Saint Exupéry

It took us thirty-two hours to get from Nantes to Paris
against the stream of refugees. I was driving the car.
Beside me was Bordier, a brothel-keeper from Nantes. He
had provided the car in exchange for the security my official pass afforded him. He did not much like teaming up
with me, but he was a meticulous business man: he wanted to put his affairs in order, that is to say recover his silver from a safe in Paris and collect the last receipts from
his fourteen slot-machines. We knew that the Germans
were approaching Paris. He looked on my naval officer's
badge of rank as a passport. No doubt he thought of the
invading army as a horde which stole silver, rifled money
from slot-machines, raped women, but respected uniforms.

It was one of the finest springtimes we had known in
years, a springtime of battle. As far as Le Mans the roads
were clear. Apart from the fact that the nation was
wearing uniforms, had surrendered to the hopelessness of
merely pretending and waiting, and apart from a few
obstacles on the roads, overturned carts laced with barbed
wire, little rows of walls forming a defile through which
one had to pass at walking pace under the eye of a bored
Territorial, there were no signs of war or of the immediate
likelihood of battle. Only the slowing down of life, caused
by the creation of an enormous administrative machine
and the sheep-like necessity of listening to the radio ten
times a day, bore witness to an exceptional period, not of
revolt or struggle, but of its resignation, egoism and fear.

. . . . We felt surprised and to a certain extent cheated at
seeing no signs of defeat: overflowing hospitals, trains of
wounded crowding the stations, units being relieved and

convoys of reinforcements going up to the line, as I had
seen at Bourges in 1914.

It was only after Le Mans, and still more after Chartres
that the signs of disaster became increasingly apparent—and these were all on the roads. In the sky, nothing. No activity or excitement in the fields; the corn
was ripening. It was only in the towns and villages that the
refugees crowded round the hotels, the cafés and the petrol
pumps. Their fear was contagious: at the sight of them
people who had never thought of leaving were suddenly
seized with the urge to go. . . .

We covered twenty kilometres in eight hours. As night
fell, our car was stuck behind a truck which was
transporting a hundred and twenty men from a technical
college to Pau. From eight o'clock to midnight they sang
and told dirty stories. At Saint-Rémy the traffic jam was
so dense that we decided, after standing still for two
hours, that at the first forward move we would park in a
side street. I went to sleep with my head on the steering
wheel, weariness and the presence of the maidservant in-
ducing an erotic dream.

At five o'clock in the morning, awakened by the chill in
the air, we took the road again. It was less crowded: the
stream flowed more rapidly. Bordier was snoring. Lambertine was sleeping in a heap, her mouth open. The sun
made me so sleepy that I could not keep awake. I came to
in a field of oats; the stalks slithering along the panels of
the car made a noise like water. The ears of corn and the
poppies cut off by the front bumper were thrown up
against the windows, drowning them in a mist of grain and
pollen. We decided to stop at the first village and sleep for
two hours. Night was falling when we reached Nantes. At
Pierrot's, the café opposite the brothel, there was so much
noise that we could not hear ourselves speak. The hubbub
was like a station. While awaiting disaster, the soldiers
and sailors of the rear areas ate, drank and had a good
time. I tried to find a room for Lambertine, who had
become a problem. Bordier suggested making her "hus-

tle". When I protested, he said, "It would be good
business. Refugees go to women like horses to a stable,
and there aren't enough to go round. However, if you in-
sist, she need only do the cleaning."

                              Emmanuel d'Astier, naval officer

RETREAT TO DUNKIRK

The 15th dawned bright and sunny, and brought orders.
The Battalion was to dig positions in the Seine Canal six
miles north of Brussels, near Vilvorde. Next day there
came a change of position and more orders, this time ominous. They were to hold a bridgehead for 3 Division to
use in their withdrawal from Louvain. Less than a week
had turned an eager advance into a withdrawal; and the
withdrawal was to turn into one of the fastest and most
disastrous of history.

17 May gave the Battalion its first view of the enemy. 3
Division had passed through, already bewildered at the
turn of events; the pontoon bridge was blown, and the
Battalion was preparing to hold the line of the Canal. A
Belgian civilian appeared on the far side of it, inspected
the wreckage of a steel bridge which had been blown some
time before, and clambered cautiously across it. Close on
his heels came the first Germans. A few shots sent them
out of sight, and the Battalion turned its attention first to
a Belgian who was claiming transport on the grounds that
he was a trusted British agent, and secondly to a couple of
messages which had just come in. The first ordered that a
certain burial ground should be reconnoitred: it was
already in enemy hands, so this message was ignored. The
second ordered withdrawal that night.

. . . . They halted at Petegem, ten miles south-west of
Ghent, on the Lys Canal. Petegem had panicked, and not
a soul was left in the village. Cigarette ends had burned
themselves away on tables, glasses had been left half-
drained, there was a game of draughts half-finished.
Despite their weariness, the Jocks went round releasing

tame rabbits and canaries—and picking up what stores they could. Petegem was a gloomy experience.

That evening—it was 19 May—the Battalion at last took up a position again, and remained in this general area for four days. The Germans arrived and deployed, and shelling developed. On the 23rd it became really heavy, as heavy as anything experienced in later years. But now the Battalion was being constantly moved to meet various threats. There was a good deal of confusion, as when they were told to leave some half-completed trenches, to move forward and to conform with some troops on the flank—who proved to be Germans.

The night of the 23rd came near to being the end of the Battalion. The enemy was round the left rear, where he announced his presence with machine-guns and emphasized it with bombers. The only wireless set to Brigade H.Q. was out of order, and messages by other means were taking an hour to bring an answer. There was little touch between Battalion H.Q. and the forward companies; but when the order finally came to disengage it was got through somehow. A long trudge of thirty miles began, with men falling asleep almost as they walked. Hitherto the direction of the withdrawal had been a little to the north of west; now it turned south-west and followed the line of the Lys to Courtrai; here some magnificent hot soup was issued, but many found that it made them sleepier than ever. At last the somnambulant Battalion stumbled into Halluin, a small town on the French frontier, and dropped off to sleep in a carpet factory. A group of officers, before doing so, tuned in to the B.B.C. and heard that the Germans were already in Boulogne.

                                        Bernard Fergusson

War Diary

Nothing but a miracle can save the B.E.F. now, and the end cannot be very far off. We carried out our withdrawal successfully last night back to the old frontier defences and by this morning we were established in the defences

we spent the winter preparing. But where the danger lies is
on our right rear. The German armoured divisions have
penetrated to the coast; Abbeville, Boulogne and Calais
have been rendered useless. We are, therefore, cut off
from our sea communications, beginning to be short of
ammunition. Supplies still all right for three days, but after that, scarcity.

Armentières has been very heavily bombed and we are
well out of it; half the town is demolished, including the
madhouse, and its inmates are now wandering about the
country.

These lunatics let loose . . . were the last straw. With
catastrophe on all sides, bombarded by rumours of every
description, flooded by refugees and a demoralized
French Army, bombed from a low altitude, and now on
top of it all lunatics in brown corduroy suits standing at
the side of the road grinning at one with an inane smile, a
flow of saliva running from the corner of their mouths,
and dripping noses! Had it not been that by then one's
senses were numbed with the magnitude of the catastrophe
that surrounded one, the situation would have been unbearable.

                              General Alan Brooke, diary 23-25 May

Not long after I received another message. Would I
report to the Battery Command Post.

One of the B.C.P. Staff went round handing each of us
a new map-sheet. I took mine without paying very much
attention. We were already up in the corner of our last
sheet, so I had expected we'd soon get a new issue.

Suddenly, glancing down at it, I noticed that a great
proportion of the new sheet was occupied by the sea.
Another look showed me a strip of coast. And the principal name on this strip was Dunkirk. It was the first time
the word had struck us with any particular significance.

Y Battery pulled out at half-past four in the afternoon.
We hadn't proceeded far when we were struck by what
seemed, at first sight, an extraordinary phenomenon. The
entire countryside was a-flutter with white. From every

house in the villages, from church steeples, farms, cottages, from everywhere where people lived there flapped a white flag, and if not a real flag, a white table-cloth, sheet, towel, or handkerchief. They were, of course, the tokens of surrender which the inhabitants were in a great hurry to have on display by the time the Germans arrived. Most of the private houses were heavily shuttered. Here and there little knots of silent people stood by the wayside. But we all had the feeling that the vast majority were peeping at us from behind the shutters with mixed emotions. Relief that the tide of war was departing from their neighbourhood, mingled with apprehensions of what troubles the entry of the Germans would bring in its train.

Approaching the bridge over the canal we once more found ourselves in a main stream of military traffic, some French but mostly British. The road narrowed here, and to add to the confusion a truck full of *poilus*, who seemed to be in a panic to get away, insisted on trying to pass all the other vehicles on the road. They were blocking up the whole procession, and causing dangerous delays as aeroplanes could be heard overhead. Shouts of, "Pull-in . . . pull-in . . . wait your turn . . . what's your hurry?" came from the angry British troops, mingled with oaths and curses. But the *poilus* took no heed. They insisted on forcing a passage through. At last they endeavoured to pass my truck. I didn't waste any words. I leaped out, drew my revolver, and told the driver that if he did not get back in line instantly I'd shoot him. He pulled in.

A few moments later, thirty yards from the bridge, the threatened air attack developed. Three bombers swooped low over the bridge and dropped their bombs. They missed the bridge but hit the banks. As the bombers swooped, everyone leaped from the vehicles and scattered over the fields on each side of the road. I crouched in a ditch. A few yards away a French soldier and a little boy had taken refuge. A bomb exploded and a fragment of it sliced head-and-shoulders off both. When the bombs finished, the machine-gunning started, the Germans from only a short distance up, emptying belt after belt of bullets

upon the troops in the fields. That over, we resumed our
journey and passed through the village of Houthem.

The face of the countryside had now undergone a complete change. Miles and miles of low-lying marshy fields
stretched far as the eye could see, all cut up by a network
of canals and highways at right-angles to each other. Each
field was below canal level, so each had its own
diminutive dyke running round it. There were few trees to
be seen anywhere, save the pollard oaks bordering the
dead-straight roads.

Into this pancake of a land it seemed as if the whole of
the B.E.F. was pouring. Every road scoring the landscape
was one thick mass of transport and troops, great long
lines of them stretching back far to the eastern horizon,
and all the lines converging towards the one focus—
Dunkirk. Ambulances, lorries, trucks, Bren gun carriers,
artillery columns—everything except tanks—all crawl-
ing along those roads in well-defined lines over the
flat, featureless country in the late afternoon sunshine,
provided an impressive and memorable picture of two
modern armies in retreat. Under their greyish camouflage
paint they resembled from a distance slow-moving rivers
of muddy-coloured lava from some far-off eruption.

It was now that I saw, for the first time, regiments in
the doleful process of wrecking their equipment. New
wireless sets, costing perhaps £20 apiece, were placed in
rows in the fields, twenty in a row, sometimes, while a soldier with a pick-axe proceeded up and down knocking
them to pieces. Trucks were being dealt with just as
drastically. Radiators and engines were smashed with
sledge-hammers; tyres slashed and sawn after they had
been deflated. Vehicles that were near the canals were
finally pushed in. Some of the canals were choked with the
wrecks, all piled on top of each other. There was more
wreck than water.

Also, from this point you encountered another novel
sight in this war-on-wheels . . . infantry marching on foot.
Having destroyed their transport they had to walk the last

ten miles to Dunkirk. This was the infantry due for immediate evacuation. Not the rearguard. They were allowed to use their transport up to a later point.

Now progress along the road, filled with pedestrians, and dusk falling, became terribly slow. The troops marched in single file along each side of the road, weary, red-eyed and dust-begrimed. But cheerful, and still able to shoot off a bit of characteristic repartee when the occasion arose.

By now we weren't altogether unaware of what was happening on the beaches. Our progress along the road had been at a snail's pace. We went forward three or four yards, then made a forced halt sometimes lasting a quarter of an hour. It was during these halts that we picked up a very good idea of the horrors going on at Dunkirk from scraps of conversation with the infantry. These gave rise to scraps of uneasy conversation among ourselves.

"Have you heard that they're gunning 'em as well as bombing 'em? . . ."

"Some have been on the beach three days before they got a boat. . . ."

"Got safely on the destroyer and it was bombed. Most of 'em blown to bits. . . ."

"Hundreds of dead and dying on the beaches. No chance for them at all. . . ."

"I've just been told that they gun the fellows as they are swimming to the lifeboats. . . ."

"What'll it be like when we get there? . . ."

"Shall we get there? . . ."

"What d'you think our chance is? . . ."

"Evens. . . ."

"I put it just under. . . ."

It will be realized from these bits of talk among us that Y Battery was having its eyes opened.

It was at one of these halts that I asked our saddler, who had been a gunner in the Mons Retreat, how it compared with the present one. His view was that Dunkirk was the worse.

"At Mons we always had the possibility of going forward again, sooner or later. Here we know we shan't.
That's what makes it bad."

                                        British gunner officer

The Beaches

Eventually we arrived at the spot on this side of the last
canal separating us from the sea, where we had to abandon the vehicles. They were smashed up in the darkness
and pushed into the canal. The men formed up by the
roadside and the roll was called for the last time. A weird
scene, the Troop sergeant-majors calling out the names of
the gunners in loud whispers, and ticking them off on their
lists by torch-light as the answers came back out of the
darkness, from nowhere it seemed.

"All present and correct, sir."

And once more the fifty of us started off, this time on
foot, formed-up in threes, the Major and I walking at the
head of the column. To our great joy we discovered that
the bridge spanning the canal had not been smashed. Once
over it, and another obstacle between us and the Unknown
had been passed. We continued towards Malo-les-Bains,
crossing the railway, and marching through the ruined
street of Rosendaal, whose skeleton walls stood around us
like the ruins of some bygone civilization. The only sound
was the crunching of the broken glass under our feet, as if
we were marching over hard ice-crystals on a winter's day.
Mysterious shadows flitted about the streets, in and out of
broken doorways, and disappearing silently round corners.
They were stray inhabitants who had been cut-off by the
swift march of events and were living in cellars. And a few
looters. And, probably, a few spies. The German gun-fire
was now incessant, the flash of the explosions continually
lighting up the scene for a second or two on every side of
us.

Now we were no longer alone. We began to meet little
batches of our infantry marching in the same direction.

Often as we approached we would be hailed out of the darkness:

"Is that A Company, King's Own Scottish Borderers? . . ." Or the name of some other unit would be shouted. These were bits of the rearguard coming back, and marching still in good formation down to the beaches.

We were now in the region of the dunes, which rose like humps of a deeper darkness. And these in their turn were dotted with the still blacker shapes of abandoned vehicles, half-sunk in the sand, fantastic twisted shapes of burned-out skeletons, and crazy-looking wreckage that had been heaped up in extraordinary piles by the explosions of bombs. All these black shapes were silhouetted against the angry red glare in the sky, which reflected down on us the agony of burning Dunkirk.

Slowly we picked our way between the wreckage, sinking ankle-deep in the loose sand, until we reached the gaunt skeletons of what had once been the houses on the promenade. The whole front was one long continuous line of blazing buildings, a high wall of fire, roaring and darting in tongues of flame, with the smoke pouring upwards and disappearing in the blackness of the sky above the roof-tops. Out seawards the darkness was as thick and smooth as black velvet, except for now and again when the shape of a sunken destroyer or paddle-steamer made a slight thickening on its impenetrable surface. Facing us, the great black wall of the Mole stretched from the beach far out into sea, the end of it almost invisible to us. The Mole had an astounding, terrifying background of giant flames leaping a hundred feet into the air from blazing oil tanks. At the shore end of the Mole stood an obelisk, and the high explosive shells burst around it with monotonous regularity.

Along the promenade, in parties of fifty, the remnants of practically all the last regiments were wearily trudging along. There was no singing, and very little talk. Everyone was far too exhausted to waste breath. Occasionally out of the darkness came a sudden shout:

"A Company, Green Howards. . . ."

"C Company, East Yorks. . . ."

These shouts came either from stragglers trying to find lost units, or guides on the look-out for the parties they were to lead on to the Mole for evacuation.

The tide was out. Over the wide stretch of sand could be dimly discerned little oblong masses of soldiers, moving in platoons and orderly groups down towards the edge of the sea. Now and again you would hear a shout:

"Alf, where are you? . . ."

"Let's hear from you, Bill. . . ."

"Over this way, George. . . ."

It was none too easy to keep contact with one's friends in the darkness, and amid so many little masses of moving men, all looking very much alike. If you stopped for a few seconds to look behind, the chances were you attached yourself to some entirely different unit.

From the margin of the sea, at fairly wide intervals, three long thin black lines protruded into the water, conveying the effect of low wooden breakwaters. These were lines of men, standing in pairs behind one another far out into the water, waiting in queues till boats arrived to transport them, a score or so at a time, to the steamers and warships that were filling up with the last survivors. The queues stood there, fixed and almost as regular as if ruled. No bunching, no pushing. Nothing like the mix-up to be seen at the turnstiles when a crowd is going into a football match. Much more orderly, even, than a waiting theatre queue.

About this time, afraid that some of our men might be tailing off, I began shouting, "2004th Field Regiment . . . 2004th Field Regiment. . . ."

A group of dead and dying soldiers on the path in front of us quickened our desire to quit the promenade. Stepping over the bodies we marched down the slope onto the dark beach. Dunkirk front was now a lurid study in red and black; flames, smoke, and the night itself all mingling together to compose a frightful panorama of death and destruction. Red and black, all the time, except for an occasional flash of white low in the sky miles away to the left and right where big shells from coastal defence guns at Calais and Nieuport were being hurled into the town.

Down on the beach you immediately felt yourself surrounded by a deadly evil atmosphere. A horrible stench of blood and mutilated flesh pervaded the place. There was no escape from it. Not a breath of air was blowing to dissipate the appalling odour that arose from the dead bodies that had been lying on the sand, in some cases for several days. We might have been walking through a slaughter-house on a hot day. The darkness, which hid some of the sights of horror from our eyes, seemed to thicken this dreadful stench. It created the impression that death was hovering around, very near at hand.

We set our faces in the direction of the sea, quickening our pace to pass through the belt of this nauseating miasma as soon as possible.

"Water . . . Water. . . ." groaned a voice from the ground just in front of us.

It was a wounded infantryman. He had been hit so badly that there was no hope for him. Our water-bottles had long been empty, but by carefully draining them all into one we managed to collect a mouthful or two. A sergeant knelt down beside the dying man and held the bottle to his lips. Then we proceeded on our way, leaving the bottle with the last few drains in it near the poor fellow's hand so that he could moisten his lips from time to time.

On either side, scattered over the sand in all sorts of positions, were the dark shapes of dead and dying men, sometimes alone, sometimes in twos and threes. Every now and then we had to pull ourselves up sharply in the darkness to avoid falling over a wooden cross erected by comrades on the spot where some soldier had been buried. No assistance that availed anything could be given to these dying men. The living themselves had nothing to offer them. They just pressed forward to the sea, hoping that the same fate would not be theirs. And still it remained a gamble all the time whether the sea, close though it was, would be reached in safety. Splinters from bursting shells were continually whizzing through the air, and occasionally a man in one of the plodding groups would fall with a groan.

British gunner officer

Small Craft at Dunkirk

Between 26 May and 4 June, 222 naval ships and 665 other vessels succeeded in bringing back to England 224,585 British and 112,546 French and Belgian troops.

Half an hour after they had left Ramsgate the yacht *Sundowner* began her crossing. *Sundowner* belonged to Commander C. H. Lightoller, D.S.C., R.N.R. (Retd.), who, as senior surviving officer of the *Titanic,* had been the principal witness at the inquiry into that disaster. She was a biggish craft, approximately sixty feet with the speed of ten knots, and with the assistance of his son and a Sea Scout, Commander Lightoller had taken her out of Cubitt's Yacht Basin at Chiswick on 31 May and had dropped down the river to Southend as part of a big convoy of forty boats which had mustered at Westminster. At dawn on 1 June he left Southend with five others and, reaching Ramsgate, was instructed in the casual manner of those days to "proceed to Dunkirk for further orders". His charts, he says, were somewhat antiquated, and he was fortunate enough to be able to obtain a new set. At ten o'clock he left by the route laid down. His account of the voyage is clear and detailed:

Half-way across we avoided a floating mine by a narrow margin, but having no firearms of any description—not even a tin hat—we had to leave its destruction to someone better equipped. A few minutes later we had our first introduction to enemy aircraft, three fighters flying high. Before they could be offensive, a British destroyer—*Worcester,* I think—overhauled us and drove them off. At 2.25 p.m. we sighted and closed

the twenty-five-foot motor-cruiser *Westerly;* broken
down and badly on fire. As the crew of two (plus three
naval ratings she had picked up in Dunkirk) wished to
abandon ship—and quickly—I went alongside and took
them aboard, giving them the additional pleasure of
again facing the hell they had only just left.

We made the fairway buoy to the Roads shortly after
the sinking of a French transport with severe loss of
life. Steaming slowly through the wreckage we entered
the Roads. For some time now we had been subject to
sporadic bombing and machine-gun fire, but as the *Sundowner* is exceptionally and extremely quick on the
helm, by waiting till the last moment and putting the
helm hard over—my son at the wheel—we easily
avoided every attack, though sometimes near lifted out
of the water.

It had been my intention to go right on to the
beaches, where my second son, Second-Lieutenant R. T.
Lightoller, had been evacuated some forty-eight hours
previously; but those of the *Westerly* informed me that
the troops were all away, so I headed up for Dunkirk
piers. By now dive-bombers seemed to be eternally
dropping out of the cloud of enemy aircraft overhead.
Within half a mile of the pierheads a two-funnelled
grey-painted transport had overhauled and was just
passing us to port when two salvoes were dropped in
quick succession right along her port side. For a few
moments she was hid in smoke and I certainly thought
they had got her. Then she reappeared, still gaily heading for the piers and entered just ahead of us.

The difficulty of taking troops on board from the
quay high above us was obvious, so I went alongside a
destroyer *(Worcester* again, I think) where they were
already embarking. I got hold of her captain and told
him I could take about a hundred (though the most I
had ever had on board was twenty-one). He, after con-
sultation with the military C.O., told me to carry on
and get the troops aboard. I may say here that before
leaving Cubitt's Yacht Basin, we had worked all night

stripping her down of everything moveable, masts included, that would tend to lighten her and make for more room.

My son, as previously arranged, was to pack the men in and use every available inch of space—which I'll say he carried out to some purpose. On deck I detailed a naval rating to tally the troops aboard. At fifty I called below, "How are you getting on?," getting the cheery reply, "Oh, plenty of room yet." At seventy-five my son admitted they were getting pretty tight—all equipment and arms being left on deck.

I now started to pack them on deck, having passed word below for every man to lie down and keep down; the same applied on deck. By the time we had fifty on deck I could feel her getting distinctly tender, so took no more. Actually we had exactly a hundred and thirty on board, including three *Sundowners* and five *Westerlys*.

During the whole embarkation we had quite a lot of attention from enemy planes, but derived an amazing degree of comfort from the fact that the *Worcester*'s A.A. guns kept up an everlasting bark overhead.

Casting off and backing out we entered the Roads again; there it was continuous and unmitigated hell. The troops were just splendid and of their own initiative detailed look-outs ahead, astern, and abeam for inquisitive planes, as my attention was pretty wholly occupied watching the steering and passing orders to Roger at the wheel. Any time an aircraft seemed inclined to try its hand on us, one of the look-outs would just call quietly, "Look out for this bloke, skipper", at the same time pointing. One bomber that had been particularly offensive, itself came under the notice of one of our fighters and suddenly plunged vertically into the sea just about fifty yards astern of us. It was the only time any man ever raised his voice above a conversational tone, but as that big black bomber hit the water they raised an echoing cheer.

My youngest son, Pilot Officer H. B. Lightoller (lost

at the outbreak of war in the first raid on Wilhelmshaven), flew a Blenheim and had at different times given me a whole lot of useful information about attack, defence and evasive tactics (at which he was apparently particularly good) and I attribute, in a great measure, our success in getting across without a single casualty to his unwitting help.

On one occasion an enemy machine came up astern at about a hundred feet with the obvious intention of raking our decks. He was coming down in a gliding dive and I knew that he must elevate some ten to fifteen degrees before his guns would bear. Telling my son "Stand by," I waited till, as near as I could judge, he was just on the point of pulling up, and then "Hard a-port." (She turns a hundred and eighty degrees in exactly her own length.) This threw his aim completely off. He banked and tried again. Then "Hard a-starboard," with the same result. After a third attempt he gave it up in disgust. Had I had a machine-gun of any sort, he was a sitter—in fact, there were at least three that I am confident we could have accounted for during the trip.

Not the least of our difficulties was contending with the wash of fast craft, such as destroyers and transports. In every instance I had to stop completely, take the way off the ship and head the heavy wash. The M.C. being where it was, to have taken one of these seas on either the quarter or beam would have at once put paid to our otherwise successful cruise. The effect of the consequent plunging on the troops below, in a stinking atmosphere with all ports and skylights closed, can well be imagined. They were literally packed like the proverbial sardines, even one in the bath and another on the W.C., so that all the poor devils could do was sit and be sick. Added were the remnants of bully beef and biscuits. So that after discharging our cargo in Ramsgate at 10 p.m., there lay before the three of us a nice clearing-up job.

Arriving off the harbour I was at first told to "lie off". But when I informed them that I had a hundred and thirty on board, permission was at once given to "come in" (I don't think the authorities believed for a minute that I had a hundred and thirty), and I put her alongside a trawler lying at the quay. Whilst entering, the men started to get to their feet and she promptly went over to a terrific angle. I got them down again in time and told those below to remain below and lying down till I gave the word. The impression ashore was that the fifty-odd lying on deck plus the mass of equipment was my full load.

After I had got rid of those on deck I gave the order, "Come up from below," and the look on the official face was amusing to behold as troops vomited up through the forward companionway, the after companionway, and the doors either side of the wheelhouse. As a stoker P.O., helping them over the bulwarks, said, "God's truth, mate! Where did you put them?" He might well ask. . . .

Dieppe: Sunk

It was a silent ship. The decks were so crowded it was impossible to form queues for the meal that was being served below. The crowd was quiet enough for Knight, wedged against the rail of the promenade deck, to hear morse from the radio cabin. In theory the promenade deck was reserved for officers, but in reality all ranks were massed there—men, N.C.O.s, officers, and even a number of nursing sisters, though so far as Knight could see he was the only R.A.F. man on board. They were not going to England, the rumour went round; they were ordered to St. Nazaire; the Allies were to hold the line of the Seine, and a new medical base area was being established in the Loire valley. A white hospital ship followed them out of the harbour. That, presumably, was making for England. Knight searched the sky but there was not an aircraft in sight.

Nevertheless the anti-aircraft gun in the stern suddenly went into action, and neat puffs of brown were seen high in the clear atmosphere. All on board felt the kick of the gun beneath their feet. The ship's siren gave a number of short, sharp blasts, a bell rang on the bridge, and the vessel changed course so rapidly the following hospital ship appeared to swing out from the land.

"All personnel below decks!" said the loudspeaker. "All personnel below decks!"

A middle-aged nursing sister with red hair peeping from beneath her steel helmet took his arm. "Come on, sonny. Grandma doesn't like this."

"Why pick on me?"

Already there was room to walk about on the deck, and the sister had merely paused to tie the strings on Knight's lifebelt when all the driving energy of the boat seeped into sound, a column of sound that was based on the bed of the sea itself. Knight tried to force the sister to the deck, but bewildered by the suddenness of the onset she fought against him and both, leaning against the rail for support, were drenched by the explosion of brine. The boat rocked on the edge of a crater. In the wildness of the moment it seemed possible for the vessel to fall to the bottom of the sea. The bomber had already pulled out of its dive. Water smacked against the hull like a hand.

"They're bombing, not gunning," said Knight. He had swallowed so much sea water that he felt hungry and sick in the same moment. "Take it from me, we're better off here than down below."

"I thought you were trying to rape me, sonny," said the sister. She lay on her belly and pressed her cheek to the deck. Drenched figures were lying all over the decks, some swearing, some laughing, but for the most part they were silent, waiting for the next attack. The ack-ack gun at the stern kicked away and the red hair, the flushed cheek and the smell of lilies of the valley were suddenly so close to Knight that he could have kissed her nose without moving. But she left him. First she lost her colour, then she looked indignant, then she rose above him, floating.

"We've been hit," he thought.

He had been turned over. If it had not been for the intense cold, he would have been perfectly comfortable, lying there on his back, gazing up at the sea. Because it was an emergency of some sort he suspected that it would be foolish to turn his head. By moving his eyes though, he could take in a great deal. There was a wave arrested at the very moment of breaking into a line of foam. Oil fumes, at the instant of combustion, froze in black and red, at right angles to the horizon. A coil of yellow rope hung in the sunshine like a flower. All the left side of his field of vision was taken up by a mountain of varnished gold that bore a delicate encrustation of elaborately worked metal; the hull of the ship, in fact, with its rust and barnacles streaming.

"Why not?" he asked himself, when the sea slipped like a carpet beneath his feet; and he set off running so lightly across the water he could feel the sharp ridges of the waves through the soles of his shoes. It was a matter of pride that he could make a quick decision and act upon it. He would go to Helen.

But in this strategem he failed. Perhaps, unwittingly, he had spoken his intentions aloud; perhaps they had read his secret from his eyes or outstretched hands. But the whole brilliant and detailed picture suddenly started into motion; the green sea yawned with all its salty breath, an underwater explosion produced a magnificent growth of liquid on the surface, flame ran like a frightened animal over the nursing sister's mop of hair, and a sudden thunder was quickly choked into silence. He was detached from the world of matter. He had lost contact. There was neither hard nor soft, and there was no sound of any kind. He opened his eyes and looked up at the golden surface of the sea. Bubbles sped from his mouth and he thought that if he could but follow they would take him to Helen. He struck out and the morning air cut him like frost.

Physically he felt splendid. Until the bombing he had been stiff from the previous day's exertions. Now, the very violence he put into his swimming restored his circulation; although the waves rolled down upon him from all sides he inhabited a new, more vigorous body which could not be defeated. After an explosion the air sang with metal. A hundred fish jumped, or so it seemed. Fragments of timber, biscuit boxes, lifebelts, a towel, a pipe, bobbed within reaching distance. He was uninjured and quite safe—of this he was never for a moment in doubt. His only anxiety was his inability to travel to Helen as quickly as he would have liked. He thought he would go out of his mind with impatience.

When he was picked up twenty minutes later, clinging to one of the emergency rafts he had fortuitously come across, his first words were, "I've got to get home quickly, you know." Then he said, "Oh, keep me out of that sea," and fainted.

He awoke to find himself swaddled like a baby, and swinging in mid-air with no obvious means of support. He could neither move his arms nor flex his legs; but he could look out over the wreckage-strewn sea to the distant white cliffs of France.

A man in a white smock tried to stuff a cigarette into his mouth, but he spat it out. "Let me out of this thing, will you? I itch like hell. I want to scratch myself, d'you understand? I want to scratch myself."

"Would you give me your number, rank, name and regiment?" said a voice. A helmeted corporal with a fountain-pen bent over him. They were unbuckling the straps that held him but they could not work fast enough for Knight.

"I'm all right. There's nothing the matter with me. I'm fine. For God's sake get me out of this thing. I'm itching, I tell you."

"Oh, and I want your religion as well," said the corporal.

                                                    P.H. Newby

THE GERMANS: POST-MORTEM

On this day (the 24th) the Supreme Command intervened in the operations in progress, with results which were to have a most disastrous influence on the whole future course of the war. *Hitler ordered the left wing to*

stop on the Aa. It was forbidden to cross that stream. We
were not informed of the reasons for this. The order contained the word, "Dunkirk is to be left to the Luftwaffe.
Should the capture of Calais prove difficult, this port too
is to be left to the Luftwaffe." (I quote here from
memory.) We were utterly speechless. But since we were
not informed of the reasons for this order, it was difficult
to argue against it. The Panzer divisions were therefore
instructed, "Hold the line of the canal. Make use of the
period of rest for general recuperation."

Fierce enemy activity met little opposition from our air
force.

Early on 25 May I went to visit the *Leibstandarte**
and to make sure that they were obeying the order to halt.
When I arrived there I found the *Leibstandarte* engaged
in crossing the Aa. On the far bank was Mont Watten, a
height of only some 235 feet, but that was enough in this
flat marshland to dominate the whole surrounding countryside. On top of the hillock, among the ruins of an old
castle, I found the divisional commander, Sepp Dietrich.
When I asked why he was disobeying orders, he replied
that the enemy on Mont Watten could "look right down
the throat" of anybody on the far bank of the canal. Sepp
Dietrich had therefore decided on 24 May to take it on his
own initiative. The *Leibstandarte* and the Infantry Regiment G.D. on its left were now continuing their advance in
the direction of Wormhoudt and Bergues. In view of the
success that they were having I approved the decision
taken by the commander on the spot and made up my
mind to order 2 Panzer Division to move up in their support.

On this day we completed the capture of Boulogne. 10
Panzer Division was fighting outside the Calais citadel.
When a demand that he surrender was addressed to the
English commandant, Brigadier Nicholson sent the
laconic reply, "The answer is no, as it is the British Ar-

---

* *Leibstandarte* Adolf Hitler: the S.S. Division which was formerly Hitler's bodyguard (Ed.)

my's duty to fight as well as it is the German's." So we had to take it by assault. . . .

On 26 May 10 Panzer Division captured Calais. At noon I was at the divisional headquarters and according to the orders I had received I asked Schaal whether he wanted to leave Calais to the Luftwaffe. He replied that he did not, since he did not believe that our bombs would be effective against the thick walls and earthworks of the old fortifications. Furthermore, if the Luftwaffe were to attack them it would mean that he would have to withdraw his troops from their advanced positions on the edge of the citadel, which would then have to be captured all over again. I was bound to agree with this. At 16.45 hours the English surrendered. We took twenty thousand prisoners, including three to four thousand British, the remainder being French, Belgian and Dutch, of whom the majority had not wanted to go on fighting and whom the English had therefore locked up in cellars.

In Calais, for the first time since 17 May, I met General von Kleist, who expressed his appreciation for the achievements of my troops.

On this day we attempted once again to attack towards Dunkirk and to close the ring about that sea fortress. But renewed orders to halt arrived. We were stopped within sight of Dunkirk! We watched the Luftwaffe attack. We also saw the armada of great and little ships by means of which the British were evacuating their forces.

General von Wietersheim appeared at my headquarters during the course of the day to discuss with me arrangements for the relief of XIX Army Corps by his XIV Army Corps. The advanced division of this corps, 20 (Motorized) Infantry Division, was placed under my command. I put it in on the right of the *Leibstandarte* Adolf Hitler. Before this discussion was over, a small incident occurred. The commander of the *Leibstandarte,* Sepp Dietrich, while driving from the front came under machine-gun fire from a party of Englishmen who were still holding out in a solitary house behind our lines. They set his car on fire and compelled him and his companions

to take shelter in the ditch. Dietrich and his adjutant
crawled into a large drain pipe, where the ditch ran under
a cross road, and in order to protect himself from the
burning petrol of his car covered his face and hands with
damp mud. A wireless truck following his command car
signalled for help and we were able to send part of the 3rd
Panzer Regiment of 2 Panzer Division, whose sector this
was, to get him out of his unpleasant predicament. He
soon appeared at my headquarters covered from head to
foot in mud and had to accept some very ribald comments
on our part.

It was not until the afternoon of 26 May that Hitler
gave permission for the advance on Dunkirk to be
resumed. By then it was too late to achieve a great victory.

The corps was sent into the attack during the night of
the 26-27th. 20 (Motorized) Infantry Division, with the
Leibstandarte Adolf Hitler and the Infantry Regiment
G.D. under command and reinforced by heavy artillery,
was given Wormhoudt as its objective. 1 Panzer Division
on its left was ordered to push forward, with point of main
effort its right wing, in accordance with the progress that
that attack should make.

The Infantry Regiment G.D. received useful support
from 4 Panzer Brigade of 10 Panzer Division and secured
its objective, the high ground Crochte-Pitgam. The Armoured Reconnaissance Battalion of 1 Panzer Division
took Brouckerque.

Heavy enemy movement of transport ships from
Dunkirk was observed.

On 28 May we reached Wormhoudt and Bourg-
bourgville. On the 29th Gravelines fell to 1 Panzer Division. But the capture of Dunkirk was after all completed without us. On 29 May XIX Army Corps was
relieved by XIV Army Corps.

The operation would have been completed very much
more quickly if Supreme Headquarters had not kept ordering XIX Army Corps to stop and thus hindered its rapid
and successful advance. What the future course of the war
would have been if we had succeeded at that time in tak-

ing the British Expeditionary Force prisoner at Dunkirk, it is now impossible to guess. In any event a military victory on that scale would have offered a great chance to capable diplomats. Unfortunately the opportunity was wasted owing to Hitler's nervousness. The reason he subsequently gave for holding back my corps—that the ground in Flanders with its many ditches and canals was not suited to tanks—was a poor one.

General Heinz Guderian

To me Dunkirk was one of the great turning-points of the war. If I had had my way the English would not have got off so lightly at Dunkirk. But my hands were tied by direct orders from Hitler himself. While the English were clambering into the ships off the beaches, I was kept uselessly outside the port unable to move. I recommended to the Supreme Command that my five Panzer divisions be immediately sent into the town and thereby completely destroy the retreating English. But I received definite orders from the Führer that under no circumstances was I to attack, and I was expressly forbidden to send any of my troops closer than ten kilometres from Dunkirk. The only weapons I was permitted to use against the English were my medium guns. At this distance I sat outside the town, watching the English escape, while my tanks and infantry were prohibited from moving.

This incredible blunder was due to Hitler's personal idea of generalship. The Führer daily received statements of tank losses incurred during the campaign, and by a simple process of arithmetic he deduced that there was not sufficient armour available at this time to attack the English. He did not realize that many of the tanks reported out of action one day could, with a little extra effort on the part of the repair squads, be able to fight in a very short time. The second reason for Hitler's decision was the fact that on the map available to him at Berlin the ground surrounding the port appeared to be flooded and unsuitable for tank warfare. With a shortage of armour and the difficult country, Hitler decided that the cost of an

attack would be too high, when the French armies to the
south had not yet been destroyed. He therefore ordered
that my forces be reserved so that they could be strong
enough to take part in the southern drive against the
French, designed to capture Paris and destroy all French
resistance.

Field-Marshal von Rundstedt, G.O.C.-in-C., Army Group

6

THE BATTLE IN THE WEST
TO VICHY

*After the evacuation of over four-fifths of the B.E.F. at
Dunkirk, France was given no respite. The final assault
began on 5 June, when the German armies in Flanders
launched their attack south-eastwards towards Paris. On
the 10th, Mussolini, anxious to be in at the kill, declared
war on the Allies. By the 16th the collapse of the French
armies was complete.*

ITALY DECLARES WAR

On 26 May, having gone to see him on a matter of
routine business, I met Marshal Balbo* in the waiting
room. He had come to Rome to discuss the unhappy state
of affairs in Libya, both from the military point of view
and from that of the civilian population, which was suffering from a lack of food.

Mussolini sent us a message to come in together; I had
hardly crossed the threshold of the vast room which he occupied when I realized that he had something of the
greatest importance to say to us. He was standing behind
his writing-table, his hands on his hips, looking intensely
serious, almost solemn. He did not speak at once but
silently transfixed us with his penetrating stare. What was
he going to say? Suddenly I found that I had difficulty in

* Translator's note: Governor and Commander-in-Chief in
Libya.

breathing. Finally he decided to speak, and then with an air of inspiration he announced, "I wish to tell you that yesterday I sent a messenger to Hitler with my written declaration that I do not intend to stand idly by with my hands in my pockets, and that after 5 June I am ready to declare war on England."

We were dumbfounded and seemed to have lost the power of speech.

Mussolini opened his eyes very widely to show his surprise at the coldness with which we had received his news.

When I was able to speak I said:

"Your Excellency, you know perfectly well that we are absolutely unprepared—you have received complete reports every week. We have about twenty divisions with seventy per cent of the necessary equipment and training; and about another twenty divisions with fifty per cent. We have no tanks. The Air Force, as you know from General Pricolo's reports, is grounded. This is to say nothing of stores—we have not even sufficient shirts for the Army. In such a state of affairs how is it possible to declare war? Our colonies lack everything. Our merchant shipping is on the high seas."

Feeling absolutely desperate, I added, "It is suicide."

Mussolini did not answer for a few minutes and then said quite calmly:

"You were right about the situation in Ethiopia in 1935. It is evident that to-day you are too excited to judge the situation correctly. I assure you the war will be over in September, and that I need a few thousand dead so as to be able to attend the peace conference as a belligerent."

General Pietro Badoglio, Chief of Staff

The Ambassador Goes Home

The fighting spirit of His British Majesty's Fleet is alive and still has the aggressive ruthlessness of the captains and pirates of the 17th century. Ambassador Bastianini, who is back from London, says that the morale of the

British is very high and that they have no doubts about victory, even though it may come only after a long time.

Count Ciano

COLLAPSE

The Anglo-French War Council: 11 June

We arrived at Briare late in the afternoon, having made a considerable detour. Aerodromes seldom give an impression of being overpopulated, but this one seemed particularly flat and deserted. Winston, in black, leaning on his stick, strolled about beaming as if he had left all his preoccupations in the plane and had reached the one spot in the world he most wished to visit at that particular moment. He conveyed the impression that the long journey had been well worth while since at last it was vouchsafed to him to walk about the aerodrome of Briare.

I, on the other hand, thought it quite a beastly place and hoped I should never see it again. The fact that my wishes have been fulfilled does not make me feel more kindly towards it.

Three or four cars drove up at intervals, and the Prime Minister left in the first with a French colonel who, from his expression, might have been welcoming poor relations at a funeral reception.

We drove a few kilometres to a hideous house, the sort of building the *nouveau riche* French *bourgeoisie* delight in, a villa expanded by successful business in groceries or indifferent champagne into a large monstrosity of red lobster-coloured brick, and stone the hue of unripe Camembert.

This was Weygand's abode, where the Prime Minister was to sleep.

The place, to which I took an instant dislike, had, I was glad to hear, a ridiculous name; it was called *Le Château du Muguet*—Lily of the Valley Castle.

As soon as we walked into the building I felt that the impression conveyed by the colonel on the aerodrome was but a projection of the attitude of our hosts. It was like walking into a house thinking one is expected, to find one had been invited for the following week. Our presence was not really desired.

It was a subtle feeling, and I may have been wrong, for every form of politeness was shown, even to the extent of giving us tea, but I do not think so. The strain caused by a situation which had greatly deteriorated since I had last seen our hosts had relaxed the bonds of friendship, even in the cause of the staunchest of our French *vis-à-vis*.

Within a few minutes we all trooped into the large dining-room where the conference was to be held. Pétain, de Gaulle, de Margerie and Colonel de Villelume, followed Reynaud. I sat near the window between Pug Ismay and de Gaulle. It was now seven o'clock.

The Frenchmen sat with set white faces, their eyes on the table. They looked for all the world like prisoners hauled up from some deep dungeon to hear an inevitable verdict.

For relief I turned to de Gaulle, whose bearing alone among his compatriots matched the calm, healthy phlegm of the British. A strange-looking man, enormously tall; sitting at the table he dominated everyone else by his height, as he had done when walking into the room. No chin, a long drooping elephantine nose over a closely-cut moustache, a shadow over a small mouth whose thick lips tended to protrude as if in a pout before speaking, a high receding forehead and pointed head surmounted by sparse black hair lying flat and neatly parted. His heavily-hooded eyes were very shrewd. When about to speak he oscillated his head slightly, like a pendulum, while searching for words. I at once remembered and understood the nickname of *"Le Connétable"* which Pétain said had been given him at St. Cyr. It was easy to imagine that head on a ruff, that secret face at Catherine de Medici's Council Chamber.

I studied him with great interest, little thinking that for a while we should be bent with such complete concentration on the same task, nor that later we would be driven so far apart.

That afternoon he had a look of confidence and self-possession which was very appealing. He had, I thought, brought it from Abbeville where he had fought a successful tank action (the only one). Fresh air had given his sallow skin a healthy colour. His cheeks were almost pink. That freshness of complexion I never saw on his face again, nor, I think, did I often see him smile as he did when he turned towards me then. It was a frank confident smile that belied his usual expression and made me feel I should greatly like this man. I perceived that afternoon what was perhaps the real de Gaulle, or maybe that part of him which might have predominated had he remained a soldier, straight, direct, even rather brutal.

. . . . There was a rather awkward pause, then, after a few words of formal welcome, Reynaud turned towards Churchill with that stiff-necked movement of his, and again raising his eyebrows asked him, with a gesture of the hands and the slight facial twitch familiar to him, to address the conference.

The Prime Minister then spoke; the words came slowly, carefully selected but hammered together sharply into a vivid mosaic. He said, in substance, that he had come to France to consider with Monsieur Reynaud and his advisers, the realities of a situation which must be faced without flinching. The matter for discussion was how best to carry on with the struggle which nothing could prevent the British from pursuing. His own impression was that as soon as the Germans had stabilized themselves on a front in France, they would turn on England. He hoped they would do so for two reasons. It would give France relief and enable the British to take a fuller and more equal share in the struggle, but above all, it would give our R.A.F. the opportunity of smashing the German air power. He had complete confidence that they would do so. Every effort was being made in Great Britain to turn out arms and re-equip the armies. At this very moment the British were sending troops to France, and a British infantry division was deployed about Le Mans.

A Canadian division and seventy-two guns were landing that night, so that there were now four British divisions in France. Another division would arrive about 20 June. The dispatch of yet a further division would depend on the guns the French could provide. Then there were the troops from Narvik. If the French Army could hold out till the spring of 1941, the British would have from twenty to twenty-five divisions to place at the disposal of the French Command, to employ anywhere. They might, for example, be used to form continental bridgeheads. He realized, he said, that the numbers he had given were small in the face of the present emergency, but if the French could hold out, the British participation would grow rapidly. The whole problem was how to tide over the present period until the potential strength of the Allies materialized.

He stopped. Reynaud thanked him, but I felt his suppressed irritation and that of the other Frenchmen at the inadequacy of these driblets to halt a conflagration whose flames were fast spreading from the Channel to the Atlantic. Reynaud added no word to his formal acknowledgement of Churchill's words and asked Weygand to report on the military situation. No one expected good news, but what we were told by the Commander-in-Chief was so bad that the sweat poured off my face as I listened. There was inescapable reality in the tale he unfolded while the light of the June evening faded under gathering clouds in the sky outside. The story had not carried the same conviction when reading reports or listened to at second hand. He appeared more intent on convincing his listeners that all was lost than on considering with them means of continuing the struggle. There was not a single battalion in reserve. The totality of the French forces were engaged. The fighting from Abbeville to Reims had been going on for more than six days without intermission. "The troops fight all day, then fall back to new positions during the night. The men have neither food nor rest. They collapse into sleep when halted and have to be shaken in the morning to open fire."

. . . . The French command had hoped to hold the Somme-Aisne line, Weygand was saying, but, although, thanks to the R.A.F., heavy losses had been inflicted on the enemy's armour as well as on his air force, the overwhelming superiority of the Germans in aircraft, tanks and manpower had compelled a withdrawal. The result was that the French armies were falling back to their last line of defence. This ran along the lower Seine and the Paris defence positions, followed the Oise and the Marne to join the north-west extremity of the Marne line, thence on to the Maginot forts. This line had been attacked at most points and broken on the lower Seine, and quite recently on the Marne. Up to this point Weygand's voice had been calm, expostulatory; it now rose a note or two as he said, "The German mechanized columns get through our lines, curl round and blow up the bridges behind our troops who, when they reach them, find themselves cut off. In other cases, as the enemy aircraft can spot French troop movements unhindered, they blow up the bridges they are making for from the air," and he told the story I had already heard of the German plane which, flying low, had blown up the French explosive charges on the Oise bridges, cutting off the troops from the positions they were withdrawing to. "It is," he said, "a race between the exhaustion of the French and the shortness of breath of the enemy divisions. . . . There is nothing to prevent the enemy reaching Paris. We are fighting on our last line and it has been breached." His tone now as dramatic as his words, he rapped out, "I am helpless, I cannot intervene for I have no reserves; there are no reserves. *C'est la dislocation*"—the break-up.

I looked around and read consternation on all the English faces. My own mouth was so dry, I could not swallow. I wrote quickly to make up for lost time as I found I had stopped to listen, for the picture evoked was slow to take shape in my mind.

I looked at Reynaud. Eyebrows raised, he was gazing at the middle of the table. Churchill, his face flushed, hunched over the table, was watching Weygand intently.

His expression was not benevolent. But Weygand was now launched on his favourite theme, the folly of having embarked on the war at all. "I wish to place on record that I consider that those responsible embarked upon the war very lightly and without any conception of the power of German armaments. As it is, we have lost something like two-fifths of our initial strength."

Weygand had finished. He was drained dry like a squeezed lemon. Not an idea, not a suggestion was to be wrung out of him. This must have been Churchill's conclusion, for he put him no questions, did not even look at him again, and merely asked that General Georges should be summoned. . . . I looked at de Gaulle. I had already noted that he had been ceaselessly smoking cigarettes, lighting one from another, his lips pursed and rounded in the characteristic movement I had already observed. Not a muscle of his face had moved. Nothing had been said that had caused his expression to change. The Prime Minister had looked at him several times. He was searching for something he had failed to find in the other French faces. The fact that he returned several times to a study of de Gaulle made me think he had detected in him the thing he was looking for.

When Georges came in he looked ghastly, but later his expression became more normal. The close similarity of his account to that already given by Weygand was very striking. They both told the same story in almost similar words. There were only differences of detail.

He told us that the Allies had lost a minimum of thirty-five divisions out of 105, as well as all the mechanized cavalry and a substantial proportion of the armoured divisions.

Georges intended to speak up for the troops, and did so. He was proud of the way many of them were fighting and was determined that where heroism had been shown it should be recognized. There was no Englishman at that table who did not understand and appreciate his intention, and his sober words carried infinitely more weight and conviction than had Weygand's discourse, which had been larded with far too many exclamations about *"troupes sans défaillances"*—an army that had fought magnificently without any exception. Such statements had exactly the contrary effect on British ears to that intended.

In his usual matter-of-fact decided way Georges said, "The fact is that some divisions have ceased to exist, they are only numbers. The Army is not in a position to oppose a powerful thrust."

Reynaud chimed in as he had done at every meeting with: "If this battle is lost, it will be through lack of aviation," uttered in a resigned voice, as he might have said, "Well, the poor chap is dead but it was his own fault." This sentence, true as are most clichés, but as unenlightening, emphasized that we were getting nowhere. Not a single positive suggestion had been made, nor had the hint of a plan emerged.

The Prime Minister may have sensed this, and felt that it was time he intervened again. His mouth had been working, an indication that he was pouring an idea into the mould of words. His voice when he spoke was warm and deep, an admirable medium for giving utterance to his generous ideas. He wished, he said, to express his admiration for the heroic resistance of the French armies, and Great Britain's grief at not being able to take a more effective part in the struggle. The inescapable fact was that the B.E.F. had come out of Flanders almost literally naked. It could only resume the struggle after it had been re-armed. Had it not been for events in the north, some thirteen or fourteen British divisions would now be fighting by the side of the French. This was the gist of his words, but they conveyed far more; the longing of the British people to help their friends in distress, their determination to do so the moment they could, and his evocation of the disaster in the north, whilst conveying no hint of reproach, nevertheless did recall facts that explained Britain's momentary helplessness.

Then, returning to his constant purpose of instilling the will to fight into the French, of demonstrating that, come what might, the struggle must continue, he evoked the past. We had been near disaster before in the last war, and had survived. Now, as then, we were losing sight of the war as a whole in the contemplation of our own immediate losses. We must not be hypnotized by our defeats, discouraged by our temporary weakness, or blind to the enemy's difficulties. The German armies must now also be in a state of extreme exhaustion and feeling the strain of their immensely long lines of communication.

The pressure might diminish in forty-eight hours. Might it not be possible, while holding the main line, to mount a counter-attack with the help of the British forces that would then be in position in the region of Rouen?

If the front held for another three or four weeks, there would be a substantial British force available to attack the enemy's flank. He was convinced the enemy was feeling his losses acutely; there was a complete absence of exultation in Germany. Every hour, every day gained tended to retrieve our fortunes. Whereupon Weygand broke in to say discouragingly but truthfully that it was a question of hours, not of days and weeks.

I ceased taking notes and watched him [Churchill], hypnotized. He found wonderful flashing words with which to express his fiery eloquence. They came in torrents, French and English phrases tumbling over each other like waves racing for the shore when driven by a storm. Something of the impression he then made comes back to me as I read this account of what occurred that afternoon. He wanted the French to fight in Paris, describing how a great city, if stubbornly defended, absorbed immense armies. And the pageant of history, the lurid glow of burning cities, some as beautiful as Paris, collapsing on garrisons who refused to accept defeat arose before our eyes. The French perceptibly froze at this.*

Incongruously perhaps, but with a slight sense of personal scorn, a half-forgotten story took shape in my memory concerning three hundred Spartans who on

---

* On this day General Weygand decided to declare Paris an open town and issued orders in consequence.

another summer day long ago sat "combing their long hair for death in the passes of Thermopylae". If such men existed in France, they were not in that room. Leonidas was there, but he was not French. But Churchill, if he had noticed the perceptible movement which had led all the French to sit back in their chairs with the tension of a motorist pressing hard on the brakes, save de Gaulle, and de Margerie who was utterly detached in his work, he did not heed it, or if he did, it merely spurred him on, for he went straight on, now counter-attacking on the subject of the Royal Air Force. Weygand had asked that every British fighting plane should be sent to France as this was the decisive battle that would settle the fate of both nations. This, Churchill declared with great force, was not so, there was a wider horizon, a vaster field to be considered.

To-day we had the battle of France, to-morrow we would have that of Britain, and it was on this field that the fate of the war would be decided. If we won that battle, all we had now lost would be retrieved. He looked very fierce, and it was quite evident that nothing would make him surrender the last air defence of Britain. And he said so. Although we were doing all we could in the air, the French could not expect us to destroy irretrievably our only hope in the present battle, the air arm. I remembered he had told me in London he would not give way on this absolutely vital issue, and he was keeping faith with himself.

The fighter force would . . . break up the attack on their island and cripple the might of Germany when it came, and it would surely come. But whatever happened we would fight on and on and on, *toujours*, all the time, everywhere, *partout, pas de grâce*, no mercy. *Puis la victoire!*

Reynaud, who had listened politely, easing his head in his collar now and then, said he fully accepted that the British fighter force should be kept in being, but he must assert that it was equally important to maintain the last line of defence in France. It was evident that British

fighters operating from England must be less effective
than those based in France. After all, where was the
danger? If the worst befell, they could always regain their
home bases. The French High Command was persuaded
that a large-scale air attack on the advancing Germans
might reverse the situation. The air force was the only
weapon left to the Allies. Great Britain could therefore
turn the scales of the present battle in favour of the Allies
if she so wished. He stopped, looked at Georges, and
made a movement of the chin in his direction. He knew
that the General had more influence on Churchill than any
other Frenchman and had observed, quick as he was, how
carefully the Prime Minister had listened to him. He
wanted his support and got it. Very solemnly Georges said
he fully agreed with Reynaud.

It was quite plain from Churchill's expression that he
had no intention of giving way. He diverted the discussion
by saying that an attack on the United Kingdom would in
all probability bring the United States into the war, since
the whole British population would resist the attack with
the utmost fierceness. The losses the German Air Force
would sustain might well be the turning-point of the
war . . .

It was of capital importance, he rapped out, to keep in
existence the instrument on which depended the intervention of the United States in the conflict. It would be folly
to ruin the only weapon capable of achieving this result.
Moreover, it was far from certain that the contrary decision would reverse the position in France.

Reynaud dryly intervened to say that nothing was less
desirable than the break-up of the British Air Force except that of the Western Front, and once more repeated
that history would no doubt say that the battle of France
had been lost because of weaknesses in the air.

As an approaching squall is heralded by choppy waters,
so the rising tone of the French Premier's voice warned of
impending trouble. Churchill perceived this, and in sen-
tences warm and soothing, emphasizing by a deeper tone
the first syllable of key words, moulded phrases rounded

and smooth that fell like drops of oil flicked on a rising sea.

The acerbity had gone from Reynaud's voice when he answered, but his theme was unchanged, for he repeated almost word for word Georges' plea that more and still more British fighters should be based in France. The Prime Minister, having got the discussion back into his own hands, was a trifle blunt as he repeated the arguments for not doing so. But easing up a little, he said that the whole position would be reviewed on his return to England. "We are always thankful, but always famished," said Reynaud in a quite friendly way. . . .

Now Weygand was speaking again: "We are at the last quarter of an hour." If he says that again, I thought, I shall do something foolish, and, by the look of my notes, I broke my pencil.

Thereupon fancy came to my rescue as it often does, and I saw Big Ben with a French general's cap on, marking time at the double, chiming the last quarter of an hour incessantly, at ever-accelerating speed, whilst the dial of the clock became Weygand's face.

My mind wandered from the discussion, but I do not think I missed much; Weygand was saying that there was conceivably still a hope of winning through, and that was why any possible help was indispensable.

The heads of Governments and the generals had met to examine what would be the consequence of the eventual dislocation of the armies. The enemy already held bridgeheads across the Seine, and his armour was manoeuvring to encircle Paris from both sides. If the present line was broken, there was no hope that it could be re-established, as there was nothing behind it. "Once this defensive battle has been lost," he said, "there is nothing to prevent the total invasion of France owing to the strength and power of penetration of the German Panzer divisions." Not only Paris but every large town in France would be occupied. Doubtless the remainder of the French forces would fight on until not a man remained, but this would be unco-ordinated warfare, and he himself, as

Commander-in-Chief, would find himself completely powerless. He found it difficult to imagine how, if the worst
happened, France could carry on with the war.

Well, now we had it. There was no mistaking the Commander-in-Chief's meaning.

I looked at Reynaud. He had bristled visibly. When he
spoke, his voice was carefully controlled and modulated,
but he was plainly very angry.

The Commander-in-Chief had given, he said in effect,
the most competent view available on the military situation, but, and here he rapped out his words, the question of whether or not the war was to continue was the
responsibility of the Government and of the Government
alone.

The two men glared at each other. Reynaud's eyebrows
were lifted so high that every wrinkle beneath them was
ironed out. But if in consequence his face was blank, his
eyes darted fury. Weygand opened and closed his mouth.
His parchment skin, tightly stretched on his Mongolian
face, looked as if it would crack under the strain of his
moving jaw. But he said nothing for a few moments whilst
all watched him. Then he recovered some control and with
the playful *bonhomie* of the dog who persists in having a
last snap at the postman's trousers, repeated that he would
be only too glad to serve under anyone who could escape
from the consequences of the present situation. His clear
intention was to indicate that he maintained his previous
statement.

The Prime Minister had been watching the two speakers
very attentively. I guessed he had learnt much from the
glimpse he had been given of the off-stage relations of the
principal actors in the tragedy. What he did was to ring
the curtain down and ask the cast if an entirely fresh approach could not be attempted in the next act.

What were the possibilities, he enquired, of establishing
one or more bridgeheads on the Atlantic? If these were
established British divisions could be put in at ever-
increasing pace. He felt certain also that the United States
would soon be taking her share. This meant Brittany. I

wondered whether the true attitude of each would now emerge.

Reynaud answered that the problem was being studied. General Altmayer (the younger) was on the spot taking stock of the situation. Certain measures in view of this eventuality had been taken on his instructions some time back. I felt, perhaps because his interest in the plan had not been apparent for some time, that Reynaud had lost faith in the idea. In any case, he spoke without conviction and seemed anxious to hand over the discussion to Weygand. Nothing loth, the General proceeded finally to demolish the project. He said the problem presented two difficulties, the first strategic, the other concerning supplies.

It was difficult to fight to the last on a given position and at the same time to withdraw troops to another. Also, seventy per cent of the armies' needs were supplied from the Paris region. Brittany certainly offered the advantage of open communications with Great Britain, but it had neither fortifications nor resources. Everything should be done to hold it, but he did not think it could be long defended. The German Air Force could make things very difficult for all those in this restricted territory. Meanwhile, the Germans would systematically destroy every town, village and factory in occupied France.

Reynaud said he could not but concur with General Weygand's conclusions. The military difficulties of such a step were immense; nevertheless he fully appreciated the great political importance it might have, which meant exactly nothing.

The Prime Minister did not pursue the subject, and to my chagrin turned to his favourite hobbyhorse, guerrilla warfare.

The Prime Minister said he put forward his proposals with diffidence in the presence of the heads of the French Army, but if only some effective means of holding up the German tanks could be devised, the tactics he suggested might lead to some secure bridgeheads being held for a few months until Britain's great strength developed, which it was doing at tremendous pace, and until American help came in full measure.

Weygand showed ill-concealed scorn at the Prime Minister's suggestion, and Pétain anger. Evidently determined the proposal should be at once squashed, "It would mean the destruction of the country," Pétain growled. He was far more moved than he had been by anything so far. Real wrath rumbled behind his words. Reynaud evidently also believed the suggestion an impossible one, and his comment showed that at some points his thought did not diverge as widely from that of the Marshal as might have been expected. He also dwelt on the suffering it would impose on the country, towns would be destroyed. . . . All this is leading nowhere, I thought. It was becoming painfully clear to me that the battle of France was lost and that no one believed in miracles. The only reality consisted in planning the next stage of the war in Africa. But no one spoke of it. I became very depressed. Hope lay in planning campaigns for the future, in establishing a new base from which attacks could be launched. But the talk was only of make-believe operations in a prostrate country with armies that had ceased to exist. This much had been made clear. If matters were left where they were, faith and confidence would be allowed to vanish from the room, absorbed by the spirit of defeat as wavelets are by sand. Darkness rather than light was being shed from the chandeliers. A miasma, a despond had fallen on the conference like a fog. No one appeared able to see his way. Then Churchill reacted explosively. As a slap in the face is considered a remedy for hysteria, or for a swoon, so he interjected violently that if the destruction of towns was an unpleasant perspective, that of falling a helpless prey to the enemy was a worse one. Britain was not only willing to suffer as France was suffering, she would gladly draw upon herself the full weight of Nazi ferocity. Meanwhile the main thing was to be able to hold out. A bridgehead on the Atlantic or some other form of resistance might achieve this. There was nothing Great Britain would not do for France except give up the struggle. She would fight

on, of that he was certain, until Hitlerism was destroyed.
She would never give in, never. She would fight on for
years, she would fight in the air, she would fight with her
navy and impose on Europe the most severe blockade.
England controlled the seas. Her Empire and that of
France were intact, the Belgian and Dutch colonies
depended on them. This war might well soon become a
war of continents. Although the collapse of France evoked
the most distressing picture, yet he felt certain that, in
spite of it, Germany could at last be brought to her knees.
"It is possible that the Nazis may dominate Europe, but it
will be a Europe in revolt, and in the end it is certain that
a regime whose victories are in the main due to its machines will collapse. Machines will one day beat machines."

The fog had gone, blown away by the great gusts of
Churchill's eloquence. All could see one thing clearly; the
path England was following. It lay straight ahead, steep,
jagged and dangerous, but leading upward to where, high
up, shone a light. I felt this so strongly that I lifted my
eyes, as in dedication, and, grateful as a thirsty man is for
a glass of water, I heard Victor Hugo's tremendous line
sing in my ears: "*L'espoir changea de camp, le combat
changea d'âme.*" Others than myself must, I think, have
seen, as Churchill spoke, a dim vista of utter ruin, dust-
clouds over collapsing cities, but in the far distance the
sun of victory rising on a silent world of dead towns and
rubble.

Major-General Sir Edward Spears

Weygand

.... Went to see Weygand at 8.30 a.m. Found him
looking very wizened and tired with a stiff neck from a car
smash on previous evening. He said he would speak very
frankly. That the French Army had ceased to be able to
offer organized resistance and was disintegrating into
disconnected groups. That Paris had been given up and
that he had no reserves whatever left. He then stated that

at the Inter-Allied Council it had been decided to hold a
position covering Brittany in front of Rennes. . . . He then
suggested that I should go with him to Georges' headquarters to draw up an agreement for this manoeuvre.

I therefore started off in the car with him for Georges'
headquarters, and, as we were trundling along, he turned
to me, and said, "This is a terrible predicament that I am
in." I was just preparing to answer that I could well understand how heavy the reponsibility must be to be entrusted with the task of saving France in her distress. To
my astonishment he continued with: "Yes, I had finished
my military career which had been a most successful one."
I remained dumb and unable to make any adequate
remark; it seemed impossible that the man destined to
minister to France in her death agonies should be thinking
of his military career.

General Alan Brooke, diary, 14 June

France From Six Miles Up

Burning is a great word when you look down from thirty-three thousand feet; for over the villages and the forests
there is nothing to be seen but a pall of motionless smoke,
a sort of ghastly whitish jelly. Below it the fires are at
work like a secret digestion. At thirty-three thousand feet
time slows down, for there is no movement here. There
are no crackling flames, no crashing beams, no spirals of
black smoke. There is only that greyish milk curdled in
the amber air. Will that forest recover? Will that village
recover? Seen from this height, France is being un-
dermined by the secret gnawing of bacteria.

About this, too, there is much to be said. "We shall not
hesitate to sacrifice our villages." I have heard these
words spoken. And it was necessary to speak them. When
a war is on, a village ceases to be a cluster of traditions.
The enemy who hold it have turned it into a nest of rats.
Things no longer mean the same. Here are trees three hundred years old that shade the home of your family. But

they obstruct the field of fire of a twenty-two-year-old lieutenant. Wherefore he sends up a squad of fifteen men to annihilate the work of time. In ten minutes he destroys three hundred years of patience and sunlight, three hundred years of the religion of the home and of betrothals in the shadows round the grounds. You say to him, "My trees!" but he does not hear you. He is right. He is fighting a war.

But how many villages have we seen burnt down only that war may be made to look like war? Burnt down exactly as trees are cut down, crews flung into the holocaust, infantry sent against tanks, merely to make war look like war. Small wonder that an unutterable disquiet hangs over the land. For nothing does any good.

One fact the enemy grasped and exploited—that men fill small space in the earth's immensity. A continuous wall of men along our front would require a hundred million soldiers. Necessarily, there were always gaps between the French units. In theory, these gaps are cancelled by the mobility of the units. Not, however, in the theory of the armoured divisions, for which an almost unmotorized army is as good as unmanoeuvrable. The gaps are real gaps. Whence this simple tactical rule: "An armoured division should move against the enemy like water. It should bear lightly against the enemy's wall of defence and advance only at the point where it meets with no resistance." The tanks operate by this rule, bear against the wall, and never fail to break through. They move as they please for want of French tanks to set against them and though the damage they do is superficial—capture of unit staffs, cutting of telephone cables, burning of villages—the consequences of their raids are irreparable. In every region through which they make their lightning sweep, a French army, even though it seem to be virtually intact, has ceased to be an army. It has been transformed into clotted segments. It has, so to say, coagulated. The armoured divisions play the part of a chemical agent precipitating a colloidal solution. Where once an organism

existed they leave a mere sum of organs whose unity has
been destroyed. Between the clots—however combative
the clots may have remained—the enemy moves at will.

Antoine de Saint-Exupéry

THE LAST OF THE B.E.F.

*On 12 June, 51 Highland Division, which was the last
major unit of the B.E.F. in France, and which had not
been involved in Flanders, was cornered at Saint-Valéry.
Five days later the last British forces in France were evacuated.*

Retreat

The weather was hot and still, gloriously blue and sunny, with fleecy white clouds high in the heavens. The
country was pleasant and pastoral, some of it cultivated
and dotted with copses, some of it hardwood forest. The
streams ran placidly to the sea, the beasts still grazed.
There is in France a cemetery of the earlier war, where
French and Scottish soldiers lie buried side by side, and
where the French, mindful of the oldest alliance in all
Europe, have put the inscription: *"Ici parmi les lilas de la
France fleurira pour toujours le chardon de l'Ecosse."* The
same will always be true of those dolorous sixty miles
from Abbeville to Saint-Valéry.

The two battalions had shaken down. There had been
little fighting in the Saar, but they had been shot over; in
the old phrase, they had smelt powder. They were now to
face disaster unprepared, underarmed, and, except for
their comrades of the Highland Division, alone.

On 5 June, 1940, when the German attack came in, the
1st Battalion held a front of two miles and a half between the pretty little villages of Lambercourt and Toeuf-
fles. On their left were the 1st Gordons, who had lost
heavily in the attack of the previous day. Beyond the Gordons were the 7th Argylls, who were even more widely
dispersed than the rest of the Division. It was against the

Argylls that the Germans moved, at dawn on the 5th; and on such a wide front it was easy for them to pass through, often unobserved and unimpeded.

What little could be done to meet this development was done at once. The Argylls stood their ground; the Gordons fell back a little to avoid being out-flanked. Their movement exposed in turn the flank of the 1st Battalion, and the enemy approached to within a few hundred yards of it, opening up with machine-guns and inflicting casualties. The 4th Battalion, under Rory Macpherson, which was some miles back, was moved across to the village of Valines, to act as long-stop to the 7th Argylls and to the 8th Argylls (a unit still farther to the left, of whose situation at this moment little was known).

The 7th Argylls still held fast, and were at length surrounded in the village of Franleu, to which their colonel, a stout-hearted officer called "Copper" Buchanan, had called in his scattered companies. The 4th Black Watch was bidden to counter-attack, with a troop of French tanks in support. An hour or two passed, but the tanks failed to arrive; and an effort to probe forward with two rifle companies was blocked before it had progressed very far. Without tanks no such attack had any hope of succeeding, and Rory Macpherson and his officers helplessly watched the enemy's assault on Franleu. At dusk, Buchanan and the few survivors left to him did their best to break out of Franleu by a desperate effort; but his battalion lost twenty-three officers and five hundred other ranks that day.

The front had now begun to crumble. It was wide, it was unsupported, it had been defied and infiltrated. The defence of the Argylls could cover one point in twenty; it could never stem the German advance, which now lapped around the 4th Black Watch in the village of Valines.

Rory Macpherson expected to be asked to hold his position around Valines . . . and was making all preparations to do so, although far from sanguine as to the eventual fate of his battalion. But soon after dark he received urgent orders to withdraw to the river Bresle. . . . But the

Battalion had hardly settled there before they were ordered to retire across the river to a new position. They
were to move at 9 p.m., but at 7 p.m. the enemy was
already nearer to the solitary bridge at Incheville than the
Battalion itself. By 7.30 p.m., a number of Germans had
actually reached it. They were driven off by the Battalion's own anti-tank guns, which were under command
of the Brigade, but which happened by chance at this moment to be on the critical spot. Most of the Battalion succeeded in crossing at the correct time and place; two
companies were cut off, crossed three miles upstream
at Gamaches, and managed to rejoin the main body
sometime on the following day.

For the next thirty-six hours the Battalion hung on by
its toe-nails, over-looking the Bresle. Its position was
again impossibly wide; the wooded and difficult country
made it easy for the enemy to infiltrate, and difficult for
Macpherson to communicate with his company commanders.

At dawn on 6 June, Major Lorne Campbell of Airds, of
the 8th Argylls (whose name will recur often in this
book), came marching in with the remnants of his company. They had been cut off two days before on the extreme left of the line near the sea at Ault; but they had
made their way back, marching among the German columns as if they had been Germans themselves. The administrative difficulties hereabouts were acute, and all that
Stuart-Fotheringham could offer Campbell as he passed
through was a glass of neat gin. The 4th Battalion stayed
all day on the Bresle, while the enemy poured through the
gaps like clear soup through a sieve. That night, the 8th,
orders were again received to withdraw at short notice,
and they marched several miles to find some buses at
Villebosc. By this time the whole brigade consisted of the
Battalion; of three hundred men who were the sole survivors of two Argyll battalions, under Lorne Campbell;
and of a battalion of the Scots Fusiliers, under Lord
Rowallan, which had hitherto been pioneers, but had now
been stepped up into the line. The enemy tried to interfere

with this withdrawal, but was stemmed by an attack, in the course of which the commander of the carrier platoon was killed.

At the Battalion's next rendezvous—in the Forest of Arques, south-east of Dieppe—a scratch force, called Ark Force, was hastily thrown together. It was given the task of hastening to Le Havre and preparing its defence, while the rest of the Highland Division withdrew more slowly to that port to prepare for embarkation. Ark Force sought to move by the coast road, but found it too congested with refugees and fugitives. It therefore moved by sideroads; and the heroes of this journey were the Quartermaster, Glasier, and the Transport Officer, Walker, whose brother was a Regular officer in the 1st Battalion a few miles away. But the 4th Battalion's task in Le Havre was sadly different to the original intention. News came through that the withdrawal of the main body of the Division had been blocked, and that an effort would be made to take it off at Saint-Valéry.

Surrender

An ominous silence prevailed. The enemy could be seen, but there was little shooting. At twenty minutes past four, Colonel Honeyman left for Brigade H.Q., leaving Bill Bradford the Adjutant in command. Almost at once tanks appeared, and the enemy opened fire with mortars and machine-guns. Some dismounted French cavalry arrived, under a veteran major with a gallant heart; and in this penultimate position of the original Black Watch, Frenchmen and Scotsmen lay side by side and fought. When the tanks appeared, Noel Jardine-Paterson, the Signal Officer, went off to try to collect the anti-tank platoon in readiness for the attack which was obviously brewing. Casualties mounted; the old French major had his arm blown off, but insisted on being carried round his position to encourage his men. We do not know his name.

Still the anti-tank platoon had not arrived, and it was not established until long after that Alastair Telfer-

Smollett, its commander, was killed, and his men either
killed or captured, in trying to get forward. In the absence
of orders, Bill Bradford decided to withdraw a little farther. He piled his wounded into the office truck, and sent
it off with Lance-Corporal Farquharson driving it. Farquharson drove across the fields to the road, and actually
reached the hospital and delivered the wounded. Then he
tried to get back, but on the way was ambushed and badly
wounded: he made his report to Bradford as a prisoner,
and died soon afterwards.

Many more wounded had to be left when Bradford succeeded in withdrawing the remnants of his two companies,
which now amounted to less than a hundred men. They
journeyed across country in the dark, and at 7.45 a.m. in
the morning of 12 June took up a position on the high
ground above the cemetery, just outside Saint-Valéry.
Bradford improvised platoons under such senior N.C.O.s
as were available, armed them with abandoned weapons
which were lying around in profusion, and formed additional sub-units from men who had become detached from
their proper companies or battalions.

By 9 a.m. his strength had almost doubled, and four officers had arrived in addition to those already with him.
The position was being heavily mortared from every direction, and a tank attack was coming into view, when Major
Thomas Rennie of the Regiment, who was serving on
General Fortune's staff, arrived. It had fallen to him to
bring the saddest news of all. The Division had
capitulated. . . .

There was nothing left to fight with, and nothing left to
fight for. The Navy was powerless to take off what little
remained of the Division; and early in the morning, acting
on orders from home, General Fortune had been forced to
surrender to the German general whose troops had surrounded him, whose name was Erwin Rommel.

When buglers blew the "Cease Fire" at Saint-Valéry,
few men could believe what they heard. They were
physically and mentally exhausted; for the last fortnight
they had never managed to win more than an hour or two

of sleep in the twenty-four. They heard the bugles, paused, and then went on with whatever they were doing: digging in on the lip of the valley where most of them were, dragging ammunition boxes from the useless lorries, or shooting at German tanks with mere Bren guns. As verbal orders reached them, they collected slowly, and under the direction of the officers destroyed everything of value which still remained to them. Then they formed up in silent and disciplined bodies.

Major Nogy Dundas addressed all those who were near him. He explained how they would soon be separated from their officers, and exhorted them not to forget who they were in the captivity that lay before them. Then they moved off; and the Brigadier—himself to die in prison —stood to attention with a long Highland crook in his left hand. As each body of troops went past, the senior N.C.O. or private gave "Eyes Left", and leaderless individuals saluted him.

Bernard Fergusson

The Victor

During the next few hours no less than twelve generals were brought in as prisoners, among them four divisional commanders. A particular joy for us was the inclusion among them of General Fortune, commander of 51 British* Division, and his staff. I now agreed divisional boundaries with my neighbour, General Cruewell, commander of 2 Motorized Division. Meanwhile, the captured generals and staff officers had been assembled in a house south of the market place. A German Luftwaffe lieutenant, who had just been liberated from captivity, was made responsible for the guard. He was visibly delighted by the change of role.

Particularly surprising to us was the *sang-froid* with which the British officers accepted their fate. The General, and even more, his staff officers, stalked round laughing in

* Highland (Ed.)

the street in front of the house. The only thing that seemed to disturb them was the frequent photographing and filming they had to endure by our Propaganda Company and some other photographers.

The captured generals were now invited to an open-air lunch at a German field kitchen, but they refused with thanks, saying that they still had supplies of their own. So we ate alone. There were still arrangements to be made for transporting away the prisoners, especially the numerous officers, for salvaging the equipment, securing the coast and evacuating Saint-Valéry. At about 20.00 hours we returned to Divisional H.Q. at Château Auberville.

It was impossible at that stage to estimate the total of prisoners and booty. Twelve thousand men, of whom eight thousand were British, were transported off by 7 Panzer Division's vehicles alone. The total number of prisoners captured at Saint-Valéry is said to have numbered forty-six thousand men.

General Erwin Rommel

Evacuation

Over three thousand men perished when the liner Lancastria *was bombed at St. Nazaire on 17 June.*

I then moved into St. Nazaire where I found "Turtle" Hamilton in charge of the naval side of the embarkation. He was most obliging and helpful in our search for the armed trawler, H.M.T. *Cambridgeshire*. She had also gone to assist in the *Lancastria* rescues, and it was some time before she could be found. When she did arrive, it was after saving nine hundred men from swimming in fuel oil, and conveying them to another transport. During their time on the trawler they had most of them stripped off their oil-soaked clothing. The whole trawler was covered in that foul-smelling black treacly substance, heaps of clothes on the decks oozed out oil, whilst in the tiny cabin below the carpet was soaked with it, the walls covered with impressions of every part of the human anatomy printed in brown on the white walls; bandages, cotton-wool, iodoform, blood and the all-permeating smell of fuel oil. Ronnie Stanyforth came to me and said, "The one reason why I like to serve you as A.D.C. is owing to the comfort and luxury that we travel in!"

. . . After embarking we lay at anchor in the harbour until 4 a.m., during which time there were several more air-raids. We were sleeping on deck and "Rusty" Eastwood had his roll of bedding alongside of mine. The A.A. Lewis guns on the bridge were firing furiously. Suddenly I heard a thump followed by a grunt of discomfort from Eastwood. I asked him if he had been hit, he replied, "Yes, by a Lewis gun drum thrown from the bridge, which landed on my stomach!"

We spent the whole of this day on the trawler, mostly lying on the deck in the sunshine and thanking God that we were safely out of France for the second time. Luckily it was a lovely calm day, and, in spite of the stink of fuel-oil, conditions were quite pleasant. Suddenly in the middle of this peaceful scene we were disturbed by piercing yells emanating from the lower parts of the trawler. The screams drew nearer and finally the individual responsible for them emerged on the deck. It was one of the stokers, a young boy who had been so seriously affected by the men of the *Lancastria* drowning in fuel-oil that he had temporarily become unhinged. He started tearing round the deck shouting, "Can't you see they are all drowning? Why are you not doing anything? Oh God, we must do something for them." We caught him and held him down, and then hunted for some bromide to give him, but there was none. We therefore got several aspirins and ground them down in some milk and poured it down his throat. He gradually quietened down and slept for a couple of hours, when the whole procedure had to be repeated.

General Alan Brooke, diary, 17-18 June

THE END

France Betrayed

We lay silent for a few minutes; then Saint-Brice asked, "What are you sighing about?"

"Did I sigh?"

"You did."

He too sighed. Then he said, "No, it's not a pretty sight."

"What do you think?" I asked. "How long are we going to keep running like this?"

"I've no idea! Maybe till the Germans occupy all France."

"And what about the Maginot Line? And the Daladier Line that's supposed to be waiting somewhere? And the resistance that's being organized on the Loire? Why shouldn't this war have its Marne, too? Don't you believe in it?"

I felt in the darkness that he had turned towards me with his head in his hands.

"No," he said, "I don't believe in it."

I did not want to ask questions, but he went on talking, as he seldom did.

"I have stopped believing," he said. "We had not prepared for this war. No, I don't speak of armaments. We could have caught up in nine months. But no Frenchman knew what he was fighting for. The Germans, over there, wrapped their foulest plans in ideological tissue-paper. And we? We did the opposite. We were really fighting for freedom and humanity, and we were ashamed of the two words. We acted as though nothing but territory were at stake. Did we hate the Germans? Our young people didn't even know what the Germans meant. Even to-day the blockheads think they'll survive a Hitler victory. Yes, they *will* survive! But as slaves. The purpose of this whole war is to bring slavery back to the world. And the world will regard us as voluntary slaves!"

His voice sounded hoarse. I stretched out on the narrow school bench. Between us lay a desk with an inkpot and drawer.

"We Frenchmen forgot the meaning of freedom long ago," he went on. "Real freedom. We were in the midst of a civil war when the Germans overran us."

"In times of war," I objected, "Frenchmen always dropped their internal quarrels."

"That was true in the past," said Saint-Brice. "Patriotism is stronger than politics. It always was in our country. But philosophy is stronger than patriotism. The Germans armed themselves with a philosophy for this war. Their philosophy is a skeleton key that lets them into a country without resistance. But God help a country once the Germans have occupied it!"

Never before had he spoken like this. Despite our intimacy, we both had preserved the distance between superior and subordinate, between Frenchman and foreigner. This time Saint-Brice seemed to be speaking to himself.

"Recently," he continued, "a captain told me that he loved France more than he loved Hitler, but that he loved Hitler more than Léon Blum. What more do you want?"

He was interrupted by a fit of coughing.

"Yes," he said at last, "I know the old story of our deficiency in arms. But do you think that was the decisive factor? Didn't we win the Great War despite our inferior armament? They say that the greatest part of our aircraft was destroyed on the ground. Do you know what that means? There were officers who prevented our pilots, at the point of a gun, from taking off. Can you conceive of such a thing?"

"No, I can't."

"I am beginning to understand, we were not sold out, but we were betrayed. And that's the worst part of it. A couple of corrupted generals can always be dealt with by a firing-squad. But we had no corrupt generals. You can't prove anything against them. There is no *bordereau* as in the Dreyfus Case. They betrayed us without having ex-

changed a single word with the Germans. They did not
want to fight against Germany. They liked Germany.
Bought by the Germans? If only they had been bought!
But they weren't even bought! Once I was told that the
people of some Balkan state were always ready to sell
their country, but never to deliver it. We did worse than
that. We delivered our country without even getting paid
for it."

"Aren't you painting too black a picture?"

I said this without conviction. But he was tormenting
me, just as he was tormenting himself. We had loved this
country and this people more than anything in the world:
each of us in his own way.

"No," he said, "it can't be painted too black."

We tried to sleep. But the day and the conversation had
been too much for us. And the thunder of the guns was
drawing nearer.

"Artillery preparation," said Saint-Brice. "They still expect resistance."

I took up the thread of his thought.

"On this lousy, clogged road resistance is unthinkable."

"Right," said the officer. "That's what they want to
show us. It's the same men who sabotaged our armament.
Always the same. They started the Dreyfus Case—and
lost it. After that they were dethroned in France. Now
they're taking revenge for the Dreyfus Case. Now they expect to stage a triumphal come-back on German bayonets.
People won't understand that. Not for a long time. Because, by accident, war was declared between Germany
and France. Because our generals were not as straight-
forward as General Franco. He, at least, openly invited
the foreigners into his country. . . . In the streets of Sainte-
Menehould, couldn't you feel that this is not a war between two states, but a civil war? You did feel it, didn't
you? And doesn't that explain everything? On the one
side, free France. Like free Spain. And against it, a gang
of bandits leaning on foreign support! Only here the plot
was much more diabolic, the whole thing was much more
subtly conceived, much more treacherously carried out. In

Spain civil war was openly proclaimed. The motives were clearly stated. No false slogans, no false banners! You could take one side or the other. Here they all sail under a false banner. They make it look as though Frenchmen are fighting Germans. Never, never, I'm telling you, would France have lost the war against Germany. We would have beaten them even with our medieval guns. But this was a war of Frenchmen against Frenchmen. And no one told us. . . ."

Hans Habe

Waiting for the Germans: Paris, 12 June

I went first to the Invalides. The only officer I found there said: "We are expecting them at any moment." Beneath our feet, the Metro had fallen silent, the buses and taxis were no doubt with the Post Office and the other vehicles on the roads to the south. All traffic had ceased; the police had been withdrawn. I tried to get news from the houses of five or six friends: but the friends and their *concierges* had gone. I left Bordier near the Opera to attend to his business. He would have considerable difficulty in tracing his machines. Then I went home.

The house was empty. On the staircase, I heard a sound of sobbing. Seated on a step, a maidservant was weeping: "I've been left behind. I've been left behind." I sat down beside her, patted her on the back and promised to take her away.

. . . . When I got up to leave the house, nothing bound me any longer to the world which had come to an end. And yet, like the little mulatto girl, who had died in my arms ten years before and wanted to take three photographs with her, I looked round for some talisman to take with me. Even though I had conquered hope and desire for possessions, books remained my weakness. I put six in my pockets.

Bordier was waiting for me at a café in the Rue Richer; it seemed to be the only one open for a kilometre around. Two metal merchants were sitting with him. A news-boy

gave us the last copy of a half-sized paper; it looked like
the newspaper of a besieged city. Two women at the bar
were questioning the cashier.

"Where are they?"

"At Saint-Denis."

"It's all over then?"

"Perhaps it's a trap."

The panic-stricken had left Paris. Those who remained
were on holiday, if somewhat bewildered. From the
Boulevards to the Porte de Châtillon, I do not believe we
passed a single car. The choice had been made. But for a
few pedestrians in the deserted streets all was still.

Emmanuel d'Astier

Paris fell on the 14th

Britain's Offer of Union with France: 16 June

As the Ambassador and I argued with Reynaud, more
acrimoniously than ever, on the subject of the Fleet, the
telephone rang. Reynaud took up the receiver. The next
moment his eyebrows went up so far they became indis-
tinguishable from his neatly brushed hair; one eyebrow to
either side of the parting. "One moment," he said. "I must
take it down," and grasping a sheet of foolscap on the slip-
pery table, he began to write, using a short gold pencil with
an enormous lead. He repeated each word as he wrote it,
and listening, I became transfixed with amazement. I was
so absorbed I did not even look at the Ambassador to see
if he shared my feelings. Reynaud was taking down in
French from de Gaulle's dictation in London, the text of
the Declaration of Union proposed by the British Government. On he wrote in a frightful scrawl, getting more excited as the message unfolded. The paper skidded on the
smooth surface of the table. I held it. As each sheet was
covered I handed him a fresh one. His pencil gave out. I
handed him mine.

Finally he stopped and said into the telephone, "'Does
he agree to this? Did Churchill give you this personally?"

There was a moment's pause and now he was speaking in English. It was evident that de Gaulle had handed the receiver to Churchill, who was assuring him that the document was a decision of the Cabinet. If there were alterations, they would be merely verbal.

Reynaud put the receiver down. He was transfigured with joy and my old friendship for him surged out in a wave of appreciation at his response, for he was happy with a great happiness in the belief that France would now remain in the war. This was his thought as it was ours, and in those first moments this was all that mattered. The sense of the generosity of the offer was overwhelming, the sincerity of the gesture completely convincing.

I was as moved as when I used to hear at some Battalion Headquarters in Flanders of a great feat of bravery and self-sacrifice. Of a man who, exhausted, wet and tired, struggled back through the mud under heavy fire to rescue a friend. For that was it. Britain, having escaped so far, now turned back to help her stricken comrade, offering to share with her everything she possessed. The one-sided sacrifice of France seemed balanced in a moment by this gesture of absolute solidarity.

The text of the proposed joint declaration was as follows:

At this most fateful moment in the history of the modern world the Governments of the United Kingdom and the French Republic make this declaration of indissoluble union and unyielding resolution in their common defence of justice and freedom against subjection to a system which reduces mankind to a life of robots and slaves.

The two Governments declare that France and Great Britain shall no longer be two nations, but one Franco-British Union.

The constitution of the Union will provide for joint organs of defence, foreign, financial, and economic policies.

Every citizen of France will enjoy immediately

citizenship of Great Britain; every British subject will become a citizen of France.

Both countries will share responsibility for the repair of the devastation of war, wherever it occurs in their territories, and the resources of both shall be equally, and as one, applied to that purpose.

During the war there shall be a single War Cabinet, and all the forces of Britain and France, whether on land, sea, or in the air, will be placed under its direction. It will govern from wherever it best can. The two Parliaments will be formally associated. The nations of the British Empire are already forming new armies. France will keep her available forces in the field, on the sea, and in the air. The Union appeals to the United States to fortify the economic resources of the Allies, and to bring her powerful material aid to the common cause.

The Union will concentrate its whole energy against the power of the enemy, no matter where the battle may be.

And thus we shall conquer.

Major-General Sir Edward Spears

The offer was rejected, and on the 17th the French Government asked the Germans for armistice terms.

General de Gaulle Appeals to the French: 18 June

The leaders who, for many years past, have been at the head of the French armed forces, have set up a Government.

Alleging the defeat of our armies, this Government has entered into negotiations with the enemy with a view to bringing about a cessation of hostilities. It is quite true that we were, and still are, overwhelmed by enemy mechanized forces, both on the ground and in the air. It was the tanks, the planes, and the tactics of the Germans, far more than the fact that we were outnumbered, that forced our armies to retreat. It was the German tanks, planes, and tactics that provided the element of surprise which brought our leaders to their present plight.

But has the last word been said? Must we abandon all hope? Is our defeat final and irremediable? To those questions I answer—No!

Speaking in full knowledge of the facts, I ask you to believe me when I say that the cause of France is not lost. The very factors that brought about our defeat may one day lead us to victory.

For, remember this, France does not stand alone. She is not isolated. Behind her is a vast Empire, and she can make common cause with the British Empire, which commands the seas and is continuing the struggle. Like England, she can draw unreservedly on the immense industrial resources of the United States.

This war is not limited to our unfortunate country. The outcome of the struggle has not been decided by the Battle of France. This is a world war. Mistakes have been made, there have been delays and untold suffering, but the fact remains that there still exists in the world everything we need to crush our enemies some day. To-day we are crushed by the sheer weight of mechanized force hurled against us, but we can still look to a future in which even greater mechanized force will bring us victory. The destiny of the world is at stake.

I, General de Gaulle, now in London, call on all French officers and men who are at present on British soil, or may be in the future, with or without their arms; I call on all engineers and skilled workmen from the armaments factories who are at present on British soil, or may be in the future, to get in touch with me.

Whatever happens, the flame of French resistance must not and shall not die.

De Gaulle

A Letter from General de Gaulle to General Weygand: 20
June

Mon Général,

I have received your order to return to France. I
therefore enquired at once about the means of doing so,
for my one determination is, of course, to serve as a com-
batant.

I therefore expect to come and report to you within
twenty-four hours if, between now and then, a capitulation
has not been signed.

If it should have been, I would join any French
resistance which might be organized no matter where. In
London, in particular, there are some military elements—and doubtless there will come others—who are
resolved to fight, whatever may happen in the Mother
Country.

I feel it my duty to tell you quite simply that I wish, for
the sake of France and for yours, *mon Général,* that you
may be willing and able to escape disaster, reach overseas
France and continue the war. There is at present no possible armistice with honour.

I add that my personal relations with the British
Government—in particular with Mr. Churchill—could
enable me to be useful to you yourself or to any other
eminent Frenchman willing to place himself at the head of
a continued French resistance.

I beg you to accept, *mon Général,* my most respectful
and devoted regards.

De Gaulle

Note.—This letter, sent on to General Weygand by
General Lelong, Military Attaché in London, was returned
from Vichy to General de Gaulle in September 1940 with
a typed slip which ran as follows: "If retired Colonel de
Gaulle wishes to enter into communication with General
Weygand, he should do so through the proper channels."

The Armistice: 22 June

When in 1918 Germany had asked for an armistice, the question arose for Marshal Foch of the place where the conditions approved by the Allied Governments should be notified to the German plenipotentiaries. Marshal Foch excluded from his choice any town and even any inhabited spot. He wanted to place the conference out of reach of indiscretions, and at the same time to spare an unfortunate adversary from a humiliation, and to avoid any manifestation of hostility towards an enemy who had made himself hated by summary executions and needless destruction. In the centre of the forest of Rethondes, the clearing in which did not then exist, there was a railway siding where the trains of the two delegations could be brought close to each other. This was the spot chosen; it was known only to M. Clemenceau and Marshal Pétain. The secret was well kept. In this way the Germans were spared all contacts or spectacles humiliating to the vanquished. This meeting in 1918 will preserve in history the character of simplicity and dignity inseparable from true greatness.

If talion law led the German Chancellor to choose the same place, the 1940 meeting was organized in a diametrically opposite spirit. In the vast clearing, nothing less than a demonstration had been provided for German vindictiveness. Every sharpening of humiliation had been devised for the one whom the fortune of war had brought low—a crowd, music, cinema, and all the paraphernalia of the taking of a film.

Nothing was spared to the representative of France, not even words to which he had no opportunity to reply. For it was in front of Hitler and in his name that General Keitel read this monument of lying and vainglory, the record of which should be preserved:

On the strength of the assurances given to the German Reich by President Wilson, and confirmed by the

Allied Powers, the German Army laid down its arms in November 1918. So ended a war which the German people and its Government had not wanted, and in the course of which it had not been given to its adversaries, in spite of a crushing superiority, to achieve a decisive victory over the German Army, Navy, or Air Force.

From the moment of the arrival of the German delegation sent to take part in the *pourparlers* for the conclusion of an armistice, there began the violations of the promise solemnly given. It was on 11 November 1918, in this same coach, that there thus began the Calvary of the German people. Every element of dishonour, moral humiliation, and material human sufferings that can be imposed on a people had its origin here. In this way violation of the pledged word and perjury crashed down upon a nation which, after a heroic resistance maintained through four years, had succumbed only through the one weakness of believing in the promises given by democratic statesmen.

On 3 September, 1939—that is to say, twenty-five years after the outbreak of the World War—England and France once more, without any reason, declared war on Germany. The decision at arms has now come.

France is beaten. The French Government has asked the Government of the Reich to make known to it the German conditions for the conclusion of an armistice.

To receive these conditions, the French delegation has been invited to come to the historic forest of Compiègne, and this spot has been chosen to efface once and for all, by an act of justice and reparation, a memory which, for France, was not an honourable page in her history, but which was considered by the German people as the deepest dishonour of all time.

France, after a heroic resistance that showed itself in an uninterrupted succession of sanguinary battles, is beaten and has collapsed. In these circumstances, Germany does not wish to give to the armistice conditions or to the *pourparlers* relating to them such a character as to humiliate so brave an adversary.

The conditions formulated by Germany aim first at preventing the resumption of hostilities, secondly at offering full security to Germany in the war against England imposed on her by this latter, and thirdly at creating the conditions necessary for the establishment of a new peace which would consist essentially in repairing the injustices done to Germany by force. . . .

Maxime Weygand

The War is Over

We really did feel that the war was over now. It looked as if we should not even have to land in England. With our U-boats blocking the sea routes, it seemed as if the British hadn't a dog's chance of getting help from the Empire or America. This meant that eventually they would simply have to throw up the sponge; all we had to do was to send in the Luftwaffe to help them make up their minds.

Lieutenant Baron Tassilo von Bogenhardt

The Truth about the Armoured Forces of the Wehrmacht

Free rein has been given to speculations about the armoured forces which faced each other in the battle.

A similar controversy has arisen about the armoured forces of the enemy. Let us examine the question.

Estimates which our specialist services gave to our Supreme Command on this subject ranged, roughly speaking, from one extreme to another. Gamelin emphasizes the divergence in this sphere between the General Staff of the north-east command and the Intelligence Service. The latter according to Gamelin . . . put the number of Panzers thrown into the fight against us at four thousand. According to the calculations of Georges' General Staff, the Wehrmacht had employed on 10 May between seven thousand and seven thousand five hundred tanks on all its fronts. . . . "These," says Major Lyet, . . . "were divided into from twelve to fourteen armoured divisions, and some

fifteen independent regiments or battalions." But he adds,
"It has often been assumed that the German Army had actually engaged in the western campaign a total of seven
thousand to seven thousand five hundred tanks." Between
these two extreme estimates lies that of our own Command of Armoured Forces which, according to Colonel
Ferré . . . "puts the number at about four thousand five
hundred or five thousand tanks".

In the confusion of defeat, imagination has still further
magnified these figures. We shall see a figure of ten thousand Panzers constantly quoted by the most authoritative
circles without it ever being contested. And Pétain, in his
speech to the nation on 25 June 1940, was to appear a
realist when he only attributed eleven Panzer divisions to
the Wehrmacht.

We now know the truth. General Guderian has told it to
us. There could be no better qualified authority. On the
eve of the war, Guderian, in actual fact, was Inspector-
General of Armoured Forces to the German Army. It was
he who, during the campaign, was to be entrusted with the
decisive movement, namely, the forcing of the Meuse at
Sedan. Guderian states that the forces thrown in against us
comprised ten Panzer divisions and six motorized. The
Panzer divisions had a total number in each ranging from
two hundred and fifteen to three hundred and twenty-four
tanks, and not four hundred to five hundred as was
estimated in 1940 by our experts. The number of Panzers
came, therefore, to 3,003 at the most. To this figure must
be added 848 heavy armoured cars. Thus there was a
grand total of 3,851 vehicles, of which a certain number
took no part in the battle. Colonel Ferré writes: . . . .
"Guderian gives a definitive figure of two thousand eight
hundred tanks and seven hundred armoured cars. Major
Lyet estimates . . . for his part that the total was three
thousand. A figure," he adds, "slightly higher than that of
the Franco-British forces."

"Thus," writes Gamelin, "is exploded the myth of a
crushing German superiority in tanks."

Is it not now a convenient time to recall once again

that, materially speaking, it was not the number of vehicles but their organization, as I had emphasized so often to the Chamber, which was the decisive factor? A collection of tanks was not, I was never tired of explaining, an armoured division. The German Army had an *armoured corps*. We had not.

Did we not see our leaders, opposed to the massive use of armoured forces, deny that these contained a danger in an assault against a continuous front? When, on the morrow of the Polish campaign, General Billotte and Colonel de Gaulle each in his turn recommended, because we were lacking armoured divisions, the integration of infantry escort tanks as armoured divisions, our Supreme Command would not listen to their proposal. It is true that this proposal would have been of no avail unless we could have been certain that the enemy would give us the necessary respite to establish the divisions, whose creation was proposed. In actual fact there could have been no question of "improvising" armoured divisions.

On this subject we also have the opinion of General Bruneau, who, as we have seen, led 1 Armoured Division into battle, the only division which, as we have also seen, was capable of standing up to the Panzer divisions. He gave his opinion to the Committee of Inquiry in his deposition, cited above of 6 July 1948. To one member who asked him if it were "technically possible" to form divisions out of battalions of escort tanks, General Bruneau replied, "No; a large armoured unit cannot be improvised."

Paul Reynaud

Vichy

It has often been charged and it is altogether likely that Pétain and others were so ready to make peace partly because they feared that the country would lapse into Communism if the unequal struggle continued, and partly because they thought that defeat would perhaps be bought not too dearly if France could be saved from herself and

remade along more godly lines. Granted the hopelessness
of the military situation, their thoughts turned quickly to
the opportunity for a national revolution. There was more
than a bit of sheer fatalism in their acceptance of defeat.

Bullitt* spoke to most of these leaders within a week of
the signing of the armistice. His report of 1 July is one of
the most remarkable and revealing documents in the entire
annals of this great war. Nothing but direct quotation will
give anything like the flavour of his comments:

"The impression which emerges from these conversa-
tions is the extraordinary one, that the French leaders
desire to cut loose from all that France has represented
during the past two generations, that their physical and
moral defeat has been so absolute that they have accepted
completely for France the fate of becoming a province of
Nazi Germany. Moreover, in order that they may have as
many companions in misery as possible they hope that
England will be rapidly and completely defeated by Germany and that the Italians will suffer the same fate. Their
hope is that France may become Germany's favourite
province—a new "Gau" which will develop into a new
Gaul. . . ."

Marshal Pétain told the ambassador in so many words
that Germany would attempt to reduce France to the
status of a province by securing complete control and by
enforcing military impotence. He was extremely bitter
about the politicians and insisted that the government of
France must be radically altered.

"In his opinion one of the chief causes for the collapse
of the French Army was that the reserve officers who had
been educated by school teachers who were Socialists and
not patriots had deserted their men and shown no fighting
spirit whatsoever. . . ."

Darlan sounded the same note. He too was convinced
that Hitler would unite all Europe in a customs union and
make France his leading vassal state: "France could do
nothing but accept such a position for the moment." The

* United States Ambassador to France (Ed.)

fault had all been with the political regime: "The entire system of parliamentary government in France had been rotten and the high commander of the army [i.e. Gamelin] had proved to be equally rotten." Chautemps, one of the leaders of the Radical Socialist Party, chimed in and remarked quite frankly to Bullitt, "Pétain, Weygand and Laval intend to abolish the present French Constitution and to introduce a semi-dictatorial state in which Parliament would play a small role." Pétain would be the Hindenburg of the new regime, and Laval the Hitler. "Pétain, Weygand and Laval," concluded the ambassador, "all believe that if a dictatorship of this kind should be introduced in France before the peace, France would obtain much better terms than could be obtained under a parliamentary regime."*

The concluding remark of Bullitt's report raises a consideration that is absolutely fundamental to an understanding of all that happened in the sequel. It must be remembered that Pétain and his followers looked upon the defeat of France as merely the prelude to the collapse of the entire resistance to Hitler and the Nazis. We know that the Führer at the time shared this view. The armistice terms as we know them betray a hastily drawn document—a document full of provisional arrangements and half-settlements that was intended only to tide over the situation until a definitive peace treaty could be drawn. We need not analyse it in detail to demonstrate the point. What is important here is the thought on the part of the French defeatists that if they at once recognized their failure and dropped out of the struggle, the whole sad business would be over so much the sooner and they might, by accepting Hitler, curry favour with him and figure in the new Nazi Europe as Germany's preferred province. Pétain and his friends saw in France's misfortune a golden opportunity to effect the national revolution and calculated that if France could be remade in the Nazi image, the conqueror would be more lenient in the terms

* Tel. (1 July, 1940) from Bullitt, at La Bourboule.

he would finally impose. Recalling the fact that Britain was given only three weeks or a month before her day of doom, it is clear that haste was indicated. Actually the new France emerged less than three weeks after the signature of the armistice.

William L. Langer

THE TRAGEDY OF THE FRENCH FLEET

Winston Churchill Speaks to the House of Commons: 4 July

I said last week that we must now look with particular attention to our own salvation. I have never in my experience seen discussed in a Cabinet so grim and sombre a question as what we were to do about the French Fleet. It shows how strong were the reasons for the course which we thought it our duty to take, that every Member of the Cabinet had the same conviction about what should be done and there was not the slightest hesitation or divergence among them, and that the three Service Ministers, as well as men like the Minister of Information* and the Secretary of State for the Colonies, particularly noted for their long friendship with France, when they were consulted were equally convinced that no other decision than that which we took was possible. We took that decision, and it was a decision to which, with aching hearts but with clear vision, we unitedly came. Accordingly early yesterday morning, 3 July, after all preparations had been made, we took the greater part of the French Fleet under our control, or else called upon them, with adequate force, to comply with our requirements. Two battleships, two light cruisers, some submarines, including a very large one, the *Surcouf*, eight destroyers and approximately two hundred smaller but extremely useful minesweeping and anti-submarine craft which lay,

* Mr. Duff Cooper.

for the most part at Portsmouth and Plymouth, though there were some at Sheerness, were boarded by superior forces, after brief notice had been given wherever possible to their captains.

This operation was successfully carried out without resistance or bloodshed except in one instance. A scuffle arose through a misunderstanding in the sub-marine *Surcouf*, in which one British leading seaman was killed and two British officers and one rating wounded and one French officer killed and one wounded. For the rest, the French sailors, in the main, cheerfully accepted the end of a period of uncertainty.

Now I turn to the Mediterranean. At Alexandria, where a strong British battle fleet is lying, there are besides a French battleship, four French cruisers, three of them modern 8-inch gun vessels, and a number of smaller ships. These have been informed that they cannot be permitted to leave harbour and thus fall within the power of the German conquerors of France. Negotiations and discussions, with the details of which I need not trouble the House, have necessarily been taking place, and measures have now been taken to ensure that those ships, which are commanded by a very gallant Admiral, shall be sunk or otherwise made to comply with our wishes. . . .

But the most serious part of the story remains. Two of the finest vessels of the French Fleet, the *Dunkerque* and the *Strasbourg*, modern battle-cruisers much superior to *Scharnhorst* and *Gneisenau*——and built for the purpose of being superior to them——lay with two battleships, several light cruisers and a number of destroyers and submarines and other vessels at Oran and at its adjacent military port of Mers-el-Kebir on the northern African shore of Morocco. Yesterday morning, a carefully chosen British officer, Captain Holland, late Naval Attaché in Paris, was sent on in a destroyer and waited upon the French Admiral Gensoul. After being refused an interview, he presented the following document, which I will read to the House. The first two paragraphs of the document deal with the general question of the armistice, which I have already explained

in my own words. The fourth paragraph begins as follows:
This is the operative paragraph:

It is impossible for us, your comrades up to now, to
allow your fine ships to fall into the power of the German or Italian enemy. We are determined to fight on to
the end, and if we win, as we think we shall, we shall
never forget that France was our ally, that our interests
are the same as hers and that our common enemy is
Germany. Should we'conquer, we solemnly declare that
we shall restore the greatness and territory of France.
For this purpose, we must make sure that the best ships
of the French Navy are not used against us by the common foe. In these circumstances, His Majesty's Government have instructed me—[that is, the British Admiral]
—to demand that the French Fleet now at Mers-
el-Kebir and Oran shall act in accordance with one of
the following alternatives:

(a) Sail with us and continue to fight for victory
against the Germans and Italians.

(b) Sail with reduced crews under our control to a
British port. The reduced crews will be repatriated at
the earliest moment.

If either of these courses is adopted by you, we will
restore your ships to France at the conclusion of the
war or pay full compensation, if they are damaged
meanwhile.

(c) Alternatively, if you feel bound to stipulate that
your ships should not be used against the Germans or
Italians unless these break the Armistice, then sail them
with us with reduced crews, to some French port in the
West Indies, Martinique, for instance, where they can be
demilitarized to our satisfaction or be perhaps entrusted
to the United States and remain safe until the end of the
war, the crews being repatriated.

If you refuse these fair offers, I must, with profound
regret, require you to sink your ships within six hours.

Finally, failing the above, I have the orders of His
Majesty's Government to use whatever force may be

necessary to prevent your ships from falling into German or Italian hands.

We had hoped that one or other of the alternatives which we presented would have been accepted, without the necessity of using the terrible force of a British battle squadron. Such a squadron arrived before Oran two hours after Captain Holland and his destroyer. This battle squadron was commanded by Vice-Admiral Somerville, an officer who distinguished himself lately in the bringing-off of over a hundred thousand Frenchmen during the evacuation from Dunkirk. Admiral Somerville was further provided, besides his battleships, with a cruiser force and strong flotillas. All day the parleys continued, and we hoped until the afternoon that our terms would be accepted without bloodshed. However, no doubt in obedience to the orders dictated by the Germans from Wiesbaden, where the Franco-German Armistice Commission is in session, Admiral Gensoul refused to comply and announced his intention of fighting. Admiral Somerville was, therefore, ordered to complete his mission before this powerful French Fleet, which was also protected by its shore batteries. At 6 p.m. he reported that he was heavily engaged. The action lasted for some ten minutes and was followed by heavy attacks from our naval aircraft, carried in the *Ark Royal*. At 7.20 p.m. Admiral Somerville forwarded a further report, which stated that a battle-cruiser of the *Strasbourg* class was damaged and ashore; that a battleship of the *Bretagne* class had been sunk, that another of the same class had been heavily damaged, and that two French destroyers and a seaplane carrier, *Commandant Teste* were also sunk or burned.

While this melancholy action was being fought either the battle-cruiser *Strasbourg* or the *Dunkerque,* one or the other, managed to slip out of harbour in a gallant effort to reach Toulon or a North African port and place herself under German control, in accordance with the Armistice terms of the Bordeaux Government—though all this her crew and captain may not have realized. She was pursued by aircraft of the Fleet Air Arm and hit by at least one torpedo. She may have been joined by other French vessels from Algiers, which were well placed to do so and to reach Toulon before we would overtake them. She will, at any rate, be out of action for many months to come.

I need hardly say that the French ships were fought, albeit in this unnatural cause, with the characteristic courage of the French Navy, and every allowance must be made for Admiral Gensoul and his officers who felt themselves obliged to obey the orders they received from their Government and could not look behind the Government to see the German dictation. I fear the loss of life among the French and in the harbour must have been very heavy, as we were compelled to use a severe measure of force and several immense explosions were heard. None of the British ships taking part in the action was in any way affected in gun-power or mobility by the heavy fire directed upon them. I have not yet received any reports of our casualties, but Admiral Somerville's fleet is, in all military respects, intact and ready for further action. . . .

A large proportion of the French Fleet has, therefore, passed into our hands or has been put out of action or otherwise withheld from Germany by yesterday's events. The House will not expect me to say anything about other French ships which are at large except that it is our inflexible resolve to do everything that is possible in order to prevent them falling into the German grip. I leave the judgment of our action, with confidence, to Parliament. I leave it to the nation, and I leave it to the United States. I leave it to the world and history.

                                                   Winston Churchill

7

THE BATTLE OF BRITAIN

The Germans were now confronted with the problem of invading Britain in the face of British naval supremacy and air cover in the Channel. The Luftwaffe was the weapon upon which the Germans relied to cow the British so that they would throw in their hand, or soften them so that a cross-Channel invasion would become easy. The Battle of Britain was therefore an air battle, with enormous consequences depending upon it. It fell into three stages, beginning on 10 July. The first and second involved the Luftwaffe's attempt to destroy British fighter strength, first by attacks on ports and coastal shipping and then by concentrated assaults on airfields. Following the failure of this plan, the Luftwaffe finally turned on the cities.

Meanwhile, in the face of his country's official state of neutrality and almost every American's dislike of involvement with any of the belligerents, President Roosevelt began his long battle to convince his people that the defence of Britain was a part of the defence of the United States and everything it stood for, and also began to do whatever could legally be done to help.

"WE SHALL NEVER SURRENDER"

TURNING once again, and this time more generally, to the question of invasion, I would observe that there has never been a period in all these long centuries of which we boast when an absolute guarantee against invasion, still less against serious raids, could have been given to our

people. In the days of Napoleon the same wind which
would have carried his transports across the Channel
might have driven away the blockading fleet. There was
always the chance, and it is that chance which has excited
and befooled the imaginations of many Continental
tyrants. Many are the tales that are told. We are assured
that novel methods will be adopted, and when we see the
originality of malice, the ingenuity of aggression, which
our enemy displays, we may certainly prepare ourselves
for every kind of novel stratagem and every kind of brutal
and treacherous manoeuvre. I think that no idea is so
outlandish that it should not be considered and viewed
with a searching, but at the same time, I hope, with a
steady eye. We must never forget the solid assurances of
sea-power and those which belong to air-power if it can be
locally exercised.

I have, myself, full confidence that if all do their duty,
if nothing is neglected, and if the best arrangements are
made, as they are being made, we shall prove ourselves
once again able to defend our island home, to ride out the
storm of war, and to outlive the menace of tyranny, if
necessary for years, if necessary alone. At any rate, that is
what we are going to try to do. That is the resolve of His
Majesty's Government—every man of them. That is the
will of Parliament and the nation. The British Empire and
the French Republic, linked together in their cause and in
their need, will defend to the death their native soil, aiding
each other like good comrades to the utmost of their
strength. Even though large tracts of Europe and many old
and famous states have fallen or may fall into the grip of
the Gestapo and all the odious apparatus of Nazi rule, we
shall not flag or fail. We shall go on to the end, we shall
fight in France, we shall fight on the seas and oceans, we
shall fight with growing confidence and growing strength in
the air, we shall defend our island, whatever the cost may
be, we shall fight on the beaches, we shall fight on the
landing grounds, we shall fight in the fields and in the
streets, we shall fight in the hills; we shall never surrender,
and even if, which I do not for a moment believe, this

island or a large part of it were subjugated and starving,
then our Empire beyond the seas, armed and guarded by
the British Fleet, would carry on the struggle, until, in
God's good time, the new world, with all its power and
might, steps forth to the rescue and the liberation of the
old.

Winston Churchill, 4 June 1940

AMERICA'S REPLY

When the second World War started the defences of the
United States consisted primarily of a scrap of paper
called the Neutrality Law, which the Congress had passed
and which President Roosevelt had signed "with reluctance". That piece of legislation, passed originally in
1936, was carefully designed to prevent us from getting
into war in 1917. It was purely retroactive, as though its
framers believed that it would restore life to the brave men
who had died at Château Thierry and in the Argonne. It
was born of the belief that we could legislate ourselves out
of the war, as we had once legislated ourselves out of the
saloons (and into the speakeasies).

Harry L. Hopkins

In our American unity, we will pursue two obvious and
simultaneous courses; we will extend to the opponents of
force the material resources of this nation; and, at the
same time, we will harness and speed up the use of those
resources in order that we ourselves in the Americas may
have equipment and training equal to the task of any
emergency and every defence.

President Roosevelt, 10 June

The President had scraped the bottom of the barrel in
American arsenals for half a million rifles, eighty thousand machine-guns, a hundred and thirty million rounds
of ammunition, nine hundred 75 mm. guns and a million
shells, as well as some bombs, T.N.T., and smokeless

powder, all to be shipped to Britain. This was done by means of more legal manipulation in a "damn the torpedoes" spirit. It was done at a moment when many men close to the White House were shouting almost hysterically that this represented suicide for Roosevelt and quite possibly for the nation——that Britain was finished and that all this material would merely fall into the hands of Hitler, who would turn it against us in our own relatively defenceless state. But it was done, and it was of inestimable value to Britain in her hour of greatest need.

Harry L. Hopkins

BEFORE THE BATTLE

. . . . I see only one sure way through now, to wit, that Hitler should attack this country, and in so doing break his air weapon. If this happens he will be left to face the winter with Europe writhing under his heel, and probably with the United States against him after the Presidential Election is over.

Winston Churchill to General Smuts, 9 June

Armed Forces Supreme Headquarters was located near our airfield, and I took advantage of this fact to visit one or two old friends now serving on Hitler's staff, including Colonel-General Keitel, who had once been my commanding officer, and Captain von Below, who had served under me in the old days and was now Hitler's air adjutant. Both these officers were convinced that England was prepared to sue for peace, and that the war was as good as finished.

Nevertheless, despite this wave of optimism in high places, the Air Force was ordered to make good its relatively light casualties in crews and machines and to prepare for the next battles which must be fought over the Channel and in the English skies. Within a few days the German Air Force was ready.

Werner Kreipe, General of the Luftwaffe

"Their Finest Hour"

What General Weygand called the Battle of France is over. I expect that the Battle of Britain is about to begin. Upon this battle depends the survival of Christian civilization. Upon it depends our own British life, and the long continuity of our institutions and our Empire. The whole fury and might of the enemy must very soon be turned on us. Hitler knows that he will have to break us in this island or lose the war. If we can stand up to him, all Europe may be free and the life of the world may move forward into broad, sunlit uplands. But if we fail, then the whole world, including the United States, including all that we have known and cared for, will sink into the abyss of a new dark age made more sinister, and perhaps more protracted, by the lights of perverted science. Let us therefore brace ourselves to our duties, and so bear ourselves that, if the British Empire and its Commonwealth last for a thousand years, men will say, "This was their finest hour".

Winston Churchill, 18 June

Hitler Addresses the Reichstag: 19 July

In this hour I feel it to be my duty before my own conscience to appeal once more to reason and common sense in Great Britain as much as elsewhere. I consider myself in a position to make this appeal, since I am not a vanquished foe begging favours, but the victor, speaking in the name of reason. I can see no reason why this war need go on. I am grieved to think of the sacrifices it must claim. . . . Possibly Mr. Churchill will brush aside this statement of mine by saying it is merely born of fear and doubt of final victory. In that case I shall have relieved my conscience in regard to the things to come.

Adolf Hitler

. . . During the evening I waited impatiently for the speech of Lord Halifax which was to be delivered at 9.0

p.m. At ten I received a telephone message to the effect that the British Government had rejected any negotiation with Germany, and had taken up the challenge. The Anglo-German war is about to begin, and if the Germans do not master England this autumn they will have lost the war.

Paul Baudouin, French Foreign Minister, 22 July

The air war will start now, and will determine our ultimate relative strength. If the results of the air war are not satisfactory, [invasion] preparations will be stopped. But if we gain the impression that the English are being crushed and that the air war is, after a certain time, taking effect, then we shall attack. An attempt must be made to prepare the operation for 15 September 1940.

Adolf Hitler, 31 July

Directive No. 17: 1 August

In order to establish the preliminary conditions required for the final conquest of Britain . . . I intend to continue the air and naval war against metropolitan Britain more intensively than heretofore. . . . The German Air Force will use all available means to destroy the British Air Force as soon as possible. Attacks will be directed primarily against the flying units, ground organization, and supply installations of the Royal Air Force, and, further, against the air armaments industry, including factories producing anti-aircraft equipment.

Adolf Hitler

The Antagonists: 10 August

. . . . The Luftwaffe had marked numerical superiority. While the Royal Air Force could put six to seven hundred fighters into the air, the serviceable aircraft of *Luftflotten* 2 and 3 consisted of 929 fighters,* 875 long-range bombers and 316 dive-bombers: *Luftflotte* 5 disposed of

* 277 of these were twin-engined fighters or fighter-bombers.

thirty-four twin-engined fighters and 123 long-range bombers.

THE BATTLE

The Luftwaffe

. . . Over the Thames Estuary we got involved in a heavy scrap with Spitfires, which were screening a convoy. Together with the Staff Flight, I selected one formation as our prey, and we made a surprise attack from a favourably higher altitude. I glued myself to the tail of the plane flying outside on the left flank and when, during a right-handed turn, I managed to get in a long burst, the Spitfire went down almost vertically. I followed it until the cockpit cover came flying towards me and the pilot baled out, then followed him down until he crashed into the water. His parachute had failed to open.

The modern Vickers Supermarine Spitfires were slower than our planes by about ten to fifteen m.p.h., but could perform steeper and tighter turns. The older Hawker Hurricane, which was at that time still frequently used by the British, compared badly with our Messerschmitt 109 as regards speed and rate of climb. Our armament and ammunition were also undoubtedly better. Another advantage was that our engines had injection pumps instead of the carburettors used by the British, and therefore did not conk out through lack of acceleration in critical moments during combat. The British fighters usually tried to shake off pursuit by a half-roll or half-roll on top of a loop, while we simply went straight for them, with wide-open throttle and eyes bulging out of their sockets.

During this first action we lost two aircraft. That was bad, although at the same time we had three confirmed kills. We were no longer in doubt that the R.A.F. would prove a most formidable opponent.

Colonel Adolf Galland, Luftwaffe

The Royal Air Force

. . . . I climbed into the cockpit of my plane and felt an
empty sensation of suspense in the pit of my stomach. For
one second time seemed to stand still and I stared blankly
in front of me. I knew that that morning I was to kill for
the first time. That I might be killed or in any way injured
did not occur to me. Later, when we were losing pilots
regularly, I did consider it in an abstract way when on the
ground; but once in the air, never. I knew it could not
happen to me. I suppose every pilot knows that, knows it
cannot happen to him; even when he is taking off for the
last time, when he will not return, he knows that he cannot
be killed. I wondered idly what he was like, this man I
would kill. Was he young, was he fat, would he die with
the Führer's name on his lips, or would he die alone, in
that last moment conscious of himself as a man? I would
never know. Then I was being strapped in, my mind
automatically checking the controls, and we were off. We
ran into them at eighteen thousand feet, twenty yellow-
nosed Messerschmitt 109s, about five hundred feet above
us. Our Squadron strength was eight, and as they came
down on us we went into line astern and turned head on to
them. Brian Carbury, who was leading the section,
dropped the nose of his machine, and I could almost feel
the leading Nazi pilot push forward on his stick to bring his
guns to bear. At the same moment Brian hauled hard back
on his own control stick and led us over them in a steep
climbing turn to the left. In two vital seconds they lost their
advantage. I saw Brian let go a burst of fire at the leading
plane, saw the pilot put his machine into a half roll, and
knew that he was mine. Automatically, I kicked the rudder
to the left to get him at right angles, turned the gun-bottom
to "Fire", and let go in a four-second burst with full deflec-
tion. He came right through my sights and I saw the tracer
from all eight guns thud home. For a second he seemed to
hang motionless; then a jet of red flame shot upwards and
he spun out of sight.

For the next few minutes I was too busy looking after myself to think of anything, but when, after a short while, they turned and made off over the Channel, and we were ordered to our base, my mind began to work again.

It had happened.

My first emotion was one of satisfaction, satisfaction at a job adequately done, at the final logical conclusion of months of specialized training. And then I had a feeling of the essential rightness of all. He was dead and I was alive; it could so easily have been the other way round; and that would somehow have been right too. I realized in that moment just how lucky a fighter pilot is. He has none of the personalized emotions of the soldier, handed a rifle and bayonet and told to charge. He does not even have to share the dangerous emotions of the bomber pilot who night after night must experience that childhood longing for smashing things. The fighter pilot's emotions are those of the duellist—cool, precise, impersonal. He is privileged to kill well. For if one must either kill or be killed, as now one must, it should, I feel, be done with dignity. Death should be given the setting it deserves; it should never be a pettiness; and for the fighter pilot it never can be.

Richard Hillary

Throughout it all the radio is never silent—shouts, oaths, exhortations and terse commands. You single out an opponent. Jockey for position. All clear behind! The bullets from your eight guns go pumping into his belly. He begins to smoke. But the wicked tracer sparkles and flashes over the top of your own cockpit and you break into a tight turn. Now you have two enemies. The 109 on your tail and your remorseless, ever-present opponent "G", the force of gravity. Over your shoulder you can still see the ugly, questing snout of the 109. You tighten the turn. The Spit protests and shudders, and when the blood drains from your eyes you "grey-out". But you keep turning, for life itself is the stake. And now your blood feels like molten lead and runs from head to legs. You black out! And you ease the turn to recover in a grey, unreal world of spinning horizons. Cautiously you climb into the sun. You have lost too much height and your opponent has gone—disappeared. You are completely alone in your own bit of sky, bounded by the blue vault above and the coloured drapery of earth below.

"Johnnie" Johnson

We made a dash for our machines and within two minutes were off the ground. Twice we circled the aerodrome to allow all twelve planes to get in formation. We were flying in four sections of three: Red Section leading, Blue and Green to right and left, and the three remaining planes forming a guard section above and behind us.

I was flying No. 2 in the Blue Section.

Over the radio came the voice of the controller, "Hullo, Red Leader", followed by instructions on course and height.

As always, for the first few minutes we flew on the reciprocal of the course given until we reached fifteen thousand feet. We then turned about and flew on 110° in an all-out climb, thus coming out of the sun and gaining height all the way.

During the climb Uncle George was in constant touch with the ground. We were to intercept about twenty enemy fighters at twenty-five thousand feet. I glanced across at Stapme and saw his mouth moving. That meant he was singing again. He would sometimes do this with his radio set on "Send", with the result that, mingled with our instructions from the ground, we would hear a raucous rendering of *Night and Day*. And then quite clearly over the radio I heard the Germans excitedly calling to each other. This was a not infrequent occurrence and it made one feel that they were right behind, although often they were some distance away. I switched my set to "Send" and called out *"Halts Maul!"* and as many other choice pieces of German invective as I could remember. To my delight I heard one of them answer, "You feelthy Englishmen, we will teach you how to speak to a German." I am aware that this sounds a tall story, but several others in the

Squadron were listening out and heard the whole thing.

I looked down. It was a completely cloudless sky and way below lay the English countryside, stretching lazily into the distance, a quite extraordinary picture of green and purple in the setting sun.

I took a glance at my altimeter. We were at twenty-eight thousand feet. At that moment Sheep yelled "Tally-ho" and dropped down in front of Uncle George in a slow dive in the direction of the approaching planes. Uncle George saw them at once.

"O.K. Line astern."

I drew in behind Stapme and took a look at them. They were about two thousand feet below us, which was a pleasant change, but they must have spotted us at the same moment, for they were forming a protective circle, one behind the other, which is a defence formation hard to break.

"Echelon starboard," came Uncle George's voice.

We spread out fanwise to the right.

"Going down!"

One after the other we peeled off in a power dive. I picked out one machine and switched my gun-button to "Fire". At three hundred yards I had him in my sights. At two hundred I opened up in a long four-second burst and saw the tracer going into his nose. Then I was pulling out, so hard that I could feel my eyes dropping through my neck. Coming round in a slow climbing turn, I saw that we had broken them up. The sky was now a mass of individual dog-fights. Several of them had already been knocked down. One I hoped was mine, but on pulling up I had not been able to see the result. To my left I saw Peter Pease make a head-on attack on a Messerschmitt. They were headed straight for each other and it looked as though the fire of both was striking home. Then at the last moment the Messerschmitt pulled up, taking Peter's fire full in the belly. It rolled on its back, yellow flames pouring from the cockpit, and vanished.

Richard Hillary

Attack on an Advanced Fighter Aerodrome: August

After about a week of Hornchurch, I woke late one morning to the noise of machines running up on the aerodrome. It irritated me: I had a headache.

Having been on every flight the previous day, the morning was mine to do with as I pleased. I got up slowly, gazed dispassionately at my tongue in the mirror, and wandered over to the Mess for breakfast. It must have been getting on for twelve o'clock when I came out on to the aerodrome to find the usual August heat haze forming a dull pall over everything. I started to walk across the aerodrome to the Dispersal Point on the far side. There were only two machines on the ground so I concluded that the Squadron was already up. Then I heard a shout, and our ground crew drew up in a lorry beside me. Sergeant Ross leaned out:

"Want a lift, sir? We're going round."

"No, thanks, Sergeant. I'm going to cut across."

This was forbidden for obvious reasons, but I felt like that.

"O. K., sir. See you round there."

The lorry trundled off down the road in a cloud of dust. I walked on across the landing ground. At that moment I heard the emotionless voice of the controller.

"Large enemy bombing formation approaching Hornchurch. All personnel not engaged in active duty take cover immediately."

I looked up. They were still not visible. At the Dispersal Point I saw Bubble and Pip Cardell make a dash for the shelter. Three Spitfires just landed, turned about and came past me with a roar to take off down-wind. Our lorry was still trundling along the road, maybe half-way round, and seemed suddenly an awfully long way from the Dispersal Point.

I looked up again, and this time I saw them—about a dozen slugs, shining in the bright sun and coming straight on. At the rising scream of the first bomb I instinctively shrugged up my shoulders and ducked my head. Out of the corner of my eye I saw the three Spitfires. One moment they were about twenty feet up in close formation; the next catapulted apart as though on elastic. The leader went over on his back and ploughed along the runway with a rending crash of tearing fabric; Number Two put a wing in and spun round on his air-screw, while the plane on the left was blasted wingless into the next field. I remember thinking stupidly, "That's the shortest flight he's ever taken," and then my feet were nearly knocked from under me, my mouth was full of dirt, and Bubble, gesticulating like a madman from the shelter entrance, was yelling, "Run, you bloody fool, run!" I ran. Suddenly awakened to the lunacy of my behaviour, I covered the distance to that shelter as if impelled by a rocket and shot through the entrance while once again the ground rose up and hit me, and my head smashed hard against one of the pillars. I subsided on a heap of rubble and massaged it.

"Who's here?" I asked, peering through the gloom.

"Cardell and I and three of our ground crew," said Bubble, "and, by the Grace of God, you!"

I could see by his mouth that he was still talking, but a sudden concentration of the scream and crump of falling bombs made it impossible to hear him.

The air was thick with dust and the shelter shook and heaved at each explosion, yet somehow held firm. For about three minutes the bedlam continued, and then suddenly ceased. In the utter silence which followed nobody moved. None of us wished to be the first to look on the devastation which we felt must be outside. Then Bubble spoke. "Praise God!" he said, "I'm not a civilian. Of all the bloody frightening things I've ever done, sitting in that shelter was the worst. Me for the air from now on!"

It broke the tension and we scrambled out of the entrance. The runways were certainly in something of a mess. Gaping holes and great gobblets of earth were everywhere. Right in front of us a bomb had landed by my Spitfire, covering it with a shower of grit and rubble.

I turned to the aircraftsman standing beside me. "Will

you get hold of Sergeant Ross and tell him to have a crew give her an inspection."

He jerked his head towards one corner of the aerodrome: "I think I'd better collect the crew myself, sir. Sergeant Ross won't be doing any more inspections."

I followed his glance and saw the lorry, the roof about twenty yards away, lying grotesquely on its side. I climbed into the cockpit, and, feeling faintly sick, tested out the switches. Bubble poked his head over the side.

"Let's go over to the Mess and see what's up: all our machines will be landing down at the reserve landing field, anyway."

I climbed out and walked over to find that the three Spitfire pilots were quite unharmed but for a few superficial scratches, in spite of being machine-gunned by the bombers. "Operations" was undamaged: no hangar had been touched and the Officers' Mess had two windows broken.

The Station Commander ordered every available man and woman on to the job of repairing the aerodrome surface and by four o'clock there was not a hole to the seen. Several unexploded bombs were marked off, and two lines of yellow flags were laid down to mark the runways. At five o'clock our Squadron, taking off for a "flap" from the reserve field, landed without incident on its home base. Thus, apart from four men killed in the lorry and a network of holes on the landing surface, there was nothing to show for ten minutes' really accurate bombing from twelve thousand feet, in which several dozen sticks of bombs had been dropped. It was a striking proof of the inefficacy of their attempts to wipe out our advance fighter aerodromes.

Richard Hillary

"Sailor" Malan on Air Strategy

Sailor would never talk freely as did the others. I found him (leaning silently against the pub mantelpiece, a pint of beer in his hand which did him the whole evening) rather difficult to know, and exceedingly uncommun-icative. As he had already established a reputation as a killer, and his silent stolidity was so much at variance with the extroversion of the others, I was at some pains to draw him out, and on one occasion devoted a whole evening to doing so.

"Tell me, Sailor, as a matter of technical interest, how exactly do you go about shooting down a bomber?"

After some rumination: "I try not to now."

"Whatever do you mean?"

"Well, I think it's a bad thing."

"Now come, Sailor. I really want to know. Don't trifle with me."

"I mean it. I think it's a thoroughly bad thing. You see, if you shoot them down they don't get back and no one in Germany is a whit the wiser. So I figure the right thing to do is to let them get back. With a dead rear gunner; a dead navigator, and the pilot coughing his lungs up as he lands . . . I think if you do that it has a better effect on their morale . . . that's what we want to aim at now. Of course, if you just mean to shoot them down, well, what I generally do is . . . knock out port and starboard engines. But, honestly, Doc, the other way is best."

Hospital Surgeon

The Few

The gratitude of every home in our island, in our Em-pire, and indeed throughout the world, except in the abodes of the guilty, goes out to the British airmen who, undaunted by odds, unwearied in their constant challenge and mortal danger, are turning the tide of the world war by their prowess and their devotion. Never in the field of human conflict was so much owed by so many to so few.

Winston Churchill, 20 August

THE BLITZ

Hitler had failed to destroy the R.A.F. in the air or on the ground. On 7 September the Blitz began. London was attacked more heavily and persistently than any other city in Britain. The Luftwaffe opened its hostilities in daylight, but by 14 November they had sustained such heavy losses that they switched to night operations and so continued until mid-1941, from which time London and the cities of Britain were generally left in peace until the beginning of the V1 raids in the summer of 1944.

The First Days

The barracks of the Middlesex Regiment are built on one of the highest pieces of ground to the north of London: the whole city lies spread out at your feet. I arrived there as a recruit in the middle of August 1940, when the sense of urgency had become almost unbearable. The Middlesex was a machine-gun regiment equipped with the .303 Vickers medium gun. They were specialists and proud of it, and the instructors were extraordinarily able. As a result, a large number of us were bulldozed into mastery of this complicated weapon in an incredibly short time. Perhaps the presence of a flying column in the barracks, ready to move at thirty minutes' notice in the event of invasion, brought home to us the perilous situation in which we and everyone else in Britain found ourselves at that time.

The weather was lovely, and we sweated day after day in our shirtsleeves as we went through the drill of: "On this spot, in that direction MOUNT GUN!" I remember one day when we were doing a platoon drill, with two D.P. guns and two which did not exist at all. Numbers One and Four were there, but were considered too old to be used in action; Numbers Two and Three were left to the imagination. One of their gunners sat on the ground

with legs crossed and hands raised in what he hoped was
the required position, to be lashed by a falsetto scream
from Sergeant Jacques: "Number One or Number Two
gun, how many times have I told you to get those fore-
fingers correctly under the safety-catch!"

Suddenly we were gaping upwards. The brilliant sky
was criss-crossed from horizon to horizon by innumerable
vapour-trails. The sight was a completely novel one. We
watched, fascinated, and all work stopped. The little silver
stars sparkling at the heads of the vapour trails turned
east. This display looked so insubstantial and harmless;
even beautiful. Then, with a dull roar which made the
ground across London shake as one stood upon it, the first
sticks of bombs hit the docks. Leisurely, enormous
mushrooms of black and brown smoke shot with crimson
expanded, for there was no wind, and the great fires below
fed more smoke into them as the hours passed.

On Friday and Saturday morning the sky grew darker
and darker as the oily smoke rose and spread in heavy,
immobile columns, shutting out the sun.

At the barracks, drill quickly became monotonous. We
had work to do, and we weren't the target. But we
couldn't keep our eyes off those sickening, solid columns
climbing up like the convolutions of a lazy snake into a
torpid sky.

I suppose our masters felt that, although the Battle of
Britain had begun, the worst might already be over—I
don't know; but they decided to put us recruits in the hat
and draw out three for week-end leave. My name came
out of the hat first, and I sent a wire to my parents in
Sevenoaks to say that I was coming home. My pass was
from midday on Saturday, and I got down to the centre of
London by Underground. Bombers were coming over at
monotonously regular intervals. I walked down to Charing
Cross. There was a lot of noise still, and a lot of smoke.
As I entered the station the loudspeakers were ordering
everyone out because planes were overhead and they were
frightened of casualties if the place were hit. I strolled out

to the top of that long flight of stone steps down into
Villiers Street and sat on the balustrade watching.

Up in the lonely sky there was still one bomber, gleam-
ing silver, and then he dropped a stick just across the
Thames from us. Back in the station the loudspeaker announced that the main line was gone and that there
wouldn't be any more trains out for hours. Hundreds of
people stood around like a flock of sheep which is
frightened and can't make up its mind which way to turn.
You could see the dead mask of indecision on their faces
as they looked about, hoping someone would tell them
what to do. I walked out of the station and decided to
hitch-hike home. I was lucky; somewhere on the south
bank of the river I met a man on a motor-cycle who was
going through Blackheath, and he took me on his pillion.

Now we were nearer to the docks. The columns of
smoke merged and became a monstrous curtain which
blocked the sky; only the billows within it and the sudden
shafts of flame which shot up hundreds of feet made one
realize that it was a living thing and not just the backdrop
of some nightmare opera. There were fire-hoses along the
side of the road, climbing over one another like a helping
of macaroni, with those sad little fountains spraying out
from the leaks, as they always seem to do from all fire-
hoses. Every two or three minutes we would pull into the
gutter as a fire-bell broke out stridently behind us and an
engine in unfamiliar livery tore past at full tilt: chocolate
or green or blue, with gold lettering—City of Birmingham
Fire Brigade, or Sheffield, or Bournemouth. The feeling
was something you had never experienced before—the excitement and dash of fire-engines arriving to help from so
far away, and the oily, evil smell of fire and destruction,
with its lazy, insolent rhythm.

It looked terrible and hopeless, but there was a kind of
Götterdämmerung grandeur about it.

I got home in one piece, and my parents welcomed me
with a splendid dinner. But that night the *Luftwaffe*,
already working round the clock, came again and dropped
a stick of bombs straight down our quiet Sevenoaks road.

They hit the town centre just by the historic Vine cricket ground with the first bomb. The last but one landed opposite our gate, and the last by the street corner. Apart from the destruction of the town hall, no damage was done, and I wonder why that particular pilot chose that particular target; I suppose he must have seen the main London-Dover railway line and his bomb-aimer let go too soon.

Sunday in Sevenoaks was the same as Sunday throughout Kent, Surrey, Sussex and Essex. The hot summer air throbbed with the steady beat of the engines of bombers which one could not see in the dazzling blue. Then the R.A.F. would arrive; the monotonous drone would be broken by the sudden snarl of a fighter turning at speed, and the vapour trails would start to form in huge circles. I lay on my back in the rose garden and watched the trails forming; as they broadened and dispersed a fresh set would be superimposed upon them. Then, no bigger than a pin's head, a white parachute would open and come down, growing slowly larger; I counted eight in the air at one time.

I had to be back in barracks on the Sunday night, and set off after supper. The twenty-three-mile journey took well over two hours, and no one could tell us what station we would be taken to. When we finally got there, it turned out to be Holborn. I stepped out into the darkness of the street, or what would have been darkness but for the fires; but as I did so a stick whistled down on the other side of the road and I ducked back inside. After a while I knew I had to begin to move. Hanging about in the station shelter wasn't doing me any good, so I started out on foot up Holborn. When I reached Gamages I was turned back: everything was cascaded down into the road as though two landslides had started simultaneously from opposite sides. There was utter silence, except for the crunch and crackle of my own feet treading a carpet of broken glass.

I was told to make a detour, and eventually got to Marble Arch, where I found a taxi. The driver said he would take me to the barracks, but we hadn't been going up the

Edgware Road for long when the next wave came in and the stuff began dropping round us all the way to Mill Hill. As I paid him, the driver said, "If I'd 'a known it was going to be like this, Guv, I'd never 'a taken the fare." I felt desperately sorry for him as he drove away into the darkness; my bed and a few hours' sleep were only two minutes' walk away, while he had a long drive back to London alone. In those early days the indifference to death and danger which became so characteristic of the civilian was as yet hardly perceptible. I, a recruit of three weeks' standing, already thought of him as a "civilian". I hope he made it.

D. F.

Firemen

I signed on at Chelsea as a member of the London Auxiliary Fire Service. The assembled recruits, aided by casual residents of Wellington Square, were already in their shirtsleeves, revelling in the lovely weather, the healthy occupation, the novelty of digging up municipal territory to fill sandbags, and the opportunity to meet strangers without introduction. Among them I found an attitude of almost incredible optimism. That it should take a war to produce this holiday-camp mood was a reflection of the dullness of people's lives and the prison of class distinction in English society. After months of brooding and preaching on the horrors of war I was astonished to find how little the prospect seemed to dismay people. There were bearded artists who talked of keeping their hands in by joining the Camouflage Corps. There were university graduates "marking time" till their chance came to join one of the Services. There were middle-aged ladies whose lonely lives had been brightened by the announcement: "Your Country Needs You." I felt happy for them. They had little to lose and great energy to give. There were society girls who could hold open the neck of a sandbag with exquisite grace, declaring that this job was more fun than Ascot. One of them—I think she was a minor actress—was so pleased with the perspiring youth who was filling her sandbag that she stagily promised to get him a commission in her uncle's regiment. Then there were old soldiers who had been in "the last lot". They would have joined the ranks to-morrow if they had been ten years younger. Their talk was full of words like "Blighty" and "Jerry"; and gave me a strange feeling of recognition. I, too, had been through it before, in a score of war books from Raymond to Remarque. Some of the old soldiers were labourers, some cab drivers, some shopkeepers. I noted at once that the "working class", if franker about their motives for joining National Service, were less public-spirited. Nor were they carried away by the community spirit the hour fostered. Many of them were there because they were out of a job, because they were lonely, or because business was bad. A few confessed that the A.F.S. was an easy alternative to the Army. "They won't get me in the Kate Karney," an unemployed truck driver declared. "My old man was four years a private in the last lot, and he brought me up a pacifist. All the same I don't mind doing my bit." He, too, seemed happy. Like everybody else, the war had provided him with a short-term object in life. We were in Civil Defence: we were firemen.

London fireman

An American Watches

All the fires were quickly brought under control. That's a common phrase in the morning communiqués. I've seen how it's done; spent a night with the London fire brigade. For three hours after the night attack got going, I shivered in a sandbag crow's-nest atop a tall building near the Thames. It was one of the many fire-observation posts. There was an old gun barrel mounted above a round table marked off like a compass. A stick of incendiaries bounced off roof-tops about three miles away. The observer took a sight on a point where the first one fell, swung his gun-sight along the line of bombs, and took another reading at the end of the line of fire. Then he picked up his telephone and shouted above the half gale that was blowing up there, "Stick of incendiaries—between 190 and 220—about three miles away." Five minutes later a German bomber came boring down the river. We could see his exhaust trail like a pale ribbon stretched straight across the sky. Half a mile downstream there were two eruptions and then a third, close together. The first two looked as though some giant had thrown a huge basket of flaming golden oranges high in the air. The third was just a balloon of fire enclosed in black smoke above the house-tops. The observer didn't bother with his gun sight and indicator for that one. Just reached for his night glasses, took one quick look, picked up his telephone, and said, "Two high explosives and one oil bomb," and named the street where they had fallen.

There was a small fire going off to our left. Suddenly sparks showered up from it as though someone had punched the middle of a huge camp-fire with a tree trunk. Again the gun sight swung around, the bearing was read, and the report went down the telephone lines: "There is something in high explosives on that fire at 59."

There was peace and quiet inside for twenty minutes. Then a shower of incendiaries came down far in the distance. They didn't fall in a line. It looked like flashes from an electric train on a wet night, only the engineer was drunk and driving his train in circles through the streets. One sight at the middle of the flashes and our observer reported laconically, "Breadbasket at 90—covers a couple of miles." Half an hour later a string of fire bombs fell right beside the Thames. Their white glare was reflected in the black, lazy water near the banks and faded out in midstream where the moon cut a golden swathe broken only by the arches of famous bridges.

We could see little men shovelling those fire bombs into the river. One burned for a few minutes like a beacon right in the middle of a bridge. Finally those white flames all went out. No one bothers about the white light, it's only when it turns yellow that a real fire has started.

I must have seen well over a hundred fire bombs come

down and only three small fires were started. The incendiaries aren't so bad if there is someone there to deal with them, but those oil bombs present more difficulties.

As I watched those white fires flame up and die down, watched the yellow blazes grow dull and disappear, I thought, what a puny effort is this to burn a great city.

Edward Murrow

Incident

The volume of noise shut out all thought, there was no lull, no second in which to breathe and follow carefully the note of an oncoming bomber. It was an orchestra of madmen playing in a cupboard. I thought, "God! what a stupid waste if I were to die now." I wished with all my heart that I was down a shelter.

"We'd be better off underground to-night, sir, and no mistake." It was my taxi-driver speaking.

"Nonsense," I said. "We couldn't be drinking this down there," and I took a long pull at my beer.

I was pushing the glass across the counter for a refill when we heard it coming. The girl in the corner was still laughing and for the first time I heard her soldier speak. "Shut up!" he said, and the laugh was cut off like the sound track in a movie. Then everyone was diving for the floor. The barmaid (she was of considerable bulk) sank from view with a desperate slowness behind the counter and I flung myself tight up against the other side, my taxi-driver beside me. He still had his glass in his hand and the beer shot across the floor, making a dark stain and setting the sawdust afloat. The soldier too had made for the bar counter and wedged the girl on his inside. One of her shoes had nearly come off. It was an inch from my nose: she had a ladder in her stocking.

My hands were tight-pressed over my ears but the detonation deafened me. The floor rose up and smashed against my face, the swing-door tore off its hinges and crashed over a table, glass splinters flew across the room, and behind the bar every bottle in the place seemed to be breaking. The lights went out, but there was no darkness. An orange glow from across the street shone through the wall and threw everything into a strong relief.

I scrambled unsteadily to my feet and was leaning over the bar to see what had happened to the unfortunate barmaid when a voice said, "Anyone hurt?" and there was an A.F.S. man shining a torch. At that everyone began to move, but slowly and reluctantly as though coming out of a dream. The girl stood white and shaken in a corner, her arm about her companion, but she was unhurt and had stopped talking. Only the barmaid failed to get up.

"I think there is someone hurt behind the bar," I said. The fireman nodded and went out, to return almost immediately with two stretcher-bearers who made a cursory inspection and discovered that she had escaped with no more than a severe cut on the head. They got her on to the stretcher and disappeared.

Together with the man in the A.F.S., the taxi-driver and I found our way out into the street. He turned to us almost apologetically. "If you have nothing very urgent on hand," he said, "I wonder if you'd help here for a bit. You see, it was the house next to you that was hit and there's someone buried in there."

I turned and looked on a heap of bricks and mortar, wooden beams and doors, and one framed picture, unbroken. It was the first time that I had seen a building newly blasted. Often had I left the flat in the morning and walked up Piccadilly, aware vaguely of the ominously tidy gap between two houses, but further my mind had not gone.

We dug, or rather pushed, pulled, heaved, and strained, I somewhat ineffectually because of my hands*; I don't know for how long, but I suppose for a short enough while. And yet it seemed endless. From time to time I was aware of figures round me: an A.R.P. warden, his face expressionless under a steel helmet; once a soldier swear-

* The writer was recovering after being badly injured in action (Ed.)

ing savagely in a quiet monotone; and the taxi-driver, his face pouring sweat.

And so we came to the woman. It was her feet that we saw first, and whereas before we had worked doggedly, now we worked with a sort of frenzy, like prospectors at the first glint of gold. She was not quite buried, and through the gap between two beams we could see that she was still alive. We got the child out first. It was passed back carefully and with an odd sort of reverence by the warden, but it was dead. She must have been holding it to her in the bed when the bomb came.

Finally we made a gap wide enough for the bed to be drawn out. The woman who lay there looked middle-aged. She lay on her back and her eyes were closed. Her face, through the dirt and streaked blood, was the face of a thousand working women; her body under the cotton nightdress was heavy. The nightdress was drawn up to her knees and one leg was twisted under her. There was no dignity about that figure.

Around me I heard voices. "Where's the ambulance?" "For Christ's sake don't move her!" "Let her have some air!"

I was at the head of the bed, and looking down into that tired, blood-streaked, work-worn face I had a sense of complete unreality. I took the brandy flask from my hip pocket and held it to her lips. Most of it ran down her chin, but a little flowed between those clenched teeth. She opened her eyes and reached out her arms instinctively for the child. Then she started to weep. Quite soundlessly, and with no sobbing, the tears were running down her cheeks when she lifted her eyes to mine.

"Thank you, sir," she said, and took my hand in hers. And then, looking at me again, she said after a pause, "I see they got you too."

Richard Hillary

Ford began to run. He ran in what he thought was the direction of the noises, along Marlow Square, past the sub-post, deciding (probably wrongly) not to go in and report first, but to go straight for the incident. It did not cross his mind that there would be any difficulty in finding it. Nor did there seem to be. He ran into Gage Street, crossed Royal Walk and the top of James Street, which he glanced down. It touched his consciousness that the outline of its houses—a quarter seen in blackness —looked unfamiliar. But he thought nothing of that. Now he saw a masked torch, switched on at the far end of Gage Street. In a moment he found Ivy Rawlings standing over a very small crater, just where the street joined the pavement. They used their torches and saw that a couple of cellars were broken in, but the houses seemed undamaged.

"It was quite a small one, then," Ford said.

A white hat came up—Mr. Strong on his bicycle.

"Come with me to Royal Walk."

"Is there another incident there?" Ford asked as they walked.

Strong said, "Considerable damage reported in Royal Walk, but no crater found yet."

Just then a car came up. Strong said, "Stay and stop the traffic." They were just back at the top of James Street. Ford stood about for a bit.

There was no traffic. He began to sense that they were on the fringe of something. He looked down James Street. He could see nothing at all. Surely even to-night one should be able to see the outline of the rows of houses? The darkness down James Street was, he now realized, something yet again. Thick, like rough woollen curtains. You looked into, or on to, total blankness. He felt that something simply wasn't there. (Nor was it.)

He began to walk down James Street. Immediately he was in another world. People were moving about and coming up. He saw that the houses opposite him were very considerably shattered. He looked farther down the street and saw that there were no houses. He became conscious of the smell. The unmistakable, indescribable, incident smell flooded into his nostrils. It is more than a smell really; it is an acute irritation of the nasal passages from the powdered rubble of dissolved houses; it is a raw, brutal smell. He realized that the particular darkness which hung over James Street was due, not to the moonless night, but to the fact that the whole of this area was still covered by an unsettled dust cloud. Here's the incident all right, he thought.

Before he had got opposite to the part of James Street that did not appear to be there, he met Miss Sterling. She pointed at the shattered-looking but still standing houses and said, "There's a good many people in there." Mrs. Morley came up, smooth and undisturbed. She said, "The mobile unit [a sort of medical advance guard consisting of doctor, nurse, and stretcher-bearers] has just gone in there," pointing to No. 50.

Ford went into the house. The ground- and first-floor rooms were more or less all right—nothing more than blown-out window frames and shattered plaster. But up from the first floor the stairs were ankle deep in rubble. He went up, passing the second-floor rooms. The two top-floor rooms and the top landing were deeply encumbered with debris, rubble, slates and roof timbers. He looked up; there was no roof overhead. There were dark clouds, picked out with momentary sparkles of shell bursts, reflected gun flashes and an uneasy search-light waving its futility.

In the first room two men of a stretcher party, a nurse and another man were bending over a figure lying on a heap of the plaster rubble. Ford saw that it was an injured man. His breathing was violent and laboured. They seemed to be trying to get something down his throat through some sort of tube. One of the stretcher-bearers saw Ford. Pointing to the back room he said, "There are two more in there." Ford looked in, cautiously using his torch, supplementing its metal hood with his hand. This room was wrecked. One side of it was heaped halfway up to the ceiling with debris. Several roof timbers lay across it. Ford began to clamber his way into it. He saw something dark lying at his feet. He put the beam of his torch on it and saw that it was a girl. She lay partly in, partly out of, the heaped-up debris of plaster and brick, her body

perhaps a third buried, like a high bas-relief. She lay in a
pleasant attitude, one hand curved behind her head, her
legs a little pulled up, to form, with her body, a gentle
shape. He had seen that attitude once before, in the little
Museum of Prehistory in the Dordogne; a skeleton of a
prehistoric girl of the Mousterian Age, from one of the
abri (they had their *abri* too). Celia had said, "I never
knew that a skeleton could be attractive and elegant; that
one's bones may be chic after twenty thousand years."
Here in the top floor back of James Street was the same
charming position.

Ford hadn't much doubt that she was dead. She looked
so small for one thing; and there was a severe head
wound. But he wondered what could have caused fatal in-
juries. The roof timbers were fairly light and had had only
a few feet to fall. With a feeling of intimacy, he took up
her unresisting hand and felt for a pulse. To his surprise
he felt, or thought he felt, a very feeble beat. He went
back to the front room and said, "Is there a doctor here?"
One of the stretcher party said: "He's a doctor, but he's
busy." He pointed at an oldish man bending over the other
casualty. Ford said, "I think the girl in here is alive. Will
you come and see?" The doctor gave no sign of having
heard. But after a time he came. He ran a hypodermic into
the grey, debris-encrusted flesh of her arm. "Just in case,"
he said. He felt for the pulse, but said, "Very improbable.
Where's the injury?" Ford said, "Her head, I think." "The
head?" said the doctor, as if astonished. Then he ran his
fingers over her skull, under her blood and rubble-matted
hair. But he said nothing. Ford said, "Shall I take her
downstairs?" The doctor said, "No." So they left her,
lying easily on the debris, looking through the roof at the
sky.

John Strachey ("Ford")

The bomb was recorded by a telephonist in the Control
Centre at 18.35. The message said that there was fire and
casualties trapped in Holy Redeemer Church in Upper
Cheyne Row. Requests followed in rapid succession for

ambulances, blankets to cover the dead, fire services and reports came in that there were many casualties.

The bomb had struck the church at an angle through a window in a most extraordinary way and had penetrated the floor and burst among the shelterers, mostly women and small children. Here George Thrope, whom we knew as "Bert," lost his life with those women and children whom he had visited to reassure them—as he always did, although he was not shelter warden. He knew that they were apt to become nervous and needed moral support in the heavy raids and he used to drop in there to boost up their courage and cheer them up. He had just despatched Jo on duty and gone there when the bomb fell. The bomb exploded right amongst the shelterers. A woman who was in the shelter told me about it when I visited her afterwards in St. Luke's Hospital. She was badly injured and said that the scene resembled a massacre—in fact, she compared it to an engraving she had seen of the massacre of the Cawnpore women and children in the Indian Mutiny, with bodies, limbs, blood and flesh mingled with little hats, coats and shoes and all the small necessities which people took to the shelters with them. She said that people were literally blown to pieces and the mess was appalling. She herself was behind a pillar or buttress which protected her somewhat—and there was a pile of bodies between her and the explosion, for it was still daylight —no one had gone to their bunks.

Jo and Len Lansdell were quickly at the scene, followed by the whole A.R.P. services. They could not get into the crypt at first because the body of a very heavy woman barred the only entrance. The explosion had set fire to the great heaps of coke stored there for heating the church and the smoke from it made it difficult to see. Jo and Len Lansdell immediately set to work with stirrup pumps to try and extinguish it before the whole place became a crematorium. The body of Bert lay there face downwards. Jo, who had spoken to him only a few minutes before the bomb fell, turned him over. She said afterwards that she wished so much that she hadn't, so that she could have remembered him as he had been when he had sent her on duty. His equipment, which was taken back to his Post, was described to me as being bright red with blood—as was everything which had been in that crypt.

The work of the A.R.P. services that night was magnificent—by nine o'clock in the evening the casualties were all extricated and were lain in the grounds of the church with the Home Guard in charge, and wonderful work was done by Dr. Castillo and Fr. Fali of Tarapore. In our F.A.P. we had numbers of casualties again, including some rare and interesting fractures which Dr. Graham Kerr commented on for the instruction of us V.A.Ds. To watch her at work, deft, neat, cheerful and competent, was a lesson in itself.

After a heavy raid with many casualties such as this one there was a task for which we were sometimes detailed from our F.A.P. and to which both our Commandants disliked having to send us. This was to help piece the bodies together in preparation for burial. The bodies—or rather the pieces—were in the mortuaries. It was a grim task and Betty Compton felt that we were too young and inexperienced for such a terrible undertaking—but someone had to do it and we were sent in pairs when it became absolutely necessary. Betty asked me if I would go as I had studied Anatomy at the Slade. The first time I went my partner was a girl I did not know very well called Sheila. It *was* pretty grim, although Mr. Leacock made it all as business-like and rapid as possible. We had somehow to form a body for burial so that the relatives (without seeing it) could imagine that their loved one was more or less intact for that purpose. But it was a very difficult task—there were so many pieces missing and, as one of the mortuary attendants said, "Proper jigsaw puzzle, ain't it, Miss?" The stench was the worst thing about it— that, and having to realize that these frightful pieces of flesh had once been living, breathing people. We went out to smoke a cigarette when we simply could not go on—and some busybody saw Sheila smoking and reported her for smoking when in uniform and on duty. Betty

Compton, who invariably supported her V.A.Ds, was most indignant about this, as indeed she was about us having to perform such a task at all. I thought myself that butchers should have done it.

After the first violent revulsion I set my mind on it as a detached, systematic task. It became a grim and ghastly satisfaction when a body was fairly constructed—but if one was too lavish in making one body almost whole, then another one would have sad gaps. There were always odd members which did not seem to fit and there were too many legs. Unless we kept a very firm grip on ourselves nausea was inevitable. The only way for me to stand it was to imagine that I was back in anatomy class again —but there the legs and arms on which we studied muscles had been carefully preserved in spirit and were difficult to associate with the human body at all. I think that this task dispelled for me the idea that human life is valuable—it could be blown to pieces by blast just as dust was blown by wind. The wardens had to gather up pieces after a bad raid—they had no choice, and someone had to assemble them into shrouds for Christian burial, but it seemed monstrous that these human beings had been reduced to this revolting indignity by so-called Christians, and that we were doing the same in Germany and other countries. The feeling uppermost in my mind after every big raid was *anger*, anger at the lengths to which humans could go to inflict injury to one another.

. . . . About twenty past eleven we decided to settle down and read for a time. Neither of us felt like going to bed—it was far too noisy and exciting. A warden raced by shouting, and suddenly we heard a shout of "lights", from the street. Richard wondered if the recent near explosion had caused the black-out curtains to shift in the studio and he said: "I'll run up and have a look."

He had scarcely gone when the lights all went out. There was a strange quiet—a dead hush, and prickles of terror went up my spine as a rustling, crackling, endless sound as of ripping, tearing paper began. I did not know what it was, and I screamed to Richard, *"Come down, come down!*" Before I could hear whether or not he was coming down the stairs, things began to drop—great masses fell—great crashes sounded all round me. I had flung myself down by the bed, hiding Vicki under my stomach, trying thus to save her and the coming baby from harm. I buried my face in the eiderdown of the bed as the rain of debris went on falling for what seemed ages . . . ages. . . . The bed was covered and so was I—I could scarcely breathe—things fell all round my head—some of it almost choked me as the stuff, whatever it was, reached my neck and my mouth.

At last there was a comparative silence and with great difficulty I raised my head and shook it free of heavy choking dusty stuff. An arm had fallen round my neck—a warm living arm—and for one moment I thought that Richard had entered in the darkness and was holding me, but when very, very cautiously I raised my hand to it, I found that it was a woman's bare arm with two rings on the third finger and it stopped short in a sticky mess. I shook myself free of it. Vicki, who had behaved absolutely perfectly, keeping so still that she could have been dead, became excited now as she smelt blood. I screamed again, "*Richard, Richard,*" and to my astonishment he answered quite near me. "Where are you?" I cried—more things had begun falling. "At the bottom of the stairs," he said. "Keep there. Keep still—there are more things falling," I cried and buried my head again as more debris fell all round me. At last it appeared to have stopped. I raised my head again—I could see the sky and the searchlights and I knew that the whole of the three upper stories of the house had gone. "We've been hit," I said. "*One in a million!*"—and the only feeling I was conscious of was furious anger.

It was pitch dark—too dangerous to move without some idea of what the position was. I had had my torch in my hand but the blast had thrown it from me—"Light a match," I said. He lit several matches, standing, as I saw by their light, in the entrance of the room. There were no ceilings, nothing above me as I crouched there. The front of the room had blown out—but the wall nearest to the one where I was crouching, the ferro-concrete one, was still there, as was the one to the hall. By the light of the matches I saw something more terrifying than the arm which was now partially covered with debris—the light lathes from the ceilings had all fallen down across me, so that their weight had not hurt me at all—but balanced on them were huge blocks and lumps of masonry. If I moved they might all crash down. "Don't come any nearer," I shouted to Richard. He said, "Keep still—I'm going to try and get out—the front door is twisted and jammed."

I had seen where my best exit passage lay when Richard had lit the matches for me, and while he was trying to shift the broken door I began wriggling very, very carefully and cautiously along the floor. It was not easy—for I was not as slim as normally, and I had Vicki. It was so perilous that I thought of loosing her and letting her find her own way out. Had she not behaved so wonderfully I would have been obliged to leave her—for the thought uppermost of anything else in my mind was to save my baby. The baby, hitherto a nebulous dream of the future, now became urgently real and my only thought was of it. I shouted again and again—for if only the Heavy Rescue would come—as they had always promised me they would if I were buried—I would not have to face this perilous crawl; but no sound came from the streets.

I have never been brave at doing dangerous things—I can only do them if I do them very quickly. As children we used to go fishing with my father in Devonshire, and had to cross some of the deep streams bridged only by a tree trunk—not even a flat one. My father always walked straight over without looking to left or right. This, he told me, was the only way. Sometimes I would not cross and he would simply leave me behind until I did.

There were constant terrific explosions and things fell each time there was a fresh thud. If I did not get out soon some of those huge blocks were bound to fall on me. I shouted again, "Help, Help," and so did Richard. The sounds echoed in the darkness and then far away I heard a

woman's voice calling, "They're coming . . . they'll come
. . ." and it died away and we didn't know if it was to us
they would come, because from the thuds and whooshes
and violent explosions all round they must have been pretty busy.

"I've got the door open enough to squeeze through,"
Richard called. "Don't light any more matches; I can
smell gas," I warned him. I could not see him—nor he
me. "I'm going to try and crawl through this space to the
door," I said, and I began doing it immediately. I remembered what Tapper told me, *"Test it first, tap it gently,"*
and his warning: "Don't go scrabbling at anything in case
it all comes down on you." Very slowly and cautiously I
squeezed my way along the tiny tunnel under the hanging
lathes on which were balanced the concrete blocks which I
had only caught sight of for a split second in the light of
the matches. It seemed a life-time. There were two awful
moments when my shoulders brushed something and there
was a fall of stuff again—and then I was at the door and
Richard had caught me and pulled me carefully up. We
stood there for a minute clinging together. "Anne's
dead—her arm is in there," I said. "I'm afraid they're all
dead—the whole storeys have gone," he said. "D'you
think you can walk?"

We now had to squeeze through the jammed door,
which he had managed to shift a little. I begged him not to
put his weight on it again in case there was another collapse of what was left standing. It was almost impossible
to get out because of the piled-up glass in the entrance to
the flats under the archway. I had to climb, and even so I
could feel the glass cutting my legs. At the back there was
a solid mass of debris—and above it nothing remained of
the Marshmans' flat—just this great pile of rubble. I
rushed at it crying frantically, "Kathleen, Kathleen! Cecil!
Cecil!" but there wasn't a sound.

                                        Frances Faviell, V.A.D.

The Germans dropped a number of huge parachute mines on London, and few who were close to one when it exploded survived to tell the tale.

On the night of 8 December 1940, I left the B.B.C. shortly after 10.45 and accompanied by a colleague . . . went to the cycle-shed in Chapel Mews. The customary nightly air-raid was in progress, and as we left the cycle-shed we could hear the distant sound of aircraft and A.A. gunfire. We were just entering Hallam Street from the mews when I heard the shrieking whistling noise like a large bomb falling. This noise continued for about three seconds, and then abruptly ceased as if in mid-air. There was no thud, explosion or vibration. I particularly remember this, as I'd heard this happen once before, and was curious as to what caused it and why it stopped. Then came the sound of something clattering down the roof of a building in the direction of Broadcasting House. I looked up, thinking that it might be incendiaries, but this was not so. . . . Whilst we were conversing I noticed a large, dark, shiny object approach the lamp-post and then recede. I concluded that it was a taxi parking. It made no noise. The night was clear, with a few small clouds. There was moonlight from a westerly direction, but Portland Place was mainly shadow.

A few seconds later I saw what seemed to be a very large tarpaulin of a drab or khaki colour fall on the same spot; the highest part of it was about ten or twelve feet above the road when I first saw it, and it seemed to be about twenty-five feet across. It fell at about the speed of a pocket handkerchief when dropped, and made no noise. . . . There were no other warnings of any imminent danger. I went towards the tarpaulin and had reached a spot . . . twenty-five to thirty feet from "the thing", when Vaughan came running towards me at high speed. He shouted something which I did not hear. At that moment there was a very loud swishing noise, as if a plane were diving with engine cut off—or like a gigantic fuse burning. It lasted about three or four seconds; it did not come from the lamp-post end of "the thing" but it may have come from the other end.

    . . . . I had a momentary glimpse of a large ball of blinding, wild, white light and two concentric rings of colour, the inner one lavender and the outer one violet, as I ducked my head. The ball seemed to be ten to twenty feet high, and was near the lamp-post. Several things happened simultaneously. My head was jerked back due to a heavy blow on the dome and rim of the back of my steel helmet, but I do not remember this, for, as my head went back, I received a severe blow on my forehead and the bridge of my nose. The blast bent up the front rim of my helmet and knocked it off my head. The explosion made an indescribable noise—something like a colossal growl —and was accompanied by a veritable tornado of air blast. I felt an excruciating pain in my ears, and all sounds were replaced by a very loud singing noise, which I was told later was when I lost my hearing and had my eardrums perforated. I felt that consciousness was slipping from me, and that moment I heard a clear loud voice shouting, "Don't let yourself go, face up to it—hold on." It rallied me, and summoning all my willpower and energy I succeeded in forcing myself down into a crouching position with my knees on the ground and my feet against the kerb behind me and my hands covering my face.

I remember having to move them over my ears because of the pain in them, doubtless due to the blast. This seemed to ease the pain. Then I received another hit on the forehead and felt weaker. The blast seemed to come in successive waves, accompanied by vibrations from the ground. I felt as if it were trying to spin me and clear me away from the kerb. Then I received a very heavy blow just in front of the right temple which knocked me down flat on my side, in the gutter. Later, in our first-aid post, they removed what they described as a piece of bomb from that wound. Whilst in the gutter I clung on to the kerb with both hands and with my feet against it. I was again hit in the right chest, and later found that my double-breasted overcoat, my coat, leather comb-case and papers had been cut through, and the watch in the top right-hand pocket of my waistcoat had the back dented in and its works broken.

Just as I felt that I could not hold out much longer I realized that the blast pressure was decreasing and a shower of dust, dirt and rubble swept past me. Pieces penetrated my face, some skin was blown off, and something pierced my left thumbnail and my knuckles were cut, causing me involuntarily to let go my hold on the kerb. Instantly, although the blast was dying down, I felt myself being slowly blown across the pavement towards the wall of the building. I tried to hold on but there was nothing to hold on to. Twice I tried to rise but seemed to be held down. Eventually I staggered to my feet. I looked around and it seemed like a scene from Dante's *Inferno*. The front of the building was lit by a reddish-yellow light; the saloon car was on fire to the left of me, and the flames from it were stretching out towards the building, and not upwards; pieces of brick, masonry and glass seemed to appear on the pavement, making, to me, no sound; a few dark huddled bodies were round about, and right in front of me were two soldiers; one, some feet from a breach in the wall of the building where a fire seemed to be raging, was propped up against the wall with his arms dangling by him, like a rag doll.

The other was nearer, about twelve feet from the burning car; he was sitting up with his knees drawn up and supporting himself by his arms—his trousers had been blown off him. I could see that his legs were bare and that he was wearing short grey underpants. He was alive and conscious.

I told him to hang on to an upright at the entrance and to shout like hell for assistance should he see or hear anyone approaching. I went back to look at the other soldier. He was still in the same posture and I fear that he was dead. I looked around. There was a long, dark body lying prone, face downwards close to the kerb in front of the building—it may have been Vaughan. There appeared to be one or two dark, huddled bodies by the wall of the

building. I had not the strength to lift any of them. I wondered where the water was coming from which I felt dripping down my face, and soon discovered that it was blood
from my head wounds.

B.B.C. employee

German Naval Staff War Diary: 14 September

From a series of reports, sent by the Military Attaché in
Washington, on the morale of the population and the situation in London, it emerges that the will to fight of the
London population is considerably affected by lack of
sleep. This physical weakness is regarded as the worst
danger to morale. As regards damage, he reports that
twenty-four large docks were totally burnt out and four
gasometers were destroyed. The stations of Sherrycross
[sic] and Waterloo, and several Underground stations are
damaged. Of ten good airfields round London, seven are
almost completely unusable.

Secret Weapon

Mr. Mallet, who in 1940 was living in Chelsea
—"carting X-ray equipment for the hospitals" is his
own description of his job—was a fire-watcher. He has
said how people at his post were always discussing strange
and weird bombs. One new weapon of which he heard tell
contained a huge coil spring, like the spring inside a
gramophone, " . . . and if you got in the way of this thing,
they said that it'd either cut your legs off, or your head
off, or cut you in half. You just laugh at things like that at
the time, you think they're talking out of the back of their
necks, you don't take any more notice of it. But those
things flash through your mind later on." One windy
night, during a raid, he was down by the Chelsea Old
Church. "They was dropping different things all over London again. Presently I heard something come down and go
with a dull thud. It may have gone in the river, I don't
know. Then I heard this noise." It was a strange, scraping,

metallic sound, which seemed to be coming closer in the semi-darkness. "Well, immediately I heard this noise it reminded me of what they were saying about this coil spring. I didn't stop to look, I just took to my heels and started to go. I went up Church Street as far and as fast as I could. All I could see was the houses on either side of me, and I didn't even bother to look whether any doors were open or not." Because, as he started up Old Church Street, he had realized that this thing, this noise was following him, rattling and scraping along the street just about as fast as he could run. It was, indeed, gaining on him. "I just belted hell for leather up the road. I thought, this darned thing, whatever it is, can't turn round a corner surely. So when I got to Paultons Street I turned the corner, and as I did this thing went by me. It stopped up the road about a hundred yards farther on." He saw it, in the half-light, a dome-shaped object in the centre of the road. For some minutes he waited at the corner of the street, ready to dodge back should it show any sign of life. After a little while curiosity won, and he made his way cautiously towards it. "And when I got up to it, what I found was this bloody dustbin lid that had chased me up the road." . . . "You can laugh at it now, but by Christ you never did then."

Constantine Fitz Gibbon

The Barrage

It was difficult for civilians to understand why there should be no more than spasmodic gunfire when hordes of enemy aircraft streamed over London most of the night. The intricate and enormous problems of night shooting were unknown to them, and impossible to explain. Londoners wanted to hear the guns hit back; they wanted to feel that, even if aircraft were not being brought down, at least the pilots were being made uncomfortable.

It was abundantly apparent that every effort must be made to defend the Londoner more effectively, and to uphold his morale in so doing.

Anti-aircraft guns take a little time to become effective after they have moved into new positions. Telephone lines have to be laid, gun positions levelled, the warning system co-ordinated, and so on. It was, however, very disappointing that, although the increase in the number of guns by the second night of the battle was very considerable, there did not appear to be much more anti-aircraft fire. And, after about three bad nights' bombing in London, in which it was obvious to me, sleeping in my bed, that our system was no good, I became both angry and frightened at the same time, and lay awake the rest of the night thinking how to deal with this business.

During the nights of 8 and 9 September my staff had been round the gun-sites and Gun Operations Rooms to try to find some more effective answer to the Hun. But, though they laid on variations of all sorts in an attempt to achieve greater accuracy, everyone was most dissatisfied with the results. So, on 10 September, we held a conference at Command Headquarters and determined that, whatever had gone before, we would meet the enemy that night with a barrage the like of which had never been seen or heard before.

The commanders of every gun position in London with their Battery, Brigade, and Divisional commanders met me in the Signals Drill-hall in the Brompton Road, and I told them personally what I wanted them to do. Every gun was to fire every possible round. Fire was not to be withheld on any account. Guns were to go to the approximate bearing and elevation and fire. Searchlights were not to expose. R.A.F. fighters were not going to operate over London, and every unseen target must be engaged without waiting to identify the aircraft as hostile.

The result was as astonishing to me as it appears to have been to the citizens of London—and, apparently, to the enemy as well. For, although few of the bursts can have been anywhere near the target, the heights of aircraft steadily increased as the night went on, and many of them turned away before entering the inner artillery zone. What, in effect, we were doing was to use our predictors, with all the information we could feed into them from any source, to engage the enemy by predicted fire from all the guns that could bear on any particular target. It was in no sense a barrage, though I think by that name it will always be known.

Anyway, it bucked people up tremendously. The midnight news said some nice things about us, and when I put through a phone call to my wife the telephone operator said, "By God, this is the stuff. All the girls here are hugging each other." Next day everyone said they had slept better, and for the first time A.A. Command hit the headlines. Apart from comforting the civilians, it stimulated the gunners, who had been feeling pretty frustrated during the long nights when they had been compelled to hear aircraft flying overhead and dropping their bombs without being engaged.

But not everyone was pleased. There were some angry voices raised, for instance, in the southern and eastern suburbs, upon which the retreating Luftwaffe jettisoned their bombs. Worse still, the council of another suburb wrote to say that lavatory pans were being cracked in the council houses by the vibration of the guns, and would we mind very much moving the barrage somewhere else.

We didn't move the barrage, and until people got used to it and could see no dead birds on the ground as a result of it, it served its purpose. As a matter of fact, almost six years to a day after the opening of the barrage, and while I was writing this chapter, I came upon a belated testimonial. In a silversmith's attic near my office I saw hanging upon the wall a pair of earplugs. There was a notice under them:

ANTIQUES OF THE FUTURE

Issued by the Ministry of Home Security to
Londoners (and never used) so that we should
not hear our guns, which were Music.

General Sir Frederick Pile, O.C. Anti-Aircraft Command

Unexploded Bomb

At 9 a.m. Archer received a message from the Assistant
Military Liaison Officer of the Regional Commissioner's
staff ordering him to take his section to Swansea where
unexploded bombs were hampering efforts to control a
fire at the Llandarcy oil refinery, at that time held to be
the largest establishment of the kind in the kingdom. Fifteen miles from the refinery, not only the smoke of the
conflagration but the huge leaping flames were clearly
visible in the morning light, and as they got nearer its appearance suggested that any operations in the immediate
area would be for the time impossible.

However, at ten o'clock when they arrived they were
met by the officer of the local bomb disposal section who
were already at work there. He guided Lieutenant Archer
to an entry into the storage area of the refinery where
there were a great many gasometer-like tanks arranged in
rows. Some were alight and others, though still intact,
fiercely hot.

In one section of this storage area there were four unexploded bombs. One had penetrated to a position directly
beneath an un-ignited tank, another was some one hundred and fifty yards away between two tanks, also un-
ignited, and the remaining pair were at a safer distance
from the stored oil. Since the first object was to prevent
further fires from breaking out, Archer decided to deal
with the bomb under the tank first.

It was a bad site to work on. Fifty yards away in one
direction and eighty in another a tank was on fire. The
heat caused by their burning was very great; as the flames
on their tops worked their way down they melted the steel
walls so that the tanks flared like gigantic Roman candles.
Smoke and flames whirled up hundreds of feet into the air,
simultaneously darkening the daylight and lighting the
place with their own unsteady glare.

The heat at the entry hole where the bomb had torn its
way diagonally into the concrete plinth at the base of the

tank was such that Archer and his men were only able to work for short periods at a time. They dug in relays, working as energetically as they could to reach the bomb before it exploded or the tank above caught fire.

At midday the bomb one hundred and fifty yards away detonated. They all threw themselves flat, none of them was struck, and no further fires were started. At two, just as they were starting to uncover the bomb case, one of the two further bombs went off. This second explosion lent even greater urgency to their efforts, and shortly afterwards they completed the uncovering.

The bomb proved to be of the 250 kg. S.C. type, and its case had split, presumably as a result of its passage through the concrete plinth. The main explosive filling was clearly visible through the break. There was only one fuse-pocket and the fuse-boss had been ripped away, disclosing a fuzz of wires and other electrical components.

Archer decided that if he was to prevent a major explosion he would have to remove the base-plate at the rear end of the bomb and then scoop out the main filling, which was the powder variety. By means of a hammer and chisel the heavy base-plate was slowly turned on its threads and eventually removed. He could then see that the fusepocket was more or less loose inside the bomb. The spot-weld by which the closed end of the tube had been fastened to the inside of the bomb-case had been completely sheared, and the weld at the open, or fuse-box end partly so. By manual force he tore the tube with its dangling wires free and removed it from the bomb. The tank was now for practical purposes safe, his men could empty the filling into sandbags and cart it and the case away. It was 2.50 p.m.; the operation had taken just over four and a half hours, during which time all concerned had been aware that it was unlikely they would see the job completed. Moreover, in addition to the heat and the perpetual extra hazard of one of the adjacent tanks exploding, they had been constantly choked and confused by smoke.

Having secured the fuse-pocket, Lieutenant Archer left

his section to complete the removal of the bomb and retired to examine it. He gripped the exposed wires with pliers and pulled until the fuse came away, disclosing the clockwork delayed-action apparatus at the rear. He unscrewed the gaine* and put the electric and clockwork components in his pocket. He then again looked into the tube. There was something else there besides the picric booster-pellets he had expected to find. He shook the tube gently and another mechanism with another gaine attached slid into view.

He had hardly unscrewed this second gaine when there was a crack and a flash from the mechanism. A small cap inside had detonated. At least he knew it would not crack again—so into his pocket it went. After destroying the booster-pellets at the bottom of the tube he next went to find the local Swansea bomb disposal officer, who told him that the immediate danger to the refinery having been overcome, he could return to his station at Cardiff.

. . . . Answers to the questions set disclosed a great range of capacities and often produced an illuminating side-light on the character of the student or his local instructor. The question—*What do you consider the ideal qualification of character for a member of a Bomb Disposal Unit?*—evoked several very different responses:

"The first and foremost qualification is caution. If a B.D.S. man is a hundred per cent careful he is a hundred per cent safe—if he is ninety-nine per cent careful he is a danger to the Squad."

"A member of the B.D.S. should be strong, unmarried, and a fast runner."

"A member of the squad should not be indispensable to the factory. He should be of excellent character and prepared for the after-life."

Major A. B. Hartley

* A type of detonator (Ed.)

MEN . . .

I was in it from the first. Like the volunteers of 1914, I
"leapt to arms unbidden"—only there were no arms to
leap to. There was nothing but an armband of white cotton crudely lettered "L.D.V." This we were instructed to
dye with tea or coffee. The drilling of the L.D.V. with
pikes and muskets instantly became a national joke. Actually it was propaganda to frighten the enemy, for in our
company, somewhere in the Home Counties, we had not
even these aids to morale. We assembled at the local drill-
hall and shot off a few precious rounds of miniature ammunition; for the rest, we drilled and marched about the
streets to inspire confidence. Eventually a few actual rifles
were distributed—I never received one of my own, or at
least not a whole one, because, although I could hit a
target, I could not master the niceties of arms drill:
presenting, sloping, shouldering, as taught by retired
sergeants of the first World War, seemed to me useless
and archaic.

Twice a week I went on patrol with two companions. It
might be at dusk, at midnight, or towards dawn. We enforced the black-out on careless house-holders, checked
cars to see that they had been properly "immobilized",
and kept our ears open for spies and fifth columnists. For
relief we occasionally retailed the latest pleasantries of
"Lord Haw-Haw", the Irishman William Joyce, whose in-
sinuating propaganda over the German radio was one of
the ingredients of that pre-invasion atmosphere. The old
soldiers returned in spirit to the Somme and Ypres; the
younger ones had to be content with speculating on the
immediate future. The dawn patrol was in some ways
the worst. The weather, that summer, seemed to be always
indescribably calm and beautiful. First the rising sun
would reveal the sensuous contours of the silver barrage
balloons that hung over a near-by aircraft factory. One of
them, which was larger than the rest and always sagged as

if from weariness, had been lovingly christened Göring.
Then I could make out the details of the little suburban
houses with their gardens full of lupins and delphiniums.

July passed with mounting anxiety but still no invasion.
We got battle-dress, boots, forage-caps. We paraded on
Sunday morning at the grammar school and were sent for
what was called a "walk", while the officers discussed
what to do with us when we came back. The whole thing
was so haphazard and impromptu that it soon became obvious that, in the mind of the central authority which
presumably was responsible for some sort of overall plan,
either our area was regarded as safe from invasion, or, as
was more likely, of no military importance since by the
time the enemy reached us we should have lost the war. I
realize of course that in coastal areas things were very different; indeed, my father-in-law, who lived near the south
coast and was twice my age, was even then undergoing a
far more rigorous training.

We were instructed in the use of new weapons. In particular, I remember one which consisted of a length of
sawn-off iron piping mounted on a sketchily constructed
tripod. This was set up behind a hedge, and imaginary
bottle-bombs were lobbed out of the tube as a deterrent to
approaching tanks. Mercifully we were never given any
ammunition, or the casualties among the gun-crews would
have been terrific. At first we evolved a very smart drill
for operating the thing with a crew of three; after that, we
unlearned it all in order to employ only two.

. . . . The climax of that autumn was the all-night stand-
to: whether this was a large-scale exercise or a genuine
false alarm we were never sure. I was lent a rifle and half-
a-dozen rounds, and despatched on my bicycle to guard a
telephone-box a quarter of a mile from my house. I stood
there all night and well on into the next day. The weather
was fine and warm, and the night was filled with a profound and unbroken calm. It will, I suppose, always seem
odd that I should have spent a whole night of my life
guarding a telephone-box with a rifle of whose precise
mode of operation I had not a perfectly clear idea. At the

time it seemed natural enough, yet even in those days I could see the humour of the situation when, at eight o'clock in the morning, another member of the company cycled past me on his way to work and asked if nobody had told me the order to dismiss had been given hours ago.

But I should not judge my company by myself: if I was not quite the most inefficient and craven member of it, I must have been pretty nearly so. We had some keen and competent men, and by mid-October, when the invasion was called off, I should think we might have put up a very fair show; by the following June, when the Germans crossed into Russia, we were almost well organized. We had a greatcoat and a service gas-mask apiece; there may even have been a few who harboured a secret regret that our mettle had never been put to the test.

J. R.

. . . AND GUNS

The vital task was to put into the hands of the troops every gun that could be found and to build up as quickly as possible a crust of artillery defence around the most threatened coasts.

The search for weapons produced the most remarkable results. The equipment that came to light in the greatest numbers was the 6-pounder Hotchkiss gun that had been fitted into the tanks of the 1914-1918 war. Some of these had already been sent to France to thicken up the anti-tank defence there, and had of course been lost, but several hundreds still remained. Some were put on pedestal mountings in the concrete pillboxes which formed the so-called "Stop Lines" across England; others were mounted on the back-axles of old motor-cars and so made mobile. Unfortunately the ammunition supply for them was hardly adequate, being about seventy rounds in all per gun. Moreover, it was always doubtful if they would have penetrated the armour of the German tanks which were likely to be opposed to them.

The Navy produced about a hundred 4-inch and 12-pounder guns. It was said that they had been concealed under a mountain of coal at one of the Royal Dockyards since they had been taken out of warships scrapped under one of the Disarmament Agreements. Of these some also were mounted on fixed bases, mostly on the coast, and some on commercial steam lorries. There were also a number of "freaks". There were two German 105 mm. guns which a medium regiment had captured complete with first-line ammunition in France and had managed to bring home. The saluting gun from Edinburgh Castle, the successor of Mons Meg, moved down and went into action near Berwick. The Navy offered the pack guns that were used in the Inter-Port obstacle race at Olympia, but as the only ammunition available for them was blank, they were reluctantly refused. One unit was said to have detached a German 5.9-inch of the 1914 war from its place on some war memorial, to have cleaned it up and to be asking for ammunition for it. At Dunbar two 6-inch guns were deployed which were reported to be two of the "Long Toms" used by the Naval Brigade in the Boer War. As for the old wooden-wheeled 13-pounders, once the equipment of the R.H.A., any unit that received one or more of these considered itself greatly favoured.

Even with all these makeshifts not all Gunners could be fully equipped at first, and in several places R.A. units were used as infantry, notably a group of medium regiments, popularly known as "John Barry's Private Army".* in Lincolnshire and Leicestershire.

Then came a great windfall. The United States of America offered to us (this was before Lease-Lend) several hundred 75 mm. guns that had been in store in America since the 1914 war. They were joyfully accepted and shipped over in haste. They proved to be of

* Brigadier J. R. Barry, C.B.E., D.S.O., was then C.C.R.A. I Corps.

three types: genuine French 75 mm. of 1897 vintage, British 18-pounders Mk I, which had been converted to take 75 mm. ammunition, and a few of more recent date, made to an American design. With them came a device by which the carriages of earlier design could quickly be converted from wooden to pneumatic wheels.

Lieutenant-Colonel C. J. Burlison

Coastal Artillery

. . . . Mr. Winston Churchill was anxious to be able to announce as soon as possible after the Germans began to shoot across the Channel that we had done the same thing. He therefore took great interest in the installations of the first of these naval 14-inch guns; and it was in consequence named "Winnie" after him. (Its mate inevitably became "Pooh".) When "Winnie" was to open fire for the first time, it was ordered that the Battery Commander should report direct to the Prime Minister, through G.H.Q. Home Forces, when and how many rounds it had fired. The following is the essence of the interchange of signals that followed:

R.M. Siege Battery to Prime Minister:
" 'Winnie' fired three rounds to-day. Two direct hits obtained."

P.M. to R.M.S.B.:
"Direct hits on what?"

R.M.S.B. to P.M.:
"Direct hits on France."

BERLIN 1940

Naturally we were all intoxicated by our victories. And if my personal life had not been sad, I too should have joined in the celebrations and victory parties. No doubt we

now and then (at least the women amongst us) thought of
our defeated enemies and were sorry for them, but the
strongest feeling of all was our pride in Germany, showing
the world that the Treaty of Versailles, with its bitter
humiliations, had been broken. I was proud to be German.
I was also proud of Hitler. Indeed, all those who formerly
had had doubts about Hitler were now carried away in
respect and admiration. He had put Germany back as a
great nation in the world.

Feverishly we waited for the invasion of England.
Some of us were astonished that it did not at once follow
the defeat of the British Army at Dunkirk. But this time I
did not become sceptical. I had learnt my lesson that I
really could not judge political or military situations at all.
We must leave these things to Hitler and trust his judgment. The Press, too, assured us daily that the day was
not far distant when we would land in England.

Else Wendel, housewife

THE STAND-TO

Autumn met me to-day as I walked over Castle Hill.
The wind that had set our corn by the ears was blowing
    still:
Autumn, who takes the leaves and the long days,
    crisped the air
With a tang of action, a taste of death; and the wind
    blew fair.

From the east for men and barges massed on the other
    side—
Men maddened by numbers or stolid by nature, they
    have their pride
As we in work and children, but now a contracting will
Crumples their meek petitions and holds them poised to
    kill.

Last night a Stand-to was ordered. Thirty men of us
    here
Came out to guard the star-lit village—my men who
    wear
Unwitting the seasons' beauty, the received truth of the
    spade—
Roadmen, farm labourers, masons, turned to another
    trade.

A dog barked over the fields, the candle stars put a
    sheen
On the rifles ready, the sandbags fronded with ever-
    green:
The dawn wind blew, the stars winked out on the posts
    where we lay,
The order came, Stand Down and thirty went away.

Since a cold wind from Europe blows back the words in
    my teeth,
Since autumn shortens the days and the odds against
    our death,
And the harvest moon is waxing and high tides threaten
    harm,
Since last night may be the last night all thirty men go
    home.

I write this verse to record the men who have watched
    with me—
Spot who is good at darts, Squibby at repartee,
Mark and Cyril, the dead shots, Ralph with a
    ploughman's gait,
Gibson, Harris and Long, old hands for the barricade.

Whiller the lorry-driver, Francis and Rattlesnake,
Fred and Charl and Stan, these nights I have lain awake
And thought of my thirty men and the autumn wind
    that blows
The apples down too early and shatters the autumn
    rose.

Destiny, History, Duty, Fortitude, Honour—all
The words of the politicians seem too big or too small
For the ragtag fighters of lane and shadow, the love that
          has grown
Familiar as working-clothes, faithful as bone to bone.

Blow, autumn wind, upon orchard and rose! Blow
          leaves along
Our lanes, but sing through me for the lives that are
          worth a song!
Narrowing days have darkened the vistas that hurt my
          eyes,
But pinned to the heart of darkness a tattered fire-flag
          flies.

                                             C. Day Lewis

OPERATION SEA LION

On 1 and 2 September, "the invasion of England" was
filmed for the German newsreels in the harbour of
Antwerp, with the bathing beach at St. Anne serving to
represent the shores of Albion. St. Anne is directly across
from Antwerp, on the opposite side of the Scheldt River
which forms the vast harbour, and is a favourite spot for
excursionists during the summer.

Here, for two days, invasion barges drew in to the shore
and men leapt into the shallow water as light tanks and
motor-cycles sped from the concrete decks to the sandy
beach, firing as they went. One of the men in charge explained to me the reason:

"You see," he said, "when we invade England it will be
at night, or very early in the morning, and there won't be
enough light to photograph it. Since this will be the
decisive event of the war, it must be covered for the
newsreel—so we're staging it here, exactly as it will be
done later on the English coast."

                                             Lars Moen

Case History

Planning for a landing in England began on 15 November 1939, when Raeder issued an order to his staff to investigate and prepare the operation. This was an order to the Naval Staff only, and neither Hitler nor the other two Services were informed. The plans were apparently prepared not so much because Raeder considered the invasion of England essential, but because he did not want to be confronted with a sudden directive from Hitler ordering the invasion at short notice.

. . . When it became obvious that, weak as she was, England had no intention of capitulating, the Supreme Command decided to investigate the possibilities of direct attack.

The three branches of the Armed Forces set to work and produced rough plans. The operation was not yet considered necessary, however, and on 11 July Raeder informed Hitler: "That for a speedy termination of the war with Britain the impact of the war must be forcibly brought home to the British public itself." He suggested that heavy air attacks should be made on the principal towns, and in particular pointed out the importance of London: "The great mass of people who cannot be evacuated, difficulties of food supply, and the fact that forty per cent of the imports come through the Port of London." On the subject of invasion, Raeder stated, "I consider that an invasion should be used only as a last resort to force Britain to sue for peace. I am convinced that Britain can be made to ask for peace simply by cutting off her import trade by means of submarine warfare, air attacks on convoys, and heavy air attacks on her main centres, Liverpool, for instance. I cannot for my part, therefore, advocate an invasion of Britain as I did in the case of Norway. The prerequisites are complete air superiority and the creation of a mine-free area for transports and disembarkation."

Hitler appeared to agree, but in the next few days he

changed his mind, and, on 16 July, issued the directive for the invasion of England—operation "Sea Lion".

Top Secret   16 July 1940

Directive No. 16

Preparations for the Invasion of England

As England, in spite of the hopelessness of her military position, has so far shown herself unwilling to come to any compromise, I have decided to begin to prepare for, and if necessary to carry out, an invasion of England.

This operation is dictated by the necessity of eliminating Great Britain as a base from which the war against Germany can be fought, and if necessary, the island will be occupied.

I therefore issue the following orders:

1. The landing operation must be a surprise crossing on a broad front extending approximately from Ramsgate to a point west of the Isle of Wight. Elements of the Air Force will do the work of the artillery and elements of the Navy the work of engineers. I ask each of the fighting services to consider the advantage from their respective point of view of preliminary operations such as the occupation of the Isle of Wight or the Duchy of Cornwall prior to the full-scale invasion, and to inform me of the result of their deliberations. I shall be responsible for the final decision.

The preparations for the large scale invasion must be completed by the middle of August. . . .

On 19 July, Raeder, through his staff, sent to the Supreme Command a long memorandum explaining the difficulties from the naval point of view:

The task allotted to the Navy in operation "Sea Lion" is out of all proportion to the Navy's strength and bears no relation to the tasks that are set the Army and the Air Force. . . .

The principal difficulties confronting the Navy are as follows:

The transport of Army troops must take place from a coast whose harbour installations and adjacent inland waterways have been extensively damaged through the fighting in the campaign against France, or are of limited capacity. . . .

The gaining of air supremacy is vital to the possibility of assembling the requisite Naval Forces and shipping in the relatively restricted area of embarkation. . . .

So far the enemy has not needed to use his fleet fully, as a matter of life and death, but the landing operations on the English coast will find him resolved to throw in fully and decisively all his naval forces. It cannot be assumed that the Luftwaffe alone will succeed in keeping the enemy naval forces clear of our shipping, as its operations are very dependent on weather conditions. . . .

These reflections cause the Naval Staff to see exceptional difficulties that cannot be assessed individually until a detailed examination of the transport problem has been made.

Meanwhile German Intelligence was trying to estimate the strength of England's defences. On 17 July an extract from the War Diary of the Naval Staff stated:

The whole foreign Press, in particular the English Press, comments that a major German attack is expected. Thousands of barges and vessels are said to be standing by on the Channel and Atlantic coast. The attack is expected in the Dover area, though the defences here are strongest.

Strong air attacks lasting several days will precede the landing.

Two days later a further report was received:

English defence measures: coastal defence by the Army. Defence is based on mobility and concentration of all available fire-power. No fixed defence line with built-in defences. The task of the fleet and the R.A.F. would be to render impossible the landing of armoured units or surprise landing by troops. The R.A.F. is so organized that strong units can be quickly concentrated at any danger spot, and also to attack the new German bases in Northern France and Holland and to search for indications of German activity, such as the assembly of ships and barges.

These reports, though lacking in definite information, impressed upon the Naval Staff the difficulties of invasion, and on 21 July Raeder reported yet again to Hitler. Only rough notes of this conference are available, but additional information shows that in Hitler's opinion the war was already won, but that England had not yet recognized the situation. From being averse to the landing the German Supreme Command (i.e. Keitel and Jodl) had entirely changed its views, and, to the alarm of the Naval Staff, now considered the landing quite a simple operation. Hitler himself was not, however, convinced:

Notes of Conference on 21 July 1940

The Führer raised the following points:
. . . The invasion of Britain is an exceptionally daring undertaking, because even if the way is short, this is not just a river crossing, but the crossing of a sea which is dominated by the enemy. This is not a case of a single crossing operation as in Norway; operational surprise cannot be expected; a defensively prepared and utterly determined enemy faces us and dominates the sea area which we must use. For the Army operation forty divisions will be required; the most difficult part will be the continued reinforcement of material and stores. We

cannot count on supplies of any kind being available to us in England. The prerequisites are complete mastery of the air, the operational use of powerful artillery in the Dover Straits, and protection by minefields. The time of year is an important factor, since the weather in the North Sea and in the Channel during the second half of September is very bad and the fogs begin by the middle of October. The main operation would therefore have to be completed by 15 September; after this date co-operation between the Luftwaffe and the heavy weapons becomes too unreliable. But as air co-operation is decisive, it must be regarded as the principal factor in fixing the date.

The following must be established:

1. How long does the Navy require for its technical preparations?
2. How soon can the guns be in place?
3. To what extent can the Navy safeguard the crossing?

If it is not certain that preparations can be completed by the beginning of September, other plans must be considered.

On the following day it was reported to Hitler that the preparations could not in any event be completed by the middle of August, and that the actual date of invasion could only be determined when air supremacy in the Channel had been achieved.

The Army then sent their theoretical demands to the Naval Staff:

The General Staff of the Army has given its intentions for carrying out the operation, as follows: about a hundred thousand men with appropriate equipment, including heavy gear, must be transported in the first wave from the area Dunkirk-Cherbourg to the area between Ramsgate and Lyme Bay. Further waves must follow in quickest succession, so that the formation of a

local bridgehead may be followed in the shortest time
by a war of movement on the island. This demands the
most rapid turn round of transports after disembarkation of the first echelon.

The amount of shipping required to carry out the Army
demands was estimated as: 1,722 barges, 471 tugs, 1,161
motor boats, 155 transports.

The assembly of this armada would impose a severe
strain on German economy and, on 25 July, Raeder again
reported to Hitler:

Conference with the Führer on 25 July 1940

Placement of batteries at the Straits of Dover:
(Report by Captain Voss.)

The guns are to be ready by 15 August. The 38 cm.
battery will not be ready until the middle of September.
Concrete covers will be built later as a protection
against air attack.

The C.-in-C., Navy, emphasizes the necessity for
making use of the batteries as soon as they are ready in
order to protect minesweepers and to close the Straits
of Dover. (The 28 cm. Kurfürst battery will be ready
about 1 August.) As British air reconnaissance is obviously closely watching the placing of the guns, firing
them will not disclose German plans to any greater
degree.

The Führer agrees.

Operation "Sea Lion":

The C.-in-C., Navy, describes forcefully once again
the effects of these preparations on the German
economy; cessation of inland shipping and a great part
of maritime shipping, strain on shipyards, etc. The C.-
in-C., Navy, requests that an order be issued that these
preparations be given preference over anything else.

The Führer and the Chief of Staff, Armed Forces High Command, agree.

There follows a report on the state of preparations on 25 July 1940. The C.-in-C., Navy, again stresses the necessity of establishing air superiority soon in order to carry out preparations. At the present time, the following can be said:

Every effort is being made to complete preparations by the end of August. Provided that there are no special difficulties and that air superiority is established soon, it will be possible to do the following:

1. Provide and convert barges.
2. Make available the necessary personnel.
3. Prepare ports for embarkation.
4. Reconnoitre the enemy coast.
5. Clear the invasion area of mines.
6. Lay protecting minefields.
7. Set up the organization.

It is still very uncertain whether a sufficient number of ships can be obtained along the Belgian-French coast and how long it will take to convert them. The C.-in-C., Navy, will try to give a clear picture by the middle of next week.

The Führer orders a conference for the middle of next week.

Preparations for "Sea Lion" now began in earnest, but the essential air superiority over the Channel was elusive.

Top Secret   14 September 1940

At the conference with the Commanders-in-Chief of the Armed Forces on 14 September the Führer has decided:

1. *"Sea Lion":*
   (*a*) The start of the operation is again postponed. A

new order follows on 17 September. All preparations are to be continued.

(*b*) As soon as preparations are complete, the Luftwaffe is to carry out attacks against the British long-range batteries.

(*c*) The measures planned for the evacuation of the coastal area are not to be set in motion to the full extent. Counter-espionage and deception measures are, however, to be increased.

2. *Air attacks against London:*

The air attacks against London are to be continued and the target area is to be expanded against military and other vital installations (e.g., railway stations).

Terror attacks against purely residential areas are reserved for use as an ultimate means of pressure, and are therefore not to be employed at present.

Heavy air attacks by both sides continued for the next two days, and on 17 September an entry in the War Diary stated:

The enemy air force is still by no means defeated; on the contrary, it shows increasing activity. The weather situation as a whole does not permit us to expect a period of calm. . . . *The Führer therefore decides to postpone "Sea Lion" indefinitely.*

On 19 September, a Supreme Command directive was issued confirming the postponement. The Naval Staff summed up the situation:

1. The preparations for a landing on the Channel coast are extensively known to the enemy, who is taking more counter-measures. Symptoms are, for example, operational use of his aircraft for attacks and reconnaissance over the German operational harbours; frequent appearance of destroyers off the South Coast of England, in the Straits of Dover, and on the Franco-

Belgian coast; stationing of his patrol vessels off the North Coast of France; Churchill's last speech, etc.

2. The main units of the Home Fleet are being held in readiness to repel the landing, though the majority of the units are still in Western bases.

3. Already a large number of destroyers (thirty) has been located by air reconnaissance in the southern and south-eastern harbours.

4. All available information indicates that the enemy's naval forces are solely occupied with this theatre of operations.

Although there was still a possibility of invading in October, shipping was dispersed to prevent further losses. By 21 September the state of the invasion armada was:

Shipping previously available		Lost or damaged
Transports	168	21 (i.e., 12.5%)
Barges	1,697	214 (i.e., 12.6%)
Tugs	360	5 (i.e., 1.4%)

Troops and ships were kept at readiness until 12 October, when the operation was postponed until the spring of 1941.

12 October 1940

Top Secret

The Führer has decided that from now until the spring, preparations for "Sea Lion" shall be continued solely for the purpose of maintaining political and military pressure on England.

Should the invasion be reconsidered in the spring or early summer of 1941, orders for a renewal of operational readiness will be issued later. In the meantime military conditions for a later invasion are to be improved. . . .

But, by the spring of 1941, Hitler and his staff were

deeply involved in the preparations for invading Russia, and Operation "Sea Lion" was shelved. It was finally cancelled in January 1942.

Anticipation

To:
SS Colonel Professor Dr. Six,
Berlin.

By virtue of *Reichsmarschall* Göring's authority I appoint you Representative of the Chief of the Security Police and S.D. in Great Britain. Your task is to combat, with the requisite means, all anti-German organizations, institutions, opposition, and opposition groups which can be seized in England, to prevent the removal of all available material, and to centralize and safeguard it for future exploitation. I designate the capital, London, as the location of your headquarters as Representative of the Chief of the Security Police and S.D.; and I authorize you to set up small action groups in other parts of Great Britain as the situation dictates and the necessity arises.
Reinhard Heydrich, Chief, German Security Service
(S.D.)

. . . . All the organs of the political and military leadership worked on the preparation of Operation "Sea Lion" at top speed and with typical Prussian thoroughness. For example, at the end of June 1940, I was ordered to prepare a small handbook for the invading troops and the political and administrative units that would accompany them, describing briefly the most important political, administrative and economic institutions of Great Britain and the leading public figures. It was also to contain instructions on the necessary measures to be taken in occupying the premises of the Foreign Office, the War Office, the Home Office and the various departments of the Secret Service, and Special Branch. This task occupied a great deal of my time, involving the collection and assembly of material from various sources by a selected staff of my own people. When it was finished an edition of twenty thousand copies was printed, and stored in a room next to my office. They were burned in 1943 in a fire started in one of the air raids.

Walter Schellenberg

LEASE-LEND

President Roosevelt's hand was strengthened by his victory in the Presidential Election of November 1940, and, in spite of opposition which was still strong, the "Lease-Lend" scheme was prepared.

I think we are doing Great Britain a great disservice in urging her to go and fight until she is exhausted. . . . Peace has got to come sometime, and I don't think there is any sane, intelligent military or naval officer . . . who thinks that England can land troops on German soil and drive the Germans back to Berlin before that time arrives. And even if our own warmongers get us into the war, as it looks now they will, I doubt that the joint efforts of Great Britain and the United States could succeed in that project.

Senator Burton K. Wheeler, Christmas 1940

On 10 January 1941 the Lease-Lend Bill was put before the United States Congress; on 11 March it was approved and signed by the President.

A NEW YEAR MESSAGE

It is the will of the democratic war inciters and their Jewish-capitalistic wire-pullers that the war must be continued. . . . We are ready! . . . The year 1941 will bring completion of the greatest victory in our history.

Adolf Hitler to his troops, New Year's Eve 1940

8

THE END OF
THE ITALIAN EMPIRE

In the late summer of 1940, Mussolini stood ready in his African domains to emulate his erstwhile pupil's sweeping victories in Europe. In North Africa over two hundred thousand men began to gather themselves for a descent on Egypt and the Suez Canal, faced only by a thin screen of British troops. In Italy's East African possessions an even stronger army, composed of her best units splendidly equipped, invaded British Somaliland on 3 August, expelling the greatly outnumbered British forces without much difficulty. The position of the Allies in Africa took a further turn for the worse towards the end of September, when General de Gaulle's efforts to rally France's colonial possessions suffered a hard knock at Dakar, on the west coast.

FOG OVER DAKAR

THE expedition left Liverpool on 31 August. I myself, with part of the French units and a small staff, was on board the *Westerland,* which flew the French flag beside the Dutch, and whose commander (Captain Plagaay), officers and crew were to prove, like those of the *Pennland,* models of friendly devotion. Spears accompanied me, delegated by Churchill as liaison officer, diplomat and informant. In England I left our forces in course of formation under the orders of Muselier, an embryo administration under the direction of Antoine, and, in the person

of Dewavrin, an element of liaison and direct information.
In addition, General Catroux was expected shortly from
Indo-China; and in a letter which was to be handed to him
as soon as he arrived I explained to him my projects as a
whole and what I had in mind for him. I reckoned that, in
spite of my absence, and provided it did not last long, the
reserves of wisdom accumulated by my companions would
prevent internal quarrels and intrigues from outside from
shaking the still very fragile edifice too profoundly! None
the less, on the deck of the *Westerland,* after leaving the
port in the middle of an air-raid warning with my small
troop and my tiny ships, I felt crushed, as it were, by the
dimensions of duty. Out in the open, in black night, on the
swell of the ocean, a poor foreign ship, with no guns, with
all lights extinguished, was carrying the fortunes of
France.

Our first destination was Freetown. . . . During the
voyage, radiograms received from London had given us a
piece of news about the Vichy forces which might well
lead to everything being reconsidered. On 11 September
three large modern cruisers, the *Georges Leygues, Gloire*
and *Montcalm,* and three light cruisers, the *Audacieux,
Fantasque* and *Malin,* having started from Toulon, had
passed the Straits of Gibraltar without being stopped by
the British fleet. But hardly had we anchored at Freetown
when a new and grave piece of information completed our
perplexity. The squadron, reinforced at Dakar by the
cruiser *Primauguet,* had just weighed anchor and was
heading southwards at full speed. A British destroyer,
detached to watch it, was keeping in touch with it at a
distance.

I could have no doubt that this powerful naval force
was bound for Equatorial Africa, where the port of
Libreville was open to it, and where it would find it easy to
retake Pointre-Noire and Duala. If such a thunder-clap
did not suffice to reverse the situation in the Congo and
Cameroons, these magnificent ships could easily cover the
transport and landing of forces of repression from Dakar,
Konakry or Abidjan. . . . It was clear that Vichy was start-

ing a large-scale operation to re-establish itself in the territories which had rallied to Free France, and that the despatch of seven cruisers towards the Equator was conceivable only with the full consent, if not at the orders, of the Germans. Admiral Cunningham fell in with my view that the Vichy squadron must be stopped at once.

In fact, the British cruisers which made contact with Admiral Bourragué, the commander of the untimely squadron, had no difficulty in making it change course when its leader learned, to his complete surprise, of the presence of a Franco-British fleet in the region. But the Vichy ships, defying all pursuit, made straight for Dakar.

In this way Free French Africa escaped a very great danger. . . . But after congratulating ourselves on having made our adversaries' plan come to nothing, we had to admit that our own was gravely compromised. In fact, the Dakar authorities were henceforward on their guard and had received a most valuable reinforcement of ships. We learned almost at once, through our intelligence agents, that to serve the shore batteries naval gunners had been substituted for the men of the colonial artillery, who were considered less reliable. In short, our chances of occupying Dakar appeared, from now on, very small.

In London Mr. Churchill and the Admiralty reckoned that, in these circumstances, it was better to do nothing. They had telegraphed this to us as early as 16 September, proposing that the fleet should simply escort our vessels as far as Duala and then move on elsewhere. I must say that to give up in this way seemed to me the worst possible solution. In fact, if we left everything at Dakar as it was, all Vichy would have to do, to resume its attempt on Equatorial Africa, would be to wait for the British ships to return northwards, as they soon would. With the sea open to them, Bourragué's cruisers would swoop once more towards the Equator. In this way the combatants under the Cross of Lorraine, including General de Gaulle, would sooner or later be mewed up in these distant territories and, even if they did not succumb to it, absorbed by a sterile struggle carried on against other Frenchmen in

the bush and forest. No prospect for them, in these conditions, of fighting Germans or Italians. I had no doubt that
those were the intentions of the enemy, of which the Vichy
puppets inevitably made themselves the instruments, conscious or not. It seemed to me that, at the stage things had
now reached, we ought in spite of everything to try to enter Dakar.

Admiral Cunningham reacted in the same way. We
telegraphed to London, arguing, most pressingly, that we
should be allowed to attempt the operation. Mr. Churchill,
as he told me later, was surprised and enchanted by this
insistence. He willingly consented and the action was
decided on.

. . . . At dawn on the 23rd,* in the midst of a very thick
fog, we were before Dakar.

The fog was bound to compromise our enterprise
seriously. In particular, the moral effect which, according
to Churchill, the sight of our fleet was to produce upon the
garrison and population would not come into play at all,
since not a thing was to be seen. But postponement was
obviously impossible. The plan as prepared was therefore
put into execution. At six o'clock I addressed the Navy,
the troops and the inhabitants by radio, announcing our
presence and our friendly intentions. Immediately afterwards two small *Lucioles*, French touring aircraft,
unarmed, took off from the deck of *Ark Royal:* they were
to land at the aerodrome of Ouakam and there set down
three officers—Gaillet, Scamaroni and Soufflet—with a
fraternization mission. In fact, I quickly learned that the
Lucioles had landed without difficulty, and that the signal
"Success" was displayed on the airfield.

Suddenly ack-ack fire was heard at various points.
Some of the guns of the *Richelieu* and of the fortress were
firing at the Free French and British machines which were
beginning to fly over the town, dropping friendly leaflets.
And yet, sinister though this cannonade might be, it
seemed to me to have something hesitant about it. I

* September (Ed.)

therefore gave the order to the two pinnaces with the
spokesmen on board to enter the port, while the Free
French sloops, together with the *Westerland* and *Pennland,*
approached in the mist as far as the entrance to the roads.

There was at first no reaction. Commander d'Argenlieu,
Major Gotscho, Captains Bécourt-Foch and Perrin and
Sub-Lieutenant Porgés ordered their boats to be moored,
landed on the quay, and asked for the port commander.
When he presented himself, d'Argenlieu told him that he
was the bearer of a letter from General de Gaulle for the
Governor-General, which letter he was instructed to
deliver to him personally. But the port commander, with
unconcealed embarrassment, informed the spokesmen that
he had orders to have them arrested. At the same time he
showed his intention of calling the guard. Seeing which,
my envoys returned to the pinnaces. As these drew away,
some machine-guns opened fire on them. D'Argenlieu and
Perrin were brought on board the *Westerland*, seriously
wounded.

Thereupon, the Dakar batteries began aiming at the
British and French ships an intermittent fire which for
several hours remained without reply. The *Richelieu*, having been moved within the harbour by tugs so that its guns
might be put to better use, began firing in its turn.
Towards eleven the cruiser *Cumberland* having been
badly hit, Admiral Cunningham addressed this message by
radio to the fortress: "I am not firing on you. Why are
you firing on me?" The reply was, "Retire to twenty miles'
distance." Upon which, the British in their turn sent some
broadsides. Meanwhile time was passing without a sign,
on one side or the other, of real fighting ardour. No Vichy
aeroplane had taken off up to midday.

From these indications as a whole I did not draw the
impression that the place was determined on a desperate
resistance. Perhaps the Navy, garrison and Governor
were waiting for something to happen which could serve
them as pretext for conciliation? Towards noon, Admiral
Cunningham sent me a signal to let me know that this was
his feeling too. Certainly, there could be no thought of get-

ting the squadron into the harbour. But would it not be possible to land the Free French somewhere near the fortress, which they would then attempt to approach by land? This alternative had been considered in advance. The small port of Rufisque, outside the range of the works, seemed suitable for the operation, provided always that this did not meet with determined resistance. In fact, while our sloops could reach Rufisque, our transports could not, because of their draught. The troops would therefore have to be disembarked by lighter, which would deprive them of their heavy weapons and make complete peace essential. However, having received from Cunningham the assurance that he was covering us from the sea, I set all in motion towards Rufisque.

Towards 3 p.m., still in the fog, we arrived at the spot. The *Commandant Duboc,* with a section of marines on board, entered the port and sent some sailors ashore in a boat to prepare the berthing. On shore a crowd of natives was already running up to welcome the patrol, when the Vichy troops in position in the neighbourhood opened fire on our sloop, killing and wounding several men. A few moments earlier, two Glenn-Martin bombers had flown over our little force at a low altitude, as if to show it that they held it at their mercy—which was indeed the case. Lastly, Admiral Cunningham signalled that the cruisers *Georges Leygues* and *Montcalm* had left Dakar roads and were in the mist at a mile's distance from us, and that the British ships, occupied elsewhere, could not protect us from them. Decidedly, the affair was a failure! Not only was the landing not possible, but, what was more, a few shots fired by the Vichy cruisers would be enough to send the whole Free French expedition to the bottom. I decided to make for the open again, which was done without further incident.

We passed the night on tenterhooks. Next morning the British Fleet, having received from Mr. Churchill a telegram inviting it to push on actively with the affair, addressed an ultimatum to the Dakar authorities. They replied that they would not surrender the place. From then on, the day was spent by the British in exchanging a rather lively cannonade with the shore batteries and ships in the roads, firing blind in the mist, which was thicker than ever. By the end of the afternoon it seemed evident that no decisive result could be obtained.

As evening fell, the *Barham* came up quite close to the *Westerland*, and Admiral Cunningham asked me to come and see him, to discuss the situation. On board the British battleship the atmosphere was gloomy and strained. They were sorry, certainly, not to have succeeded. But the dominant feeling was that of surprise. The British, being practical people, could not understand how and why the authorities, naval forces and troops at Dakar expended such energy upon fighting against their compatriots and against their allies at a time when France lay beneath the invader's boot. As for me, I had from that moment given up being astonished at it. What had just happened showed me, once for all, that the Vichy rulers would never fail to misuse, against the interests of France, the courage and discipline of those who were in subjection to them.

Admiral Cunningham summed up the situation. "Given," he declared, "the attitude of the place and of the squadron supporting it, I do not think bombardment can result in a solution." General Irwin, who commanded the landing units, added that he was ready to send his troops ashore to assault the fortifications, but that it must be clearly understood that this would mean a great risk for each boat and each soldier. Both of them asked me what would become of the Free France "movement" if an end were put to the expedition.

"Up to now," I said, "we have not made an all-out attack on Dakar. The attempt to enter the harbour peaceably has failed. Bombardment will decide nothing. Lastly, a landing against opposition and an assault on the fortifications would lead to a pitched battle which, for my part, I desire to avoid and of which, as you yourselves indicate, the issue would be very doubtful. We must, therefore, for the moment, give up the idea of taking Dakar. I propose to Admiral Cunningham that he should announce that he is stopping the bombardment at the request of General de Gaulle. But the blockade must be maintained in order not to allow the ships now at Dakar their liberty of action. Next, we shall have to prepare a fresh attempt by marching against the place by land, after disembarking at undefended or lightly defended points, for instance at Saint-Louis. In any case, and whatever happens, Free France will continue."

The British admiral and general fell in with my view as regards the immediate future. In the falling night I left the *Barham* on board a launch which danced on the waves, while the officers and crew, drawn up along the handrails, sadly gave me a ceremonial send-off.

But during the night two facts were to make Admiral Cunningham go back on what we had agreed. First, a fresh telegram from Mr. Churchill expressly called upon him to pursue the enterprise. In it the Prime Minister showed astonishment and irritation at the idea of the affair coming to nothing—the more so because, already, political circles in London and, above all, in Washington, were beginning to grow agitated, impressed by the Vichy and Berlin radios. At the same time the fog was lifting, and this at once seemed to give the bombardment another chance. The fighting therefore began again at dawn—this time without my having been consulted—with an exchange of gunfire between the fortress and the British. But towards evening the battleship *Resolution,* torpedoed by a submarine and in danger of sinking, had to be taken in tow. Several other British ships had been badly hit. Four aircraft from the *Ark Royal* had been shot down. On the other side, the *Richelieu* and various other ships had taken some hard punishment. The destroyer *Audacieux,* the submarines *Persée* and *Ajax* had been sunk; a British destroyer had managed to pick up the latter's crew. But the stalwarts of the fortress still went on firing. Admiral Cunningham decided to cut the losses. I could not but agree. We headed for Freetown.

The days which followed were cruel for me. I went through what a man must feel when an earthquake shakes his house brutally and he receives on his head the rain of tiles falling from the roof.

In London a tempest of anger, in Washington a hurricane of sarcasms were let loose against me. For the American Press and many English newspapers it was immediately a matter of course that the failure of the attempt was due to de Gaulle. "It was he," the echoes repeated, "who thought of this absurd adventure, misled the British by imaginative reports on the situation at Dakar, and insisted, out of Don Quixotism, that the place be attacked when the reinforcements sent by Darlan made any success impossible. . . . Besides, the cruisers from Toulon had come only as the result of the incessant indiscretions of the Free French, which had put Vichy on the alert. . . . Once for all, it was clear that no reliance could be placed on people incapable of keeping a secret." Soon Mr. Churchill, too, was roughly handled for having, so it was said, so easily let himself be carried away. Spears, with a long face, kept bringing me telegraphed reports from his correspondents suggesting it as probable that de Gaulle in despair, abandoned by his partisans, dropped by the British into the bargain, would renounce all activity, while the British Government would take up afresh with Catroux or Muselier, on a much more modest scale, the recruitment of French auxiliaries.

As for the Vichy propaganda, it triumphed without restraint. The Dakar communiqués gave the impression that the thing had been a great naval victory. Innumerable messages of congratulation, addressed to Governor-General Boisson and to the heroic fighters of Dakar, were published and commented upon by newspapers of both zones and by the so-called "French" radios. And I, in my narrow cabin, in a harbour crushed by the heat, was completing my education in what the reactions of fear could be, both among adversaries taking revenge for having felt it and among allies suddenly alarmed by a set-back.

General de Gaulle

COLLAPSE IN EAST AFRICA

In East and North Africa troops were assembling under the command of General Wavell who were to win the first land victories achieved by the Allies in the second World War. In January 1941 a mixed force of British and Commonwealth units took the offensive from the Sudan, driving in the Italian forces which had occupied Kassala and Gallabat, just over the frontier from Eritrea and Abyssinia.

Compared with the subsequent campaigns in the Western Desert, Italy, North-West Europe and Burma, the campaign in Eritrea in the early part of 1941 was probably very small beer. But to those who took part in it from January to March 1941 it seemed a big and important show. Important it certainly was as a means of preventing any interference by the Italians with our communications through the Red Sea and Suez Canal and with our bases in Egypt. From a prestige point of view also it was important. After all, it was the only completely successful campaign in the second World War until 1943, when the North African campaign was finished.

Those who advanced into Eritrea in January 1941 and expected to meet the same sort of opposition as they met in Wavell's Sidi Barrani campaign in December 1940 got a rude shock. The Italian army in Eritrea and Abyssinia were much stouter fighters than Graziani's troops in Libya. Their black troops, too, fought well right up to the moment they decided to come in and surrender.

Lieutenant-Colonel J. L. Gardner-Brown

Gallabat

. . . . Patrolling in the tall elephant grass was a nervy procedure, and small patrols might well come unexpectedly face to face with an Italian party. Then the men in front would shoot it out while their companions behind tried to outflank the opposite side. Already the vultures were feasting in Gallabat, or what remained of it, after the fighting and bombardments. Care was essential when approaching the fort, because the sudden rising of a flock of these sinister birds could reveal our presence to a watchful foe. False alarms were many, and often caused by the baboons which abounded in the district.

The tinder-like elephant grass was also a problem to the Gunners. Several fires started in the gun-pits when fragments of burning cordite set the grass alight. Buckets of water had constantly to be kept at hand, and smoking was strictly forbidden. Because of the visits of hostile aircraft day after day, these gun-pits were elaborate with their camouflage nets draped on poles. The Gunners went to the length of cutting sods with the grass attached and of "planting" these on top of the camouflage nets to simulate the normal jungle grass growing on every side. As these covers had to be taken down every time the guns were fired, and then replaced immediately afterwards, the trouble involved was great, but amply repaid. Never once were the Gunners spotted by Italian pilots.

The local superiority enjoyed by the enemy in the air was a salutary training in care and concealment to our men. Track discipline was rigorously enforced. Trucks of all kinds were parked under trees and liberally draped with foliage. The troops lived in huts constructed of boughs and named *tukis*. These had to be dug in, for protection against the "egg-basket" type of Italian bomb, a series of anti-personnel grenades that were virtually shovelled out of the enemy bombers. Along the banks of the local *khors* the trees were particularly heavy and green. At this season the streams were mostly dry, with an occasional pool, and away from their proximity the bush was scorched by heat and drought, the leaves burnt off, and the landscape consequently more open than a few months earlier when the vegetation had been dense and tall.

The mirage whose outline faded and then vanished as

you drew near, the heat shimmer from which tree-ringed
lakes and the likeness of still water might be stared at,
were a frequent memorable feature of many a drive over
the desert. Wells became important and recognizable by
the swarms of flies as well as by the camels, cows, goats
and donkeys that watered there in daylight. To pick out
the one camel track to be followed among many such
tracks was often perplexing, and a glance at the sun or a
compass would be necessary to avoid taking the wrong
route. Patches of long *tubbas* grass grew on the sand now
that the rains were falling, and camel-thorn bushes studded the ground. Where these bushes flourished, particularly round Gedaref, men found it difficult to walk any
distance without getting caught up in thorns like fish-
hooks. The scratches festered into septic sores, and in certain units there was hardly a man without bandages on
one or both arms and knees.

Antony Brett-James

Keren

*Fighting back doggedly, the Italian retired on Keren,
the formidable position covering Asmara, capital of
Eritrea. Here they concentrated their strength for a
decisive stand.*

The town of Keren, which lies over four thousand feet
above sea-level, is protected on all sides, except on the
east, by a formidable barrier of gaunt and rugged mountains. From the direction of Agordat, the only gap is the
narrow, winding Dongolaas Gorge that takes both road
and railway through to Keren. High on the left of the
Gorge are Mounts Samanna and Amba and also the
towering Mount Sanchil, which appears to dominate the
entire range. On the outer side of the Gorge are the high
jagged formations of Falestoh and Zeban, before and
below which lies the fortified feature of Dologorodoc. In
front of the fort, in the direction of Agordat, lies the long,
wide bed of the "Happy Valley", from which the sur-

rounding features shoot heavenwards some two thousand feet. Rising sharply in the east corner of the valley stands the Aqua Col.

The strategic value of this mass of natural defences had long since been fully appreciated by the Italian High Command, and it was here that General Luigi Frusci, Governor of Eritrea and Commander-in-Chief of the Italian Northern Army, decided to concentrate the bulk of his forces in one final effort to hold Eritrea.

The Key

The Italian stronghold of Fort Dologorodoc, the key position covering Keren and the main approach road to Asmara, capital of Eritrea, provided one of the bloodiest of battlegrounds, and its capture was largely responsible for the sudden and total collapse of Italy's mighty colonial empire, comprising Abyssinia, Somaliland and Eritrea.

The Battleground

Since the Gallabat showdown, we had concentrated largely on marching and assaulting the precipitous heights round Sabderat, which lies between Kassala and Keren. As intended, the latter form of activity obviously fitted us well for the Keren operations. Lord, how we sweated and toiled to master those monstrous heights, and yet the dry humour common to the sturdy Yorkshireman continued to flow freely. Between their puffs and grunts, one caught such apt and expressive remarks as: "Think we're bloody mountain goats" and "We'll be sprouting horns soon."

One felt that to scale those almost unclimbable heights, fully armed and equipped for battle, was a feat in itself, requiring supreme physical effort. It was not surprising therefore that one of the major problems with which we were faced at Keren was that of arriving high up on the enemy strongpoints in a fit state to fight.

The soil between the hard, jagged boulders crumbled underfoot, and many of the smaller rocks were so easily dislodged that they proved to be an extremely risky aid to climbing. One had also to contend with the thick, thorny scrub and the hard sharp-pointed grass that, together with the boulder-studded slopes, made up the general pattern of the Eritrean countryside around Keren.

The enemy, on the other hand, held every advantage. He could sit tight in comparative comfort and await the approaching mass of struggling humanity. As a general rule, the greater proportion of his forces were established behind and just below the crest of whatever height they occupied. It was only when our artillery barrage lifted, and they thought that an assault on their position was imminent, that their defences were fully manned and their full strength exposed. Time and time again our troops got to within a stone's throw of the enemy strongpoints, only to be literally blasted back by automatic fire and showers of the comparatively small, red, tinny grenades with which the Italians were well supplied.

. . . . On the night of 15-16 March the battle was joined. We moved off quietly with the object of making a wide detour to the right and crossing into the immediate battle zone at a point known as White Ridge.

We had already been told of the magnificent display of courage by the 3rd/5th Mahrattas, who had advanced to the attack at last light. After fierce hand-to-hand fighting, and at least four spirited attacks, they had finally succeeded in driving the enemy from the summit of "Pimple". In doing so, they had expended their entire reserves. We were later to learn that the task of taking "Pimple", the next and final objective before the Fort, had been taken over by the 3rd/12th Frontier Force.

Throughout our advance the noise was deafening. We scrambled forward and upwards at a good if erratic pace among the scrub and between the juts of jagged rock. The roar of our guns, now seemingly well behind us, was relieved only by the blinding flashes and the crashing of our shells immediately in front. So close to us were many of these shells that I gained the impression that we were not regulating the pace of our advance to timed artillery concentrations, but that we were following closely in the wake of a creeping barrage.

We passed through the 3rd/12th Frontier Force on "Pimple" soon after they had beaten off an exceptionally fierce counter-attack. It was first light, and we passed on at staggering pace past many of that gallant regiment, who appeared to be half-standing and half-lying against the large sloping rocks as if in momentary repose. To all appearances these men, with their rifles in the immediate-action position, were keeping vigilant watch towards Dologorodoc: it was only on hurrying past that one realized that they would see no further action.

Supported by the guns of the 144th and the 28th Field Regiments, we passed on along the knife-edged ridge between "Pimple" and Fort Dologorodoc. The going was tough and the fighting hard but spasmodic. Small, independent pockets of resistance were soon overcome at the point of the bayonet. The last hundred yards or so up to the Fort were difficult to negotiate, owing to the crumbling and powdery nature of the ground—a state our artillery had undoubtedly helped to produce. At about 6.30 a.m. the success signal, in the form of Verey lights, indicated that we were at last in possession of Fort Dologorodoc.

The Fort consisted of a concrete trench running most of the way round and just below the rock-faced summit of the hill. As the concreted half of the newly-won dug-outs now faced away from the enemy, we were set the immediate task of building sand-bag walls on the reverse side of Dologorodoc, from which direction the enemy would surely counter-attack.

The fighting which followed our capture of Fort Dologorodoc was close and bitter in the extreme. Between counter-attacks the enemy pumped shells and mortar bombs into the Fort by day and by night.

That the enemy considered Fort Dologorodoc to be the key position in his defence system was indicated by the ferocity and determination of his attempts to oust us from it. These heavy and costly attacks with such crack troops as the Savoy Grenadiers and the Alpini and Bersaglieri Regiments eventually sapped his strength and cracked his morale.

In the early hours of 25 March, attacks were successfully pressed home by the West Yorks and the 3rd/12th Frontier Force on three small features which lay just forward and to the left of the Fort between Falestoh and Zeban.

On the night of 26-27 March, 29 Brigade passed through the newly-won 9 Brigade positions and assaulted Falestoh and Zeban. By dawn we had occupied both features.

At first light on 27 March a white flag was to be seen flying from the impregnable Mount Sanchil, and a little later others appeared on "Brigs Peak" and Mounts Amba and Samanna.

British infantry officer

So Keren fell after fifty-three days of siege. It is estimated that the Italians employed in battle a total of thirty-nine battalions and thirty-six batteries, and that during the period of operations they disposed in all of something over thirty thousand infantry, supported by 144 guns. Many of these were fresh troops, and although the British forces never succeeded in driving their opponents from the main peaks on either side of the Dongolaas Gorge, and suffered over four thousand casualties in their attempts to do so, it is true to say that the enemy brought defeat on himself and finally wore himself out in his eight fierce but fruitless attempts to retake Dologorodoc Fort. It was here that his best and freshest units were driven back with crippling losses. In General Frusci's own situation reports, which were captured, he reveals that three thousand dead were left in Keren, including General Lorenzini and five senior officers. Practically all had been staked in holding this natural fortress, with the result that, at the end, there were but three battalions and a few batteries uncommitted between Keren and Asmara. The fall of Keren was the beginning of the end of Italian influence and power in East Africa. The road lay open to the capital city of Eritrea. On 1 March our troops marched into Asmara. Massawa, the enemy's principal port on the Red Sea coast, surrendered with ten thousand prisoners on 8 April.

Lieutenant-Colonel J. E. B. Barton

Meanwhile East and South African forces under General Cunningham had executed a rapid and brilliant advance northward, overrunning Italian Somaliland, and, in conjunction with troops landed from Aden, had by mid-March cleared British Somaliland of the enemy. By April the Italians were being driven from Abyssinia. On the 6th of the month General Cunningham's soldiers entered Addis Ababa. The remnants of the Italian armies in East Africa, under the Duke of Aosta, were hemmed in at Amba Alagi by General Mayne.

Indians at Amba Alagi

I had puffed and panted my way to the top of a sheer peak which afforded the best available observation of the enemy's position at Toselli. The Garhwali tactical headquarters were there, and so was an important O.P. from the 28th Field Regiment. As I arrived exhausted at my destination, a party of British gunners caught me up and were hailed with obvious enthusiasm by some Garhwali signallers, who were brewing tea in a dugout. I stopped for a breather before scaling the last fifty feet to the look-out, and saw out of the tail of my eye much hand-shaking and then the Englishmen squatting down beside the Indians and accepting the tea and cigarettes that they offered.

Having finished my own business in half an hour or so, I began stumbling down the hill again, only to be stopped by the same Garhwali signallers and led into the dugout. There I, too, was given tea, biscuits, and a cigarette. I took them thankfully, but with mild protest, knowing that every half-pint of water and morsel of everything else had to be carried by hand from a water point over a mile away and nearly a thousand feet lower down, and I asked the Garhwalis whether it was their habit to entertain every Tom, Dick and Harry who came their way. Their answer was a flat denial. Not a bit of it. It was business enough to keep their own tummies full, and normal hospitality had to go hang. But in my case it was different. I was, after all, the Divisional Commander and a very old man too! Then what about the British soldiers, I asked. "Oh, that's quite different," they replied, "they belong to the 28th. They belong to us."

General Mayne

At about 7.30 a.m. on 6 May, when plans for an all-out assault on the enemy's main defences were almost complete, envoys from the Duke of Aosta arrived at General Mayne's headquarters. They first asked for an armistice, in order that they might hand over to us their many casualties. It was also requested that they should be given access to fresh water supplies. When a truce was refused, General Mayne was asked to receive one of the Duke of Aosta's senior officers, with the object of discussing surrender terms. To this he agreed.

The reason for this sudden desire to capitulate was soon evident. On the night before the Duke sent his envoys to General Mayne, a burst from our artillery had hit an Italian fuel dump high up on Amba Alagi. The contents of the dump had cascaded downhill and contaminated the enemy's only source of drinking water.

British infantry officer

Surrender with Honour

"Surrender with Honour" was an idea that had never occurred to me and nothing of the kind was included in the terms of surrender which I sent by hand of Colonel Russell to the Duke of Aosta. The suggestion originated with the Duke himself, and as soon as it was communicated to me I felt that I could make capital out of it—that it was I who would benefit much more than the

Italians. This is why I thought of it that way.

Amongst my terms of surrender, which Colonel Russell was to elaborate verbally, was a demand that the battle-field should be handed over "clean"; all mines, booby traps and such like were to be clearly defined and their location shown to those troops of mine who were to take over the area; there was to be no sabotage or destruction of any kind of guns, equipment and stores; none were to be hidden and all were to be handed over intact to my rep-resentatives. All that was very easy to say and equally easy for the Italians to accept. But would they play up honestly? Obviously not, I thought. It would be nothing else than normal, underhand, war-time practice for them to spend the intervening hours between now and the march-out hiding or sabotaging the breech-blocks of valuable guns and anything else that might be of use to us; and it would be only natural for an enemy conveniently to forget to show us some of the places where mines and booby-traps had been laid, and many of our men would be blown up for the price of their "forgetfulness".

But if I put the Duke of Aosta "on his honour" it might, I thought, put things on an entirely different foot-ing. He was, as I knew, an honourable man and, as a popular Prince, his word ought to be unbreakable law to every single soldier in his army. So, for the price of allow-ing the Italian troops to march out in military forma-tion—handing over their arms a couple of miles away from the battlefield instead of on the battlefield itself—I should, as I hoped, get a clean and complete hand-over of valuable equipment and stores. And, more important still to my way of thinking, I should save the lives of men who might otherwise stroll over ground that looked harmless, but, in fact, concealed death-dealing contraptions of many kinds.

As events proved, I was quite right. The Duke of Aosta was delighted with my concession and, as he told me, gave a rigid and unmistakable edict that the hand-over was to be complete and clean, making it quite clear that any breach of his orders would mean that he had broken his own word. So the Italians did play up. We got everything intact and no one, save Abyssinian patriots who broke all bounds in their search for loot and deserved their fate, suffered so much as a scratch from a hidden mine, although there were plenty of them about.

General Mayne

A Message to the Emperor: 9 May

It is with deep and universal pleasure that the British nation and Empire have learned of Your Imperial Majesty's welcome home to your capital at Addis Ababa. Your Majesty was the first of the lawful sovereigns to be driven from his throne and country by the Fascist-Nazi criminals, and you are now the first to return in triumph.

Winston Churchill to the Emperor
Haile Selassie of Abyssinia

THE WESTERN DESERT

During the long months needed to conquer Italian East Africa, the deserts of the north had been the scene of spectacular attack and counter-attack. After three months of skirmishing, the main Italian army advanced into Egypt on 13 September 1940, but so successfully were they harried by the inferior British forces slowly retiring before them that they halted at Sidi Barrani only four days and sixty-odd miles later.

Introduction to the Desert

The desert has been described, acidly but with no little justice, as "miles and miles and bloody miles of absolutely damn all". There was a seeming eternity of barren, inhospitable nothingness. And this lack of physical features and recognizable landmarks by which to find your way made navigation a problem to all, and was particularly baffling to the newcomer to the desert. You learned to move by map, compass and speedometer. You were never really certain that you were actually at the point from which you thought you were starting, and you had to take your map reference on trust: there was no guarantee. It was hard to tell how far away the horizon was. Your sense of direction became befuddled, you were haunted by the constant risk of losing your way. After a time you developed a sense of direction in daylight; but at night, though to proceed in a general direction was tolerably simple, it was no light matter to pin-point a unit or a rendezvous. You might search for a group of tanks reported to be leaguered at a certain map reference, and you might spend hours driving round the sand, when all the time the tanks were only a mile distant. Unless it was extremely urgent that they be found, it was wiser to camp down for the night and wait until daybreak. Usually the tanks were then visible towards the horizon.

You had to step out of your truck or jeep, lorry or staff car whenever you needed to take a new compass bearing. You kept a watchful eye on the speedometer. And you found your way back by observation of tiny details: a pile of stones or jerry cans that someone had dropped, or a strip of red flag on a hillside, or a tin of bully-beef lying in the sand. All vehicles looked alike, and to search for your unit was sometimes like looking at a sea of transport as though in a nightmare. You gazed upon acres of flat desert studded with scores of trucks, and these were poor landmarks—they might move at any time.

All vehicles could be seen moving from afar because of the trail of dust that billowed up behind or to one side. When two trucks did meet, each driver tried desperately to steer to windward and so avoid the dust of the other vehicle. You might wear sand goggles, but your face was coated with sand that caked itself into a beige mask, clinging to the sweat of your countenance, collecting in the corners of your eyes. Hands and arms, necks and knees became coated with this same sand, which penetrated under your shirt, and caught in your throat, and made your eyes smart. Your hair became matted and bistre. Along your limbs the trickling sweat would cleave little rivulets through the sandy coating.

All day long thousands of vehicles shod with balloon tyres or with tracks were moving about, each with its plume of sand that poured up over the mud-guards, penetrated into the carburettor, came through chinks in the truck's body, or round the edge of a staff car's window. The tanks cut deep ruts in the sand. Half the surface of the desert might appear to be in the air at one time, and drivers would keep their windscreen-wipers going in order to clear the dust and so see a few yards ahead. For in a sandstorm, with its blown and gritty sand that lashed the human body and was blasted everywhere that particles of sand can go, there was an opaque yellowish fog ahead, into which you could peer for but a yard or two. It was as though some shuddering beige curtain had been drawn across the face of the desert; the light of day became unreal in its strange hues; you stumbled over tent ropes and into slit trenches; minefields became a still greater source of danger; while maps were invisible beneath the layer of dust. . . .

Although you were permanently coated with sand when driving or when the wind blew up, baths were impossible and you grew accustomed to being dirty, to washing seldom. Water was short in the desert, scarcer by far than petrol. On a gallon a day for all purposes it became an art to wash, shave, clean your teeth, wash your feet, all in a mug of water, with the resultant glutinous fluid being strained and poured into the radiator of your truck. Some men planned to wash a third of their bodies each day, for the sand became matted in the hairy parts of the body, and they felt the imperative need for washing it away, even though a fresh lot of sand was picked up at once.

Antony Brett-James

The Art of War

It was after we had left the coastal road that Templeton stopped the truck and said, "Now, if you two are going to learn to drive in the desert, you might as well start now. You'll find it's not so easy as you may think. Stannard, you take first crack."

He allowed each of us a turn and, being novices at what we later recognized as something of an art, our efforts were exhausting. It was not so much that we lacked practice in driving, but that with unfailing regularity each of us had managed to pick just those soft patches of sand into which the truck sank axle-deep each time. Then followed the business of digging out the wheels, placing the sand channels and driving forward or backward to the limit of the channels, so that, repeating the process time after time until firm ground was reached again, we could drive on until we struck the next patch of soft sand. It was after yet another of these incidents that Egerton, his normal cheerfulness somewhat subdued, was heard to remark, "If the whole —— desert's like this, it's going to be a bloody long war."

This was almost despair from Egerton, for nothing in our so far brief association had ever seemed to worry him unduly. But we were all feeling tired and irritable by now and were thankful when Templeton decided on a meal halt.

We now made our first attempt at the recognized Desert Army method of a "brew-up" of tea. We cut in half one of the thin sheet-metal four-gallon petrol tins used at that time, punched it with holes and filled it with sand and gravel. We then poured on a generous splash of petrol and set it alight. The tea was brewed in the other half of the tin. When the water was boiling, tea, sugar and milk were all added and the whole potion was vigorously stirred. The resulting brew was strong and sweet, like no other tea that we had tasted before.

Cyril Joly

.

THE ITALIANS ADVANCE

At last, on 13 September, the Italians advanced into

Egypt. It was with a fanfare of triumphant threats that they launched the new campaign.

For three days before the advance actually began the indications had been so clear that we had already started to take the preliminary action before withdrawal. The track down the escarpment at Halfaya Pass had been torn up and mined, as had the coastal track from Sollum to the east. Mines had been sown, too, at various vital places in the desert and the available water supplies had been salted.

The Italians' advance was entirely down "Hellfire" Pass and along the coastal road.

The move down the pass was bombed by the R.A.F., shelled by our artillery and hampered by exploding mines, until such confusion reigned that the Italian troops were forced to dismount from their lorries and scrambled down on foot. The subsequent advance along the coast was preceded, as usual, by motor-cyclists to reconnoitre, supported by groups of tanks to execute the main thrusts and assaults, backed by guns to clear each new objective and disperse opposition, and finally reinforced by the infantry, whose task it was to occupy the ground captured and to repel any counter-attacks.

For four days, from the 13th to the 16th of September, the slow, fumbling, hesitant advance continued until it had reached Sidi Barrani, sixty-five miles from the Italian starting positions. Each small ridge was contested. The Italian columns were bombed by day by the R.A.F. and by night were shelled by the guns, who found it easy to locate and hit the Italian night leaguers, since their positions were given away by searchlights which continually swept the surrounding desert.

At Sidi Barrani the advance halted and, to our surprise and indignation, the Italians started to dig in and prepare defended positions—surprise because till then the Italians had not had to overcome any prepared positions nor had they suffered excessive losses; indignation because a strong counter-thrust had been prepared farther east and the remainder of 7 Armoured Division was lying in wait.

From the beginning of the war in June the Italians had suffered some three thousand five hundred killed and wounded and had lost seven hundred prisoners; many guns, tanks and lorries also had been destroyed. Our losses had been a hundred and fifty men killed, wounded and missing and not more than fifty tanks and lorries destroyed or captured. Despite the disparity in numbers and the distance from the base, we had, for three months, not only contained a vastly superior enemy, but had also made ourselves such masters of the open desert that, even with five divisions, the Italians now felt obliged to bring their ponderous advance to a grinding halt, to secure the sixty-five miles of communications against the mere threat of action which might have cut them off from their base.

Cyril Joly

THE DESERT GALLOP

The Italians remained inactive for nearly three months, a breathing-space which allowed the British forces in Egypt to be built up for a counter-offensive. On 8 December 1940 General O'Connor's assault was launched.

All through the night of Sunday, 8 December, the R.A.F. bombed Sidi Barrani and aerodromes to the west, the Navy bombarded Maktila and the guns of 7 Armoured Division shelled the camps of Nibeiwa and Rabia. Under cover of this noise the final moves to complete the concentration were made. Guided by specially posted marker lights organized by the Support Group, the Matilda tanks and 11 Indian Infantry Brigade moved until they were in position to the west and north-west of Nibeiwa, facing the less heavily defended portion of the perimeter and a gap through which, the previous evening, twenty-three Italian M. 11 light tanks had been seen to move—a reassuring sign that it had not been mined.

Punctually at 07.00 hours the next morning the guns

began to register their targets. At 07.15 the bombardment by about two hundred guns started, and the Matildas and the infantry moved in to attack Nibeiwa.

Meanwhile we in 4 Armoured Brigade had begun our advance to the coastal road some thirty-five miles away. As the sky lightened in the east and the guns started their bombardment, I could not help feeling awed and exhilarated. To my right, as we moved, the desert was bare and deserted, but it was from here that in due course the enemy might attack or the desert might become filled with enemy surprised by our move. However empty and tranquil it looked then, there was the lurking threat of sudden action, and action on a scale that I had not experienced before.

However preoccupied I was with the stark, ominous desert to my right, I could not resist occasionally glancing at the scene on my left. As far as the eye could see, stretching across the horizon to my left front and flank and rear, there were vehicles moving: the tanks of the leading and the other flanking regiment to my front and left, and behind me the other two squadrons of my own regiment. Each tank was followed by a plume of sand, lit and highlighted by the slanting rays of the early sun, as it pitched and rolled and tossed over the uneven, stony surface of the desert. Within the three-sided box formed by the tanks were the supply vehicles, the fitters' lorries, the doctors' trucks, the ambulances. In the centre of the whole array I could see the few vehicles of the Brigade Headquarters. In front of them, and behind the centre of the leading regiment, was the small group of tanks from which I knew the Brigadier was controlling the whole move and ready to give instant orders the moment the enemy was met. The contrast between the scene on my left and that on my right continued to enthral me as we advanced towards the coast.

As the light spread over the sky to the east I felt, rather than heard, the dull concussion of the guns as they fired on Nibeiwa. I could imagine the consternation of the unsuspecting Italians and the confusion which would follow. In my mind's eye I followed the Matildas in their attack.

Cyril Joly

The fall of Sidi Barrani, Sollum, Fort Capuzzo, Bardia, Tobruk and Benghazi were the landmarks in the breathless onset of General O'Connor's mobile forces. At the end of two months, five hundred miles of territory had been won and an enemy army destroyed.

We were all desperately tired, until sometime during the siege of Tobruk, when I, for one, got my second wind. Starting with the sandstorm during the attack on Sidi Barrani, the weather had been persistently bad. High winds had either lashed the desert sand into storms of unusual intensity or had brought torrential downpours of rain, which had swamped the pits we dug for shelter or penetrated the hastily rigged bivouacs and seeped through every crack and crevice in tank or lorry. After the intense heat of the summer I found that I took time to get used to the cold and wet. Nor, to begin with, was I accustomed to the endless lack of sleep and the inadequate food. Eighteen hours of intense watchfulness and alert wakefulness, followed by six hours of so-called rest disturbed by a tour of guard duty and the ceaseless turmoil and noise of the leaguer, for forty days at a stretch—that had been our lot. When, at last, at the end of each day I crept into my blankets to get what sleep I could, I found that my earlier life of ease and luxury made it difficult for me to sleep soundly in these conditions. Either the blankets were wet from the day's heavy rain, or, muffled beneath a ground-sheet as protection against more night rain, the air was too close for comfort; or the ground was hard and pebbly; or it was just too cold for the blankets to afford enough warmth for sound repose. Whatever the reasons, I found that each night it was an effort to sleep.

Cyril Joly

Tobruk: 22 January 1941

The morning after the battle ended, smoke from smouldering dumps and ships still drifted over the town and harbour of Tobruk, though the front had already jumped a hundred miles westward to the heights above Derna. Before continuing their advance the Australian and British troops who had stormed Tobruk could rest, swim and look around. Only a few were supposed to have access to the town, but several hundred spirited themselves inside.

Driving in that morning, we turned up Via Mussolini, already renamed "Pitt Street", and past "Albergo Tobruch", which now bore the sign "Young and Jackson's". Down the road swaggered a party of Diggers, Italian national and regimental pennants flying from their bayonets, gay Fascist badges, cockades and ribbons stuck in their hats or pinned to their jackets. Their pockets bulged with miscellaneous souvenirs—monogrammed ashtrays, and cutlery from "Albergo Tobruch", knick-knacks from officers' house, revolvers, Fascist badges, sashes, swords, whistles and knives from Italian ordnance stores. They reminded me of an incident that occurred earlier in the campaign. A Digger who was escorting some prisoners had acquired an Italian captain's insignia and badges of rank. I asked him how he got them and he said: "I swapped 'em—for a coupla fags; for 'arf a bloody packet, I coulda been a blasted general."

Further down the road I saw some Australians with a pile of Italian paper money and it soon became fashionable to light a cigarette with a fifty or a hundred lire or to post an autographed note back to Australia. Useless in Tobruk, these same notes were real money in Benghazi, as the troops ruefully discovered a few weeks later. Through the streets troops were driving anything that moved; little Fiats, big Lancias, captured motorcycles and Diesel trucks. Some of these and a number of British trucks were drawn up in front of the Italian Navy and Army stores, where there was all the food the troops wanted—and they lost no time in supplementing their rations.

.... Tobruk was stocked with enough tinned food for a garrison of twenty-five thousand for two months—a windfall for our troops who had been existing on little but bully-beef, biscuits, butter, jam and tea. The Italian tinned fruit and vegetables were as good as Australia's best. In one store in Tobruk there were supplies of tinned cherries, strawberries, pears, apricots, beans, peas and carrots, and these were soon being issued along with regular British rations. Most welcome of all were square two-gallon tins of pulped tomatoes and great boxes of spaghetti; but packets of powdered garlic had few takers. Even the cool-store was well stocked with meat, and in one dump there were several hundred tons of flour which went straight to our field bakeries.

Chester Wilmot, war correspondent

Victory

On 7 February 1941 the remains of the Italian army in Cyrenaica were trapped near Beda Fomm, beyond Benghazi, and there they surrendered.

The battlefield was an amazing sight. It was strewn with broken and abandoned equipment, tattered uniforms, piles of empty shell and cartridge cases. It was littered with paper, rifles and bedding. Here and there small groups of men tended the wounded who had been gathered together. Others were collecting and burying the dead. Others still, less eager to surrender than the majority, stood or lay waiting to be captured. Some equipment was still burning furiously, more was smouldering. There were many oil and petrol fires emitting clouds of black smoke.

There were few incidents. Soon the generals and the high-ranking officers had been discovered and taken away. The remaining officers were piled unceremoniously into Italian lorries and driven off. The thousands of men were formed into long columns guarded at head and tail by only one or two of our impassive, imperturbable and perpetually cheerful soldiers, who shouldered the unaccustomed new duties with the same confident assurance with which they had met and mastered all the other trials of the campaign.

It was the work of some days to clear the battlefield of all that was worth salvaging and to muster and despatch on their long march to the prison camps in Egypt the thousands of prisoners. At Benghazi, which had fallen into Australian hands on the same day as the surrender to us farther south, and at Beda Fomm, the Italians had lost some twenty thousand men killed and captured, as well as fifteen hundred lorries, 112 tanks and 216 guns.

                                                                                Cyril Joly

During February, 7 Armoured Division pushed ahead as far as El Agheila, on the borders of Tripolitania, but by now General O'Connor's little army had reached the end of its endurance. The "gallop" was over.

9

GERMANY STRIKES SOUTH

*Even while the Italian Empire crumbled before Wa-
vell's forces, storm-clouds were gathering to the north.
Hitler was preparing to overrun the Balkans, in order to
cover his preparations for an assault on Russia, to
establish himself on the Mediterranean and thus threaten
the Middle East, and incidentally to afford succour to the
battered Italians, who had been faring as badly in their
war with Greece as elsewhere. The victorious British
forces in Africa were hurriedly depleted so as to allow aid
to be sent to Greece. However ill-fated this was, Germany's intervention in Greece led to a delay which was to
prove fatal to Hitler's designs on Russia.*

THE GREEK ADVENTURE

THE more we examined the problem, the more unsound
the venture appeared. There were so many uncertain
quantities. What would Turkey do? Would Jugoslavia
resist an Axis move through her country? Would Germany
attack Turkey before Greece? The answer to any of these
questions would have a decided influence upon our plans.
One thing was quite certain, and that was if Germany
decided to attack Greece it would be in full strength, and
by all practicable routes.

In February, 1941, a very high-powered party arrived
in Cairo. There were Eden (then Secretary of State for
War), Dill (Chief of the Imperial General Staff), and
their advisers. Discussions took place behind closed doors

and we on the lower levels were all agog to know what
was happening, and what decisions were being made. As
far as I can remember the Planners were not asked to produce a paper giving their views as to the feasibility of the
project. We certainly held some very decided ones.

The D.M.I., Brigadier Shearer, did produce a paper
drawing attention to the great dangers of this campaign in
view of the German resources and methods. I remember
this paper coming back from the C.-in-C., General Wavell.
There was a short note written in his own hand across the
top—it said:

" 'War is an option of difficulties.'—Wolfe, A.P.W."

Major-General Sir Francis de Guingand

Winston Churchill to General Smuts: 28 February

We have taken a grave and hazardous decision to sustain the Greeks and try to make a Balkan Front.

Landing in Greece: March

Because of a bad bloomer on someone's part, we were
issued with tropical kit of "Bombay bloomers" (those
frightful turned-up shorts), "Bombay bowlers" (pith helmets) and shirts. As practical kit for crossing the Med.
and fighting in a Greek spring, the clothing was just fantastic, and the "bowler" an unmitigated bloody nuisance. I
threw mine into a snowdrift on Mount Olympus. Despite
instructions to hand in battle-dress, all Kiwis wore it,
packing the tropical gear, except the helmet. Only place
for the confounded thing was on the head—hence the extraordinary spectacle of British and New Zealand troops
disembarking at Piraeus in battle-dress and pith helmets.
That must have shaken the German Embassy, as they
watched us pass.

Another point worth mentioning is the secrecy of our
move to Greece. Officially, the verdict is that the destination was not known to the bulk of the troops. My im-

pression is rather different. Anyone who was interested knew perfectly well, including the enemy! There were Gyppo and other money changers at most dock gates, and in Amiriya, peddling drachmae notes: "Very good money —veree cheap! You need, Kiwi—in Athens!"

Brigadier George Clifton

We landed at the Piraeus and for a few days camped in the pines on Mount Hymettos, on the outskirts of Athens. Our camp was inspected by some smart-looking Evzones, the German Consul, and a number of half-starved citizens. The 18th Battalion, the first to land, had already gone forward. It was impossible to do any serious training, and we waited impatiently. At last orders arrived for us to entrain and also for me to leave six out of my forty officers and forty-six of my 813 other ranks. This meant more painful selections and I had to withstand some most urgent protests. But I was determined to have good people in the reinforcements and made no concessions, promising them all plenty of fighting in the good time to come. After a church parade I told the battalion what I could remember about Greece and what it stood for, and we marched through Athens past the crowded balcony of the German Embassy and entrained for the front, now being built up north of Mount Olympus.

Brigadier Kippenberger

Retreat—Break-up

The British forces, consisting of the New Zealand Division, 6 Australian Division and 1 Armoured Brigade, were to help seven weak Greek divisions to hold the Aliakhmon line, which ran across northern Greece from the Jugoslav frontier on the west to the Aegean on the east. In Bulgaria the Germans had massed fifteen divisions and ten times the Allies' strength in aircraft for their assault, which could fall on both Greece and Jugoslavia.

Two days after the Germans attacked on 6 April the Jugoslav armies crumbled, leaving the western flank of the

Aliakhmon line completely exposed, and five days later the withdrawal from this position began. As the Germans poured down into Greece the Greek forces disintegrated, rendering the British plan of making a stand at Thermopylae impracticable. Evacuation was then the only course left open to the British troops.

Germany declared war on Greece,* and to our surprise we still made no move forward. Across the bay one evening we heard the faint rolling thunder of distant bombing and saw the dull glow of fires in Salonika. It could not be long now.

Next day there was rain. About four in the afternoon I was ordered to report to Brigade Headquaters. On the way down I saw the 6th Field Regiment hauling and winding and manhandling its guns out of their muddy pits on to the equally muddy road. Obviously we were going forward. The Brigadier, to my extreme surprise, said that we were giving up the Aliakhmon position, 6 Brigade going back behind 5 Brigade somewhere, 4 Brigade to move through the Olympus pass and up to Servia to cover the left of the army. There had been disaster in Jugoslavia and the position might become serious.

Brigadier Kippenberger

We had been preparing a defensive position in support of the Rangers, the motor battalion of 1 Armoured Brigade, to meet the expected German attack from Bulgaria to our north-east. As usual our gunpits were to be wasted. For on the evening of 8 April came a message that the Germans had smashed their way across southern Jugoslavia and were pushing south through the Florina Gap behind us, threatening to cut us off. Our orders were to move at once forty miles west into the mountains and join the rest of 1 Armoured Brigade on a line south of Florina. The position of the Germans was unknown and there were rumours that they had already cut our route at

* 6 April (Ed.)

the road junction of Veve. If so, our prospects would not be cheerful.

It was a long, cold, wet drive. As we passed through the villages in the dark, Greek soldiers and civilians came out to cheer us, thinking that we were on our way north to attack the enemy. Little did they know that the retreat had already begun. Their enthusiasm brought back memories of the "triumphant" march into Belgium in May 1940, and we hoped that this time there would be a less dismal ending. We reached Veve about 1 a.m. As we wound down into the village we could see a long line of pinpricks of light moving slowly along the road from Florina. Luckily for us we soon discovered that it was not the enemy, but a column of mules and bullock-carts of the Greek and Jugoslav armies, mixed up with civilian refugees. A few minutes later we were hailed out of the darkness by a cheery Aussie voice and we knew that the Australians had arrived from the south and we were not cut off.

. . . . We moved back thirty-five miles, across the Aliakhmon river, leaving a small brigade rearguard to follow us later. There had been much talk of the Aliakhmon as the main line of defence in Greece. When we crossed the river in bright moonlight and saw not a sign of troops, not even a list trench dug, we realized that our retreat was very far from going according to plan. We were on the extreme left of the Imperial forces in Greece. The only Greek troops we saw were by now thoroughly disorganized, for with horsed transport they hadn't a chance of getting away. Next day we spent lying up just north of Grevena. The scrub-covered valleys offered little concealment and the first morning flight of Messerschmitts spotted us.

That evening we got orders for a further fifteen-mile retreat to a position behind the river Venetikos. A message from our C.O., Lieutenant-Colonel Aikenhead, prepared us for the worst: "You will hold your positions at all costs till the flanks are turned, when you will extricate your troops as best you can and, unless other or-

ders are received, move to rejoin the British troops in
Greece, in a south-easterly direction. I am confident that
the Regiment will continue to give a fine account of itself.
. . . Good luck." Much later we were to hear that G.H.Q.
had given the Brigade up for lost and never expected us to
emerge from the mountains.

After dark we started on a nightmare drive. Grevena
was full of burning dumps and lorries and houses, bewildered Greek troops and confused columns of mules and
bullock carts. The road on to the Venetikos was narrow
and twisting, sometimes with steep ravines or precipices
on both sides. We were a mixed cavalcade. Vehicles were
jammed nose to tail for miles, double- and even treble-
banked wherever the road was wide enough. Buses and
private cars, Greeks on horseback and foot, were all
jumbled in between our guns. Halts were interminable and
we crawled forward a few hundred yards at a time. Weary
drivers fell asleep in their cabs and had to be roused by
cursing officers and N.C.Os. Our route was strewn with all
the litter of a retreat: discarded clothing, ammunition and
harness, dead mules and horses, sodden papers and office
files, and dozens of abandoned vehicles—ramshackle req-
uisitioned lorries from every province of Greece, British
three-tonners side by side with Italian tractors and mobile
workshops captured by the Greek Army in Albania and
now waiting for their original owners; some bogged down
in the ditches, some tipped at crazy angles into bomb
craters, others burnt out or shattered by machine-gun
bullets. All the time dawn was getting nearer and we could
look forward to being caught by the first air sortie like rats
in a trap, unable to disperse off the narrow road. But at
first light the miracle occurred and the column began to
move. As we twisted down into the Venetikos valley, a
single Messerschmitt flew along the bottom of the gorge
below us. But we were safely in action across the river and
well camouflaged before the first air attacks began. It had
taken us twelve hours to cover fifteen miles.

We never fired a round on the Venetikos, for the enemy

found more to interest him in our flanks and was slow to follow down our road. But the Luftwaffe showed no lack of interest in us, treating us every few hours to a display of machine-gunning and dive-bombing which brought home to us as never before what monopoly of the air meant. Our guns were well off the road and were not attacked, but our B Echelons had a grim day. On the 16th we woke to grey skies and clouds low down over the hills. The rain saved us, and for thirty-six hours we didn't see a single enemy plane. But our road became a morass of potholes, mud and slime. About 3 p.m. we were on the move southwards again, wondering whether we would get through. The track was a new one, unmarked on our maps, and it was not certain whether it had ever been completed. There were also rumours that the Germans had cut it a few miles ahead. Working parties travelling in front of each unit performed wonders. They felled pine-trees to fill the axle-deep ruts, put down wire-netting, filled in craters and pushed crocks and abandoned lorries off the road. The rain poured steadily down. But we met no Germans and our skid chains got us through. Next day the pace quickened, and at midday on the 17th we emerged from the misty, wooded mountains and reached the plains, sunshine and a metalled road. We had regained contact with the main Imperial forces—and simultaneously with the Luftwaffe.

Major C. I. W. Seton-Watson

When to "blow" and who orders the engineer firer to press his exploder handle are two problems which have given many soldiers and staff officers headaches in many wars. Coming back down Greece, whenever New Zealanders tailed the withdrawal, a squadron of the Divisional Cavalry were last men out. They had a Demolition Officer, who stood by each successive firing party, tallied his squadron past like sheep through a drafting race, and when either the last vehicle or the first enemy appeared said, "O.K. Let her go!" And she went. Simple but most

effective. My engineers blew up ninety-five bits and pieces
of Greece and we only slipped once.

                                                Brigadier Clifton

My idea was the obvious one: to travel south during the
day, cross the road down which the German army would
be pouring by night, and then head east for the coast. First
we must get some food and perhaps help from the
villagers, and so two of the party set off for a village near
by. We were out of sight of the road and all the countryside was bright and silent. Before they had gone out of
earshot we heard, startlingly, the thudding of guns far to
the south. I jumped up. "That's our rearguard at Elassona;
they are certain to have orders to stay till night," I said.
And at once we all started southwards as fast as we could
walk.

For an hour we plodded on. Small groups of peasants
were tramping towards high hills to the west and we
passed a few shepherds with little flocks. We said
"Elassona?" to one, and he pointed the way we were
going. The thudding and rumble of guns continued, almost
seemed a little nearer, and we began to have hope. I called
a halt and said that we would observe the regulation ten
minutes' halt before every clock hour, and otherwise
would walk on all day; that we had a chance, just a
chance. We were very weary and hungry, the ground was
rough and tumbled; but we trudged on hour after hour,
crossing little streams, scrambling through scrub, literally
over hill and dale. Soon after midday we came in sight of
the road again, packed solid with German transport, head
to tail, tanks and guns, lorry-loads of infantry, all halted,
with the men strolling about. We turned out of sight,
crossed a difficult ravine very slowly, and started to
climb up a steep valley leading to the crest of a distinct
line of low hills. The guns were undoubtedly nearer,
though muffled by the hills, and I thought I could distinguish the nearer crumps of shell-bursts. The valley was
steep and we were desperately tired, but we were hopeful
now and somehow kept going.

From there on we alternated formations, moving as a clump when the ground concealed us from the Germans and we could be seen by our own gunners, extending to forty paces when the Germans could see us, and moving in bounds from one piece of cover to the next. It was a slow business; we were all tired out and starving, the day was hot, and at each halt half the party would fall asleep and have to be kicked awake for the next bound. The ground was covered with spring flowers and the birds were singing. Evidently we puzzled the gunners of both sides, for sometimes we would make our move in peace, the next time be fired on, and once both parties joined in to fire on us.

Brigadier Kippenberger

Then came three busy days under command of the New Zealand Division at Molos, on the east coast near Thermopylae. On the third day the enemy pressure was becoming formidable and the shelling and dive-bombing were the most intense of the whole campaign. But the New Zealanders held them and the final withdrawal went magnificently according to plan. At 11 p.m. on the 24th we fired off our last rounds with buffers and recuperators drained, left our wrecked guns in their pits and started south for the last time. Next day when we drove through Athens the Greeks lined the streets in thousands, many of them in tears, yet cheering and throwing flowers and shouting, "You will be back; we'll be waiting for you." Few retreating armies can have had such a send-off.

Major C. I. W. Seton-Watson

Evacuation: 21-29 April

Anzac Corps allotted 6 Australian Division the honour of following Leonidas and his Spartans in holding the famous Pass of Thermopylae where the main bitumen road zigzagged up nearly three thousand feet of mountain wall. The New Zealanders were spread out for probably ten miles along the coastal sector among the pines, olive groves, and occasional villages fringed by small bays and lovely blue sea. Across a narrow inlet were more hills, and the road winding round from Volos down which some of us had withdrawn. Easy enough to cross by boat, as many of our stragglers did—and as the Boche could do too, if he was so minded. So part of the plot involved coast watchers and even sea patrols in borrowed power-craft. For nearly forty-eight hours everyone worked hell for leather on defences, which the first orders from Force H.Q. decreed would be held for at least one month. Then sometime on 21 April, the unfortunate Greeks finally gave up the unequal struggle and surrendered,* but insisted on two days' grace for the British forces to leave their beautiful country! Easy enough to plan but not so easy to execute. My diary speaks for everyone—"22 Apr.—Called to Div. Conference about 11 hrs. regarding plot for withdrawal and embarkation. Move by night by brigades. Lie up by day. Embark by night. All nicely worked out by Anzac Corps. Only disturbing factors are enemy and Force H.Q. who will change scheme for certain. Found Kiwis providing rear-guard, and as demolitions were the vital factor asked for command and got it—to my astonishment. Wrote my first complete Engineer Order to take Companies out; saw them all and said good-bye. Then started on my first fighting job."

Brigadier Clifton

The Peloponnese

. . . . As the light went, the Sunderland crept round the far headland at nought feet to make a perfect landing, perfectly timed. Then a motley collection from Generals to batmen spilled out of various vehicles on to the jetty and prepared to depart. Limited to one suitcase each, great men, accustomed to settle the lives and destinies of thousands by quick snappy decisions, rummaged over masses of kit, trying to decide what should be jettisoned. Having

* Actually 24 April (Ed.)

already taken similar action back at Thermopylae, we stood round sardonic-like and vulturish, waiting for the pickings. A pathetic sight. They took so long and fussed so much that finally the skipper of the Sunderland climbed on to a bollard and roared out: "Gentlemen! If you don't make up your bloody minds and get aboard the tender, I'm leaving in ten minutes time, otherwise we'll be shot down in daylight to-morrow morning. For God's sake, make it snappy." Nobody arrested him and they made it very snappy. Within five minutes sixty of them were aboard and away. Not many minutes later we had transferred our gear into a sleek Humber Pullman and gladly jettisoned an historic, battered Utility, veteran of two campaigns. The transfer included four tins of an excellent brand of smoking mixture and two boxes of good cigars which the late, unknown owner had left behind, doubtless with regret.

Brigadier Clifton

By 2 May a total of 43,000 Imperial troops had been evacuated, many of them going to Crete, where on 5 May Major-General Freyberg, the most famous of all New Zealand soldiers, took up his appointment as Commander-in-Chief. Eleven thousand men together with the whole of the army's matériel remained on Greek soil.

CRETE

For about a fortnight there was an uneasy lull.

It was the end of April 1941, in Germany.
A bright spring day dawned over the moorland, and across the broad tracts of the artillery range the young grass sparkled in the morning dew. It felt like the first Sunday after the creation of the world: everything was new and clean and good. A group of young soldiers had fallen in, the early sunlight glinting on their fresh faces. They were wearing the rimless helmets and copious, ap-

parently ill-fitting jumping suits of German parachutists, and their variegated apparel—a mixture of green, grey, brown, and black patches—gave them the appearance of harlequins.

In my capacity of commander of the 1st Battalion of the 3rd Parachute Regiment, it was my duty, on that beautiful spring morning, to decorate each of the twelve young men in the group with a parachutist's badge, for they had just completed their jumping course.

. . . . The small black cases, in which the gilt bronze badges depicting a plunging eagle in an oval garland of oak and laurel leaves lay upon dark blue velvet, were handed to me one by one by my adjutant (who happened to have been a student of theology in civilian life). When I had affixed the last badge, it was up to me to say a few words to the men. I spoke of the obligations which the wearing of this decoration entailed. "Our formation is young. We have not yet any traditions. We must create tradition by our actions in the future. It depends upon us whether or not the sign of the plunging eagle—the badge which unites us—will go down in history as a symbol of military honour and valour."

Baron von der Heydte, O.C. 1st Battalion, 3rd Parachute Regiment

Winston Churchill to General Wavell: 28 April

It seems clear from our information that a heavy airborne attack by German troops and bombers will soon be made on Crete. Let me know what forces you have in the island and what your plans are. It ought to be a fine opportunity for killing the parachute troops. The island must be stubbornly defended.

General Freyberg to General Wavell: 1 May

Forces at my disposal are totally inadequate to meet attack envisaged. Unless fighter aircraft are greatly increased and naval forces made available to deal with sea-

orne attack I cannot hope to hold out with land forces
alone, which as result of campaign in Greece are now de-
void of any artillery, have insufficient tools for digging,
very little transport, and inadequate war reserves of equipment and ammunition. Force here can and will fight, but
without full support from Navy and Air Force cannot
hope to repel invasion. If for other reasons these cannot
be made available at once, urge that question of holding
Crete should be reconsidered.

Plans for Invasion

One look at the hermetically-sealed and shuttered room
in the Hotel Grande Bretagne,* where the commanders of
all the paratroop regiments and battalions were gathered
to receive their orders, was sufficient to dispel the secret
of our target: a large map of Crete was prominently
displayed upon the wall.

In a quiet but clear and slightly vibrant voice, General
Student explained the plan of attack. It was his own, personal plan. He had devised it, had struggled against heavy
opposition for its acceptance, and had worked out all the
details. One could perceive that this plan had become a
part of him, a part of his life. He believed in it and lived
for it and in it.

. . . . When the General had finished, the corps intelligence officer rose to speak. He sketched a broad picture
of the enemy's situation. On the island were the remnants of two or three Greek divisions, much weakened by
the battles on the mainland, and a British force of divisional strength consisting mainly of Dominion troops
under command of the well-known General Freyberg. A
portion of the population would be sympathetic towards a
German attack. There was also on the island a secret
resistance group which would be prepared to fight
alongside the Germans and would make itself known to us
by the code-words *"Major Bock"*.

* In Athens (Ed.)

Next, the quartermaster dealt with the question of supplies, the medical officer with that of hospital arrangements, the commander of the air-transport fleet with matters relating to the air sortie, an admiral with nautical plans, and finally, when it came to the turn of unit commanders to ask questions, there were still some whose egos would not permit them to lose the opportunity of posing questions either which they could well have answered themselves or to which no one could provide any answers at all.

It was already afternoon when the conference came to an end. Before we dispersed, our regimental commander called his three battalion commanders together and ordered us to visit his headquarters in the early evening to receive his operational instructions. Only a short time was left to us in which to snatch a hasty luncheon before returning to our troops. And I was in Athens, no more than a few hundred yards from the foot of the Acropolis. . . . But there was no time for that sort of enjoyment. I felt like a child at the open door of a room full of toys and not being allowed to enter.

Baron von der Heydte

General Freyberg to General Wavell: 16 May

Have completed plan for defence of Crete and have just returned from final tour of defences. I feel greatly encouraged by my visit. Everywhere all ranks are fit and morale is high. All defences have been extended, and positions wired as much as possible. We have forty-five field guns placed, with adequate ammunition dumped. Two infantry tanks are at each aerodrome. Carriers and transport still being unloaded and delivered. 2nd Leicesters have arrived, and will make Heraklion stronger. I do not wish to be overconfident, but I feel that at least we will give excellent account of ourselves. With help of Royal Navy I trust Crete will be held.

20 May

As it grew dark we were transported in lorries to the
airfield, where we were greeted by the ear-splitting roar of
a hundred and twenty air-transports as they tested their
engines in preparation for the take-off. Through clouds of
dust we could see red glowing sparks flaring from the ex-
hausts of the machines, and only by this light was it possible to discern the silhouettes of our men. Flashing the
pale green beams of their torches in order to indicate
their whereabouts, the hundred and twenty officers and
N.C.O.s of my battalion tried their best to make themselves heard above the thundering of the engines. The picture reminded me of glow-worms in August.

During the hours which precede a sortie everything
seems to become bewitched. Arms containers being
hoisted into the racks spill open, aircraft are not where
they should be, and the most important machine is liable,
for some reason or another, to pack up. But the most extraordinary thing is that despite these numerous hitches the
take-off invariably seems to proceed satisfactorily.

Later:

I was roused by my adjutant and started awake, still
drowsy, to hear a roar of engines growing louder and
louder, as if coming from a great distance. It took me a
moment or two to remember where I was and what lay
before me.

"We are nearing Crete, sir."

I got up and moved towards the open door, beside
which the dispatcher whose duty it was to see that all final
preparations for the jump were ready was seated. Our
plane was poised steady in the air, almost as though motionless. Looking out, beyond the silver-grey wing with its
black cross marking, I could see our target—still small,
like a cliff rising out of the glittering sea to meet us—the
island of Crete.

Slowly, infinitely slowly, like the last drops wrung from
a drying well, the minutes passed. Again and again I

glanced stealthily at my wristwatch. There is nothing so
awful, so exhausting, as this waiting for the moment of a
jump. In vain I tried to compel myself to be calm and pa-
tient. A strange unrest had also gripped most of those who
were flying with me.

. . . . Scarcely able to bear it any longer, I stepped once
again to the open door. We were just flying over the
beaches. The thin strip of surf which looked from above
like a glinting white ribbon, separated the blue waters from
the yellow-green of the shore. The mountains reared up
before us, and the planes approaching them looked like
giant birds trying to reach their eyries in the rocks.

We were still flying inland as if to run against a dark
mountainside. It seemed almost as though we could touch
the steep slopes upon which trees and solitary buildings
appeared like toys. Then our left wing dipped and we
swung away from the mountain and the plane started to
circle; but soon we straightened out again, and at that moment there came the pilot's order, "Prepare to jump!"

Everyone rose and started to fasten his hook to the
static line which ran down the centre of the body of the
plane. And while we stood there, securing our hooks, we
noticed that we were losing height, and the pressure of air
became hard, almost painful, to the ear.

Next came the order, "Ready to jump!"

In two strides I was at the door, my men pressing close
behind me, and grasped the supports on either side of it.
The slipstream clutched at my cheeks, and I felt as though
they were fluttering like small flags in the wind.

Suddenly, a lot of little white clouds appeared from
nowhere and stood poised in the air about us. They looked
harmless enough, like puffs of cotton-wool, for the roar of
the plane's engines had drowned the sound of the ack-ack
shells' detonation.

Below me was the village of Alikianou. I could see
people in the streets staring up at us, others running away
and disappearing into doorways. The shadows of our
planes swept like ghostly hands over the sun-drenched

white houses, while behind the village there gleamed a large mirror—the reservoir—with single coloured parachutes, like autumn leaves, drifting down towards it.

Our plane slowed down. The moment had come.

"Go!"

I pushed with hands and feet, throwing my arms forward as if trying to clutch the black cross on the wing. And then the slipstream caught me, and I was swirling through space with the air roaring in my ears. A sudden jerk upon the webbing, a pressure on the chest which knocked the breath out of my lungs, and then—I looked upwards and saw, spread above me, the wide-open, motley hood of my parachute. In relation to this giant umbrella I felt small and insignificant.

Baron von der Heydte

The morning of 20 May was calm and cloudless, as was every day during the battle. Before the sunlight had reached the valleys the German reconnaissance plane appeared. Shortly afterwards a fighter arrived and started to roar up and down the main street of Galatos firing bursts at anything it could see. This struck me as a bit unusual so I hurriedly finished shaving and looked with some caution out of my first-floor window. Other fighters were swooping over the Canea road and there was a great deal of noise from aeroplane engines. Nothing appeared imminent, however, so I finished dressing and went down for breakfast under the trees outside. The plane was still tearing up and down the street and maybe the cooks were busied, for the porridge was mere oatmeal and water. I was grumbling about this when someone gave an exclamation that might have been an oath or a prayer or both. Almost over our heads were four gliders, the first we had ever seen, in their silence inexpressibly menacing and frightening. Northwards was a growing thunder. I shouted, "Stand to your arms!", and ran upstairs for my rifle and binoculars. I noticed my diary lying open on the table. Four years later it was returned to me, having meanwhile been concealed by some Cretan girl.

When I reached the courtyard again the thunder had become deafening, the troop-carriers were passing low overhead in every direction one looked, not more than four hundred feet up, in scores. As I ran down the Prison road to my battle headquarters the parachutists were dropping out over the valley, hundreds of them, and floating quietly down.

                                         Brigadier Kippenberger

More like a tramp than a soldier at war I walked along the road towards the white wall before me. And now, as the last of the aircraft turned north towards base, the sound of engines grew fainter and fainter, more and more distant. Somewhere on the high ground ahead of me, to the left of the road, where the village of Galatos was situated, a machine-gun started stuttering. Another answered, followed by rifle-shots. Part of the 2nd Battalion must have contacted the enemy. I registered this fact appreciatively, yet practically without concern, for I was not responsible for what happened over there. Then suddenly, from the mountains behind me, there came a screech of engines—not the ponderous roar of a transport plane, but a sound more like a siren—followed by a fierce crackle of machine-gun fire. Automatically I hurled myself into the ditch—a deep, concrete ditch bordering a large field of corn—and at that moment a German fighter with all guns blazing swept over within a few feet of where I lay. A stream of bullets threw up fountains of dust on the road, and ricochets sang away into the distance. Then as suddenly as it had appeared, the apparition passed. The fighter pulled up high and disappeared over the olive groves in the direction of what I took to be Canea. So the first shots to be aimed at me during this attack had been fired by one of my own countrymen! No one could have thought of laying out identification signals so soon after landing, and the fighter-pilot, whose task it was to support our attack, had obviously never imagined that this lackadaisical figure wandering in such unmilitary fashion down the centre of the road could possibly have been the commanding officer of a German battalion. . . .

Baron von der Heydte

General Freyberg to General Wavell: 10 p.m., 20 May

To-day has been a hard one. We have been hard pressed. So far, I believe, we hold aerodromes at Retimo, Heraklion, and Maleme, and the two harbours. Margin by which we hold them is a bare one, and it would be wrong of me to paint optimistic picture. Fighting has been heavy and we have killed large numbers of Germans. Communications are most difficult. Scale of air attacks upon Canea has been severe. Everybody here realizes vital issue and we will fight it out.

The Battle

The third day dawned—Thursday, 22 May 1941. In the early morning I went once again with Willi Riese to visit the positions. Nothing had changed during the past twenty-four hours. The ammunition and food situation had not improved. What little ammunition we had received during the previous day had already been used up, and food was virtually unobtainable. According to plan, each company had started to explore the backward areas for supplies. In the abandoned British and Greek positions one would find a tin here, a packet of cigarettes there, and in some deserted farmhouse there might be bread and cheese; but there was nothing like enough to go round. The soldiers were hungry, and in the awful monotony of waiting their morale sank. They tried to make themselves more comfortable by utilizing the paraphernalia which they had found in the abandoned enemy positions. One of the men in 3 Company discovered a most welcome piece of loot in a deserted British dug-out: a gramophone and several records. A sound of dance music was consequently to be heard all day long in the region of "Little Castle Hill", where 3

Company was in position, and the men took an especial
delight in playing English numbers whenever the enemy
artillery opened up. A barrage would usually last for
about the same length of time as it took to play a record;
but once, when the firing continued rather longer, one of
the men shouted over the parapet, "Wait a moment while
I change the record!"

Baron von der Heydte

During the day the valley would ring to the volleys of rifle and machine-gun fire sent hurtling across it by both
sides, but after darkness set in shooting ceased; for, by a
tacit and mute understanding, no firing took place at
night; it would have inconvenienced both sides equally.
For this was the time when whatever had to be done was
done, when the casualties were evacuated, the dead were
buried, the rations and ammunition distributed, and the
men were able to walk and stretch their legs.

Before dawn we would all be back in our trenches, the
hum of aeroplanes would fill the sky, and so would start
another day.

After breakfast there was nothing to do except go to
sleep, or try to, all except one who acted as sentry. But it
was not usually long before someone would cock an ear
and exclaim, "Listen! Here they come!" Whereupon we
would scramble to our feet and gaze out towards the sea
near the promontory a mile or two up the coast. Then the
faintly audible drone that we knew so well came floating
towards us from over the sea, followed by the dark shapes
of troop transports flying in low over the water. Punctually at nine o'clock every morning the armada arrived.

At the end of each day, when I visited the posts and
talked with the soldiers, it was always the same question
they asked me: how was the battle going, and what was
the news? Their high spirits had been replaced by a grim
determination; for they were now playing that hardest of
all games—namely, sitting tight, under orders to defend
their positions to the last man, and with no prospect of
relief.

And so the cycle of days continued. Relief was out of the question: there was no one to relieve us. Not a man had taken off his boots during this past week, or had been able to have a proper wash; but fortunately the nights had been cool, thus preventing bodies from attaining that unhygienic state they would have done in a hotter climate.

British infantry officer

About four o'clock a dozen Stukas dive-bombed Galatos. We had no anti-aircraft defences and they must have enjoyed it. My headquarters had one or two very near misses. At this stage I was standing on a table looking through a window that gave a view over the line from the village to the sea, and every few minutes I had to stand aside to avoid being seen by one of the planes continuously cruising over the tree-tops shooting at everything in sight. Fountaine, O'Callaghan and Carson were with me, waiting the order to counter-attack. Carson's batman kept us all going with cups of tea.

Immediately after the bombing the main infantry attack started against the 18th, and the crackle of musketry swelled to a roar, heavily punctuated by mortar bursts. Inglis rang and asked what all the noise was about and I could only say that things were getting warm. I estimated the mortar bursts at six a minute on one company sector alone. "Overs" from the German machine-guns were crackling all round our building in the most alarming manner. The telephone system had been almost destroyed by the bombing; the line to Brigade now went out and, though the linesmen worked gallantly, was never restored. I went a few hundred yards forward to get a view of Wheat Hill, and for a few minutes watched, fascinated, the rain of mortar bursts. In a hollow, nearly covered by undergrowth, I came on a party of women and children huddled together like little birds. They looked at me silently, with black, terrified eyes.

Brigadier Kippenberger

Suddenly—almost frighteningly, like a rifle-shot—there sounded from the bushes all around us a loud, joyous tremolo. The birds were greeting the dawn. From every side there came an answer, and the air was filled with the echo of their song. Lucky creatures, I thought, they did not know about the murder in their midst. Their polyphonic concert was almost painful with its cruel sweetness, for the contrast between the carefree singing and all the inhuman and terrible things which we had experienced, and which still lay before us, was almost too much to bear. And then the bird-song stopped almost as suddenly as it had started, and the dawn of the new day broke in eerie silence. Only the recollection of the choral greeting still hung in the air, just as alien as, but not less real than, the stench of decomposing bodies.

And now it was day—Monday, 26 May 1941. Since early morning the sounds of heavy fighting on the heights of Galatos had indicated that our alpine troops had renewed their assault on the positions of the New Zealanders.

Baron von der Heydte

General Freyberg to General Wavell: 26 May

I regret to have to report that in my opinion the limit of endurance has been reached by the troops under my command here at Suda Bay. No matter what decision is taken by the Commanders-in-Chief from a military point of view, our position here is hopeless. A small, ill-equipped and immobile force such as ours cannot stand up against the concentrated bombing that we have been faced with during the last seven days. I feel I should tell you that from an administrative point of view the difficulties of extricating this force in full are insuperable. Provided a decision is reached at once, a certain proportion of the force might be embarked.

The End

It was one of the strangest quirks of fortune of the war that on the very day that the British decided that they must evacuate Crete, General Student, his men exhausted and with little ammunition, saw his dive-bombers taken from him for use in another theatre. His assault on Canea on 27 May was his last despairing throw, but it was enough.

The Victors

The garden suburb of Chaleppas on the coast was reported by our scouts to have escaped the bombardment, so my adjutant sensibly suggested that we should transfer our headquarters there.

"The battle for Canea is over, sir," he said. "The fight for comfortable billets has now begun."

I agreed to his proposal, and selected as my headquarters a small villa of the coast near the building which, until now, had housed the British Consulate. The villa, like most of the other houses in the district, had been evacuated. It had a pleasant terrace and a well in the garden from which we were able to draw delicious cold water. Since we had nothing better to do for the moment I suggested to my staff that we should take advantage of the lull to have a bathe. We undressed and started splashing each other like fifteen-year-olds, and it was while we were thus disporting ourselves that a British soldier suddenly appeared at the garden gate. The villa had apparently been used as a British headquarters, and I suppose the soldier, in his ignorance, had arrived with a message for the staff. I do not know who was the more astonished, he or ourselves, but in any event he realized his mistake more quickly than we and hastily beat a retreat.

He was the last British soldier I saw in the battle for Canea.

General Student visited us almost immediately after the fall of Canea. Had fourteen days really elapsed since I had

last seen him issuing orders in Athens? He had visibly altered. He seemed much graver, more reserved, and older.
There was no evidence in his features that he was joyful
over the victory—his victory—and proud at the success of
his daring scheme. The cost of victory had evidently
proved too much for him. Some of the battalions had lost
all their officers, and in several companies there were only
a few men left alive.

. . . . The battle for Crete was to prove the overture to
the great tragedy which reached its climax at El Alamein
and Stalingrad. For the first time there had stood against
us a brave and relentless opponent on a battleground
which favoured him. On this occasion things had gone well
with us, but it seemed almost a miracle that our great and
hazardous enterprise had succeeded. How it did, I cannot
say to this day. Success had suddenly come to us at a moment when, as so often happens in war, we had ceased to
believe in the possibility of success.

My interview with General Student was brief and to the
point. In answer to his questions I concisely reported our
experiences in the attack and told him of our losses. When
I had finished he grasped me firmly by the hand and held
it for a long time.

"I thank you," was all he said; but the grasp of his hand
and those three short words were quite sufficient for me.

Once the action was over, one of our primary tasks was
to collect and bury our dead. I ordered that a common
cemetery should be made on the road from Alikianou to
Canea, near the spot where my first company had been
held up, for the dead of both my own battalion and the
British and Greek troops who had opposed us. At the entrance to the cemetery we erected a large cross. On one
side of its pedestal was the following inscription:

In these olive groves and on the heights of Perivolia
these men of the 1st Battalion of the 3rd Regiment fought, and won and died.

On tablets to the left and right of this inscription the
names of our dead were engraved, while the reverse side
of the pedestal carried an inscription as follows:

In valiant combat against the Battalion one hundred and fifty-six members of the following British regiments died for their King and Country.

Beneath were inscribed the names of the units to which the British troops who had fought against us had belonged.

Once the bodies of the dead had been retrieved and the cemetery been completed, I invited the British officers who had fought in our sector and been taken prisoner to attend the consecration of the memorial.

The survivors of my battalion paraded at the cemetery. I spoke first to them in German, then added a few words in English. The senior British officer replied. And at that moment we did not consider ourselves enemies, but friends who had been defeated by the same harsh fate.

. . . . During that very same evening the sentry at my headquarters reported that a young Greek lady had arrived and wished to speak to me. Automatically I thought of Ariadne; but this young woman did not bear a sword. She had brought a large bunch of white flowers which she asked me to lay on the graves of the German, British and Greek soldiers who had been buried in the cemetery.

Baron von der Heydte

Evacuation Again.

The companies made their selections and Jim Burrows started to organize his rear-party and to take over water and food from those who were to go. Fountaine's company came back, very hot and tired. When they were collected, Fountaine told them how many were to stay and asked for volunteers. There was a gasp and then Grooby, the C.S.M., stepped forward. He was followed at once by Fraser, the C.Q.M.S., and by Kirk and Vincent, the two sergeants, and then the remaining forty men. The N.C.Os insisted on staying, and after much argument lots had to be drawn for the men.

The afternoon wore miserably on, but at last there was nothing for it but to say good-bye and go. I spoke as reassuringly as I could to the rear-party, shook hands with Jim, and went off very sadly.

We had a tramp of some miles to the beach, the last part lined with men who had lost their units and were hoping for a place with us. Some begged and implored, most simply watched stonily, so that we felt bitterly ashamed. There was a cordon round the beach with orders to shoot any man who tried to break in. I had to count my men through. We were the last unit to pass, and on the principle that there is always room for one more, I bullied the cordon officer into letting me take Frank Davis, with some of Divisional Headquarters as well. I had Brian Basset with me, and just before embarking found that John Russell was in an A.D.S. on the beach and insisted on taking him also.

We embarked on the Australian destroyer *Napier* and were at once led to great piles of bread and butter, jugs of cold water, and urns of coffee. We ate and drank incredible quantities. An Australian colonel and his adjutant got aboard, but just before sailing discovered that their battalion had not embarked and went hurriedly ashore again. We sailed after midnight and made for Alexandria at full speed.

Brigadier Kippenberger

It has been said that the losses suffered by the German airborne troops in their Cretan landings were so severe that Hitler was discouraged from ever again undertaking a similar venture. If that was the case, all those who fought on the island—including nearly six thousand New Zealand casualties—had struggled not only manfully but with success—however clouded their glory may have seemed at the time.

THE MIDDLE EAST

While the Germans overran Greece and Crete and (as will be told) turned the tide in the Western Desert, they were also planning to gain control of Syria, Iraq and Persia through puppet governments. Here was a deadly threat to Suez and Britain's communications with India, and to her Middle Eastern oil supplies.

During March Rashid Ali's pro-German party seized power in Iraq. German and Italian aircraft were actually being landed on Iraqi airfields when British forces, advancing from the Persian Gulf and across the desert from Palestine, forestalled them and forced Rashid Ali to flee on 30 May.

Syria

Syria was strongly held for Vichy France, and thus was a potential base for German bombers and airborne troops now established in the Balkans. To avert such a disastrous situation, British and Free French forces entered Syria on 8 June 1941. The Vichy French, better equipped, more numerous and supported by German aircraft, resisted with determination and skill, and the fighting, complicated by the uncomfortable feeling that each side should have been the ally, not the enemy, of the other, was bitter and costly. One of the Allied columns, under Major-General William Slim, invaded Syria from the east.

.... About the middle of June, my division was suddenly transferred from the Iraq to the Syrian Command, and I was told to advance as speedily as possible up the Euphrates into Syria. My objective, a hundred miles inside the French frontier, was the town of Deir-ez-Zor, the capital of Eastern Syria, where desert routes from all directions converged on the only bridge spanning the river for the five hundred miles between Habbaniyeh and the

Turkish Frontier. Once there, I should outflank the
French line across Syria and might menace Aleppo, far in
their rear. At the moment the British and Australian
forces were fighting slowly northward against strong opposition in a two-pronged drive on Damascus and on Pal-
myra. My division would make a third prong a hundred
miles to the east.

Major-General William Slim

*For the attack on Deir-ez-Zor, General Slim divided his
force into two parts, one to make a frontal assault while
the other, a flying column, set off into the desert to make
a long flanking march which would take the defenders in
the rear.*

Towards us flowed the winding Euphrates, broad,
placid and now beginning to reflect the sun. East and west
on either side stretched, mile after mile, the desert, flat
and featureless, a muddy brown. To the north, a low *café-
au-lait* ridge ran obliquely away from us to the north-west.
We saw only its rounded end, coming down in a steep but
even slope to within a few hundred yards of the river
bank. Through the gap between ridge and river the white
thread of the road ran on past the airfield into Deir-ez-
Zor. The ridge screened a large part of the town and all
but a corner of the aerodrome from our view. Judging by
the size and height of the flat-topped houses we could see,
the town promised to be bigger and more imposing than I
had expected. If we got our small force involved in fighting through those streets, it would be soaked up like water
in a sponge—not a very comforting thought.

It was now full daylight. Weld and I walked slowly up
and down, waiting. I looked surreptitiously at my watch,
six-thirty—surely the column *must* be there! Soon it would
break silence and call up! The hands of my watch
crawled on. *Seven.* French could not have failed to locate
the column by now. Still no signal came. *Seven-thirty . . .
eight.* If the column was ever going to reach the Aleppo
road it must have done so already and, wherever it was,

he enemy must have seen it! I told the Signal Officer to all it up. No answer; obviously something had gone rrong—very wrong.

We resumed our measured pacing, stopping every now nd then to gaze through field-glasses at the enemy posions. No visible movement there and a silence broken nly once by the French guns firing again at their first ove, the wrecked trucks on the road. As we walked, to onceal our mounting anxiety we spoke of old days in India, of our friends, of casual things, yet our minds were lsewhere. What had gone wrong? Where *was* that blasted olumn? If only I had an aeroplane, just one aeroplane, to end out to look for it! A couple of armoured cars? No, ley would take too long. I glanced sideways at Weld; I oped I appeared as unperturbed as he did.

Nine . . . conversation languished; we walked in silence. *Tine-thirty!* As at a signal, we stopped and faced one nother. I was quite sure my plan had failed. We had ushed Weld and his brigade into a far worse position lan they had been at the end of their first attempt. Then e could reunite his force; now the flank column could not ossibly get back—it would have no petrol left. Should I rder a frontal attack with what we had in hand or call the hole thing off and concentrate on an attempt to rescue le column?—how, I had no idea. It is always a nasty moent when one faces a disaster knowing it has been aused by one's own obstinacy in persisting in a plan gainst advice. I was having such a moment now.

Weld's common-sense came to my rescue. "We haven't eard any firing north of the town," he pointed out. "If e French had spotted the column there would have been n enough. Better hang on a bit. All the chaps down there ave their orders—we can start an attack in a matter of inutes if we want to."

"All right," I agreed, grateful to him for this excuse to ut off decision. "We'll wait another half-hour."

We resumed our silent promenade.

No gun fired, no aeroplane flew, no bomb crumped -all was quiet. Quiet except that it required an increasing effort of will to continue this steady march up and down, up and down. . . .

Footsteps behind us. We turned and there, charging towards us, waving a signal form in his hand, was the Brigade Signals Officer.

"The column's come through," he gasped. "They're on the Aleppo road a couple of miles north of Deir-ez-Zor and advancing. Leading troops nearing town. No opposition so far!"

Ten years and a ton of weight dropped off my shoulders. I turned to Weld to say "Let battle begin" or words to that effect, but he and the Signals Officer were already sliding down the mound to the signal truck.

A quarter of an hour later, our guns started with a grand and simultaneous crash. I dare say there have been bigger and better bombardments, before and since, but no general ever listened to one with more relief than I did on that mound. The upper part of the ridge vanished in rolling clouds of fawn dust. The racket grew as rifles and automatics joined in and the French guns thumped away at ours.

The bombardment of the ridge was at its height when uneven lines of Gurkhas began to move forward across the flat ground at its foot. Luckily for them the billowing curtain of dust half way up the slope blinded the French earthworks. The distant lines of little figures pushed on up the steep incline at a real hillman's pace and disappeared into the smoke and dust. Our guns had by now lifted and were firing over the ridge; I could see some of their shell bursting beyond the aerodrome.

The cloud on the ridge thinned rapidly and drifted away. The Gurkhas were half way up, some of them shooting from the hip. Suddenly, on the top of the ridge, silhouetted against the smoke and sky, appeared an agitated figure or two, arms waving, bodies bent. Then more, then a crowd of them, scrambling wildly over the crest and vanishing down the other side. The French native troops were abandoning their entrenchments. A few moments later the Gurkhas reached the top of the ridge and plunged out of sight after them.

The noise of gun and rifle fire died away except for the chattering of light automatics from the aerodome. I turned my glasses in that direction and could see our men advancing each side of the road, some already at the corner of the airfield. As the din wavered towards silence, I heard for the first time a strange confused murmur from the town itself, punctuated by bursts of machine-gun fire, rifle shots and the crump of shells—the column! A vehicle, leaving a trail of dust behind it, fled madly down the road from the aerodrome into the town; others followed it and rifle fire started again. Coloured Verey lights—success signals—leapt up from the ridge and from the aerodrome. The enemy was on the run. The double attack had been too much for his nerves. We were into Deir-ez-Zor!

General Slim

The Enemies

In the earlier stages of the engagement, before heat and tiredness had worn the edge off enthusiasm, I crawled forward to an outpost to see what I could of our enemy. At dawn, when we had reached the mountain-top, we had seen a few unidentifiable figures silhouetted against the rising sun. Since then the enemy had been invisible, shooting at us through loopholes in the fort or from the neighbouring hillsides. I lay down beside a trooper. More for the fun of the thing than because he had a target, he was firing a Hotchkiss sporadically at a low built-in stone parapet about fifty yards away. Suddenly, behind the parapet, two black French soldiers (Senegalese, I believe) popped their heads up. Their two faces, under steel helmets, grinned at us, and I can still see the whiteness of their teeth and eyeballs. God knows what they thought they were doing. Probably they had never been in a battle before and, like myself, they were childishly curious to have a look at their enemy.

Or were they attempting to do something more? If men
are ever to cease destroying one another, if the everlasting
tit-for-tat process is ever to be halted, it will perhaps only
come by an individual, a simple black man, for example,
standing up suddenly in the face of bullets and crying out:
"See, here I am. I don't want to kill you. Why kill me?
Let us stop the battle and be friends."

The trooper beside me was so astonished by the apparition of the two black men that he never thought of firing
his Hotchkiss.

"Shoot!" I hissed at him.

He pressed the trigger and nothing happened. A cartridge had jammed. There was a simple drill for curing the
stoppage, but now, in his excitement, the trooper bungled
it. I pushed him out of the way, grabbed the gun and
ejected the cartridge.

Over the sights, I saw my burst hit the top of the
parapet. The two grinning faces vanished like puppets. A
little dust lingered in the air where they had been. Thus,
with the wantonness of a boy destroying some harmless
bird for "sport", I contributed my share towards the
never-ending story of man's inhumanity to man. But at
the time I thought I had behaved rather splendidly and the
trooper was impressed too.

John Verney

*By 11 June this unhappy campaign was over. Syria was
lost to Vichy France, and to Germany.*

Persia

*Thousands of German agents flourished in Persia, har-
boured by a government which refused to expel them.
General Slim was appointed to command the British force
which on 25 August 1941 entered Persia to enforce Allied
demands. By this time the situation had become doubly
dangerous, for on 22 June Germany had invaded Russia,
and a pro-Axis Persia on her southern flank could not be
tolerated.*

. . . . I was fully occupied going over with Aizlewood, the Brigadier of the Armoured Brigade, the plans he had already prepared for the first phase of our invasion —the forcing of the formidable Pai Tak Pass, which within thiry miles of our crossing the frontier would bar our way. With time so short it was fortunate that I could heartily approve his plans, and I decided to act on them without serious alteration.

Accordingly, before dawn on 25 August, led by the Hussars in their always gallant but decrepit and slightly ridiculous old Mark VII tanks, whose only armament was a single Vickers machine-gun apiece and whose armour almost anything could pierce, we crossed the frontier. By that time I was becoming accustomed to invasions; this was the fifth frontier I had crossed in the past year. All the same, there was a thrill about it. But very little happened. A few harmless shots from vanishing frontier guards greeted us as we encircled the village of Qasr-i-Shirin, about ten miles inside Persia, but we met no real opposition. As it grew lighter, Aizlewood and I pushed on with the advance guard, and by mid-morning we were almost at the entrance to the Pai Tak Pass. Here we stopped and, covered by a screen of light tanks, stood on the roof of my station wagon to study this historic gate through which, over the centuries, so many armies had passed or tried to pass.

Viewed from below it was a most formidable and threatening obstacle. The interminable flat plains of the Tigris and Euphrates which stretched behind us for hundreds of miles here came to an abrupt end at the great boundary wall of a mighty escarpment stretching from north to south across our path. The road to Kermanshah which we must follow rose sharply into the mouth of the Pass and, climbing in curves and loops, vanished among cliffs and gorges to emerge, three thousand feet higher, on to the plateau of Gilan. It looked as if a handful of men could hold it against an army many times the size of mine. At the moment there was no sign of even the proverbial handful in the Pass or on the crest of the escarpment. Both appeared completely deserted. Yet our intelligence was quite firm that there was a Persian force, reliably reported to have been reinforced to a strength of five thousand, well dug in on and around the Pass. It was so still and deserted that we began to wonder if there really were any enemy at all. Curiously but cautiously we drove on a few hundred yards and again searched the hills and cliffs. Not a sign of movement; not the sound of a shot. Proceeding in this way, growing bolder with continued impunity, we reached the point where the road entered a sinister and narrowing gorge, the jaws of the Pass itself. The road, quite empty, ran uphill from us to disappear with surprising suddenness round a sharp corner a couple of hundred yards farther on. At this corner stood a white-washed *chai khana,* a tea shop, the Persian equivalent of a tavern, with a few small trees growing at the roadside in front of it; all utterly peaceful, drowsing deserted in the sunlight.

The irresistible urge to look round the corner that comes on every winding road fell upon us. Why not? It looked safe enough! Standing boldly upright, our heads and shoulders through the open roof, we drove slowly to the corner, cautiously poked our bonnet round it and peered up the Pass. I had just spotted above the road what I took to be the oil pumping station marked on our map when a bang, well behind us and off to one side, made me jump.

"What's that?" I asked Aizlewood.

His reply was emphasized by a much louder and nearer *crump* and a cloud of dust, smoke and stones level with us but some way off the road. Almost simultaneously with it came the *crack* of a gun ahead.

"By God, they're shooting at us!" exclaimed the Brigadier in an aggrieved voice.

Our driver had already realized this unpleasant fact, and we jerked in reverse round the corner as a couple more shells from the anti-tank gun smacked into the road at the spot we had just left. The driver needed no orders to turn the car behind the *chai khana,* and we left the Pa

Tak Pass a good deal more briskly than we had entered it.

There was an interesting postscript to this incident. Some days later the anti-tank battery fell into our hands and we were told that just as it was ordered to the Pai Tak Pass it had been issued with brand-new guns. The first shot its crew had ever fired from one of these was the opening round at us and, as a Persian gunner wistfully remarked, a little more practice would have made them shoot better!

We could now, at any rate, be sure there were enemy on the Pass and that they meant to hold it against us. The idea of a frontal attack up the rugged and in places almost vertical escarpment was not attractive, but the Brigadier when studying his map before my arrival had spotted a route by which any position at the Pai Tak itself could be by-passed. This was a track which crossed the escarpment some twenty miles further south and went via the village of Gilan to Shahabad on the main Kermanshah road, about thirty miles south-east of the main pass. It was a long—about ninety miles—and rough track but it was said to be passable by wheels. Although we could hardly expect it not to be blocked by the enemy, all reports agreed that their strength there was small and, even if we were delayed, the threat to the Persian rear would, we could hope, at least divide their force. I therefore decided to send the Armoured Brigade by this track and, as soon as the enemy began to feel the threat against their rear, to attack on each side of the Pai Tak Pass with the rest of my force.

On the 26th, the R.A.F. located enemy defences in the Pass and along the escarpment, and later in the afternoon bombed them. Throughout the day the infantry carried out their reconnaissances and preparations for the attack while the Armoured Brigade began its arduous and hazardous march, the first stages of which were to be completed before daylight. About Gilan the column was delayed for a time by road blocks and some infantry and machine-gun fire. An overheard radio conversation when this skirmish was at its height, while it did not diminish our fear that the column might be seriously held up, did at least give us a smile:

First Signaller: "This is getting a bit too hot! I'm going under my truck. Over."

Second Signaller: "I *am* under my truck! Out!"

Before dawn on the 27th, two Gurkha battalions, one each side of the Pai Tak Pass, began in real mountain warfare style to scramble up the escarpment. Hardly had they got going when I was most relieved to receive a signal from the flank column that it had taken Shahabad. The news of this had proved too much for the Persians, already shaken by the bombing, and they had pulled out hurriedly across country north of the road while it was still dark.

General Slim

No other opposition was offered to the British troops, and within three days the Persian Government had agreed to expel German influence from Persia.

KEY TO THE SOURCES
OF EXTRACTS

For an explanation of how to use this Key and the following section entitled *Sources*, see page xvi

Heading or first words

SOURCES

SOURCES

The Editors wish to express their gratitude to all the publishers, authors, literary agents and others who so kindly granted permission for the reproduction of the extracts in this anthology.

1. *Ack-Ack: Britain's Defense Against Air Attack During the Second World War*, by General Sir Frederick Pile. Harrap, 1949; British Book Centre, 1950.
2 *American Treasury, 1455-1955, The*, by Clifton Fadiman. Harper, 1955.
3. *Ball of Fire: The Fifth Indian Division in the Second World War*, by Antony Brett-James, Gale & Polden, 1951.
4. *Battle of the River Plate, The (Graf Spee)*, by Dudley Pope. Kimber, 1956; Lippincott, 1957.
5. *Black Watch and the King's Enemies, The*, by Bernard Fergusson. Collins; Crowell, 1950.
6. *Blitz, The (The Winter of the Bombs)*, by Constantine FitzGibbon. Wingate, 1957; Norton, 1958.
7. *Bombed But Unbeaten*, by Beatrice L. Warde. Friends of Freedom, 1941.
8. *Bomber Offensive*, by Marshal of the Royal Air Force Sir Arthur Harris. Collins; Macmillan, 1947.
9. *Call to Honour, 1940-1942, The*, by Charles de Gaulle. Collins; Viking, 1955.
10. *Chelsea Concerto, The*, by Francis Faviell. Cassell, 1959.
11. *Collected Poems*, by C. Day Lewis. Hogarth Press and Cape, 1949.
12. *Daedalus Returned*, by Baron von der Heydte. Hutchinson, 1958.
13. *Defeat in the West*, by Milton Shulman. Secker & Warburg, 1947; Dutton, 1948.

14. *Documents on International Affairs: Norway,* by M. Curtis. Oxford, 1941.

15. *Drive: A Chronicle of Patton's Army,* by Charles Codman. Little, Brown, © 1957 by Theodora Duer Codman.

16. *Dunkirk,* by A. D. Divine. Faber, 1945; Dutton, 1948.

17. *Fall of France, The,* by Major-General Sir Edward Spears. Heinemann; Wyn, 1954.

18. *Fatal Decisions, The,* by Werner Kreipe and others, edited by Seymour Freidin and William Richardson. Joseph; Sloane, 1956.

19. *First and the Last, The,* by Adolf Galland. Holt, 1954; Methuen, 1955.

20. *Flight to Arras,* by Antoine de St.-Exupéry. Heinemann; Harcourt, 1942.

21. *Follow My Leader,* by Louis Hagan. Wingate, 1951.

22. *German Military Intelligence,* by Paul Leverkuehn. Weidenfeld & Nicolson; Praeger, 1954.

23. *Going to the Wars,* by John Verney. Collins; Dodd, 1955.

24. *Happy Hunted, The,* by Brigadier George Clifton. Cassell, 1952.

25. *Happy Odyssey,* by Sir Adrian Carton de Wiart. Cape, 1950.

26. *Hausfrau at War,* by Else Wendel. Odhams, 1957.

27. *Hitler and His Admirals,* by Anthony Martienssen. Secker & Warburg, 1948; Dutton, 1949.

28. *Infantry Brigadier,* by Major-General Sir Howard Kippenberger. Oxford, 1949.

29. *In the Thick of the Fight,* by Paul Reynaud. Cassell, 1955; Simon & Schuster, 1956.

30. *Italy in the Second World War,* by Pietro Badoglio. Oxford, 1948.

31. *I Was Graf Spee's Prisoner,* by Captain Patrick Dove. Withy Grove, 1940.

32. *Journal of the War Years,* by Anthony Weymouth. Littlebury, Worcester, 1948. Acknowledgements to the Public Trustee and the Society of Authors.

33. *Last Enemy, The (Falling Through Space),* by

Richard Hillary. Macmillan. Acknowledgements to the Estate of Richard Hillary; St. Martin's, 1942.

34. *Lost Victories*, by Field-Marshal Erich von Manstein. Methuen; Regnery, 1958.

35. *Memoirs of Field-Marshal the Viscount Montgomery of Alamein*. Collins; World, 1958.

36. *Memoirs of Marshal Mannerheim, The*. Cassell, 1953; Dutton, 1954.

37. *Merchantman Re-armed*, by Sir David W. Bone. Chatto & Windus, 1949.

38. *My Sister and I: The Diary of a Dutch Boy Refugee*, by 'Dirk van der Heide'. Harcourt, 1941.

39. *Operation Sea Lion*, by Ronald Wheatley. Oxford, 1958, Crown Copyright.

40. *Operation Victory*, by Major-General Sir Francis de Guingand. Hodder; Scribner, 1947.

41. *Our Vichy Gamble*, by William H. Langer. Knopf, 1947.

42. *Panzer Battles, 1939-1945*, by F. W. von Mellenthin. Cassell, 1955; U. of Okla. Press, 1956.

43. *Panzer Leader*, by Heinz Guderian. Joseph; Dutton, 1952.

44. *Post D (Digging for Mrs. Miller)*, by John Strachey. Gollancz; Random, 1941.

45. *Private Diaries of Paul Baudouin, The*, Eyre & Spottiswoode, 1948.

46. *Recalled to Service*, by Maxime Weygand. Heinemann; Doubleday, 1952.

47. *Retreat, The*, by P. H. Newby. Cape; Knopf, 1953.

48. *Return Via Dunkirk*, by Gun Buster. Hodder & Stoughton, 1940.

49. *Rommel Papers, The*, edited by B. H. Liddell Hart. Collins; Harcourt, 1953.

50. *Royal Artillery Commemoration Book, 1939-1945, The*. Bell, 1950.

51. *Sailor Malan*, by Oliver Walker. Cassell, 1953.

52. *Schellenberg Memoirs, The (The Labyrinth)*, edited by Louis Hagen. Deutsch, 1956; Harper, 1957.

53. *Sea Wolves, The*, by Wolfgang Frank. Weidenfeld; Rinehart, 1955.

54. *Second World War, The,* by Winston Churchill, Vol. 1. Houghton, 1948.

55. *Second World War, The,* by Winston Churchill, Vol. 2. Houghton, 1949.

56. *Second World War, The,* by Winston Churchill, Vol. 3. Houghton, 1950.

57. *Seven Times Seven Days,* by Emmanuel d'Astier. MacGibbon & Kee, 1958.

58. *Small Back Room, The,* by Nigel Balchin. Collins, 1943; Houghton, 1945.

59. *Take These Men,* by Cyril Joly. Constable, 1955.

60. *This is London,* by Edward Murrow. Cassell; Simon & Schuster, 1941.

61. *This is Pearl!,* by Walter Millis. Morrow, copyright 1947 by Walter Millis.

62. *Thousand Shall Fall, A,* by Hans Habe. Harcourt, 1941; Harrap, 1942.

63. *Through the Dark Night,* by J. L. Hobson. Gollancz, 1941.

64. *Time for Decision, The,* by Sumner Welles. Hamilton; Harper, 1944.

65. *Times, The,* 9 April 1940, statement by British and French Governments

66. *Tobruk 1941,* by Chester Wilmot. Angus & Robertson, 1945.

67. *Trial of German Major War Criminals, The: Proceedings of the International Military Tribunal at Nuremburg, 1946.* H. M. S. O.

68. *Turn of the Tide, The,* by Sir Arthur Bryant. Collins; Doubleday, 1957.

69. *Under the Iron Heel,* by Lars Moen. Hale; Lippincott, 1941.

70. *Unexploded Bomb,* by Major A. B. Hartley. Cassell, 1958; Norton, 1959.

71. *Unfinished Man, The,* by James Byrom. Chatto & Windus, 1957.

72. *Unofficial History,* by Field-Marshal Sir Willaim Slim. Cassell, 1959.

73. *Venlo Incident, The,* by Captain S. Payne Best. Hutchinson, 1950.

74. *Voices From Britain*, edited by Henning Krabbe. Allen & Unwin, 1947; Macmillan, 1948.
75. *War Begins at Home*, edited by Tom Harrisson and Charles Madge. Chatto & Windus, 1940.
76. *War Speeches of the Rt. Hon. Winston S. Churchill, The*, Definitive Edition, Vol. 1. Cassell, 1951; Houghton, 1953.
77. *We Shall March Again*, by Gerhard Kramer. Cape; Putnam, 1955.
78. *White House Papers of Harry L. Hopkins, The (Roosevelt and Hopkins)*, by Robert E. Sherwood. Eyre & Spottiswoode; Harper, 1948.
79. *Wing Leader*, by Johnnie Johnson. Chatto & Windus, 1956; Ballantine, 1957.

MAPS

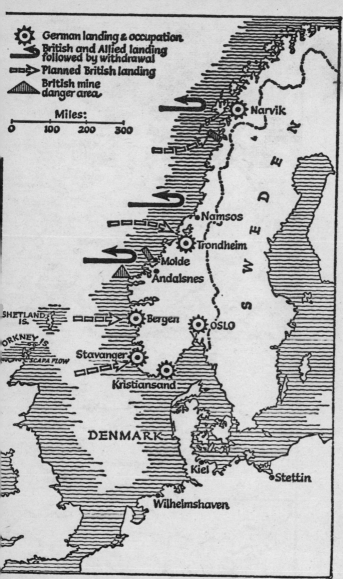

Legend

⚙ German landing & occupation
→ British and Allied landing followed by withdrawal
▭▭▷ Planned British landing
◭ British mine danger area

Miles:
0   100   200   300

Narvik

S W E D E N

Namsos

Trondheim

Molde

Åndalsnes

SHETLAND IS.

ORKNEY IS
SCAPA FLOW

Bergen

OSLO

Stavanger

Kristiansand

DENMARK

Kiel

Stettin

Wilhelmshaven

The Allied Campaign in Norway - 1940

Walcheren
Middelburg

Zeebrugge

Ostend ●Bruges

B

Dover
Dunkirk Nieuport
Furnes Dixmude ●Thielt
Strait of Dover Gravelines Bergues R.Yser
Calais Poperinghe Ypres Courtrai
Cap Wormhoudt Menin Tourcoing
Griz Nez St.Omer Cassel Comines Roubaix
Boulogne Bailleul Armentières
Hazebrouck Merville Lille Tournai
R.Lys
Aire La Bassée Maulde
Etaples Béthune Carvin
Montreuil Hesdin St.Pol Lens Scarpe Douai
Mont St. Arleux Denain
Éloi Arras R.Sense Cambrai
Doullens Bapaume Ruyaulcourt
Abbeville C
F R A N
R.Somme Albert
Amiens Péronne
Peix R.Avre St.Quentin
Roye
Montdidier Chauny
Gournay ●Beauvais Compiègne Noyon
R.Oise Soissons
●les Andelys ●Marœil
R.Seine Pontoise R.Marne
Meaux
PARIS

NORTHERN FRANCE & THE

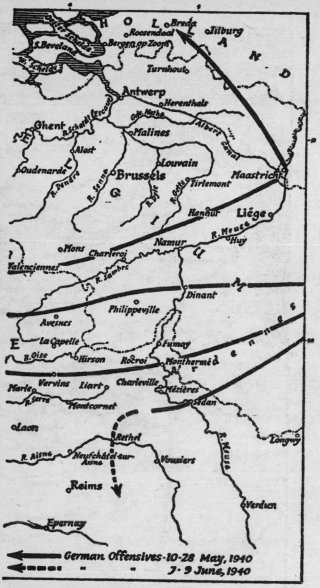

German Offensives—10-28 May, 1940
" " 7-9 June, 1940

LOW COUNTRIES — 1940

Lines of British invasion ➡
Railways ---

Pt Soudan
Atbara
Khartoum
Agordat Keren
Kassala
Massawa
Asmara
Adowa
Gallabat
Gondar
Amba Alagi
Assab
SOUDAN
White Nile
Blue Nile
Debra Tabor
FR. SOMALILD
Dessie
Aden
Djibuti
GOJJAM
Debra Markos
Addis Ababa
Berbera
Jijiga
BRITISH
SOMALILND
Diredawa
Harrar
Jimma
ABYSSINIA
ITALIAN SOMALILAND
Dolo
Ferfer
L. Rudolf
Juba
UGANDA
KENYA
Jelib
Mogadishu
Nairobi
Kismayu
Lake Victoria
TANGANYIKA
Mombasa
500 MILES

THE CAMPAIGN IN EAST AFRICA 1941

GREECE & CRETE 1941

INDEX

INDEX

THE TASTE OF COURAGE: THE WAR, 1939-1945
edited by Desmond Flower and James Reeves

A MAJOR FIVE-VOLUME SERIES
ON WORLD WAR II
FROM BERKLEY

The drama, the humor, the horror, and sometimes the tenderness of men and women confronting their greatest ordeal speak through this absorbing narrative of World War II, told in eyewitness accounts by soldiers, housewives and journalists in the many countries involved.

VOLUME II: *THE AXIS TRIUMPHANT*

deals with the Axis nations at the height of their power. Germany invades Russia in Operation Barbarossa, and quickly reaches the outskirts of Moscow, Leningrad and Stalingrad. In the Atlantic, German U-boats dominate the vital trade routes. In the Far East, Japan celebrates the bombing of Pearl Harbor by sweeping through Indonesia, the Philippines, Malaya and Burma, and is poised to invade India. In North Africa, the British Eighth Army is in full retreat before Rommel's Afrika Korps.

(Z1976—$1.25)

VOLUME III: *THE TIDE TURNS*

is the story of the first Allied victories of the war, victories which followed endless defeats. In Russia, the Wehrmacht suffered its first major setback when the German 6th Army, commanded by von Paulus, was first held, then smashed, at Stalingrad. In North Africa, Montgomery and the British Eighth Army defeated the hitherto invincible Afrika Korps at El Alamein. At sea, the victorious Japanese Navy was stopped at Midway. The Allied Air Forces were carrying the bombing war to Germany. For the first time, it seemed that the Allies had a real chance of victory.

(Z1991—$1.25)

(Please turn page)

VOLUME IV: *THE ALLIES ADVANCE*

describes the slogging advance of the Allied armies through Italy; and the Italian surrender; the painful island-hopping by the Americans as they beat the Japanese in the Pacific; and the slow attrition of the Japanese armies in Burma under the British onslaught.   (Z2008—$1.25)

VOLUME V: *VICTORY AND DEFEAT*

carries the story to its dramatic conclusion, in the collapse of Germany under the twin pressures of the sweeping Russian victories in the East, and the relentless advance of the British and American armies in the West; and the final surrender of the Japanese, demoralised by the atomic holocausts of Hiroshima and Nagasaki. (Z2018—$1.25)

Send for a *free* list of all our books in print

These books are available at your local bookstore, or send price indicated plus 30¢ per copy to cover mailing costs to
Berkley Publishing Corporation
200 Madison Avenue
New York, New York 10016